THE PUREST BOND

THE PUREST BOND

UNDERSTANDING THE

HUMAN–CANINE CONNECTION

Jen Golbeck, PhD, and
Stacey Colino, MS

ATRIA BOOKS

New York   London   Toronto   Sydney   New Delhi

ATRIA
B O O K S

An Imprint of Simon & Schuster, Inc.
1230 Avenue of the Americas
New York, NY 10020

First Atria Books hardcover edition November 2023

ATRIA B O O K S and colophon are trademarks of Simon & Schuster, Inc.

For information about special discounts for bulk purchases, please contact Simon & Schuster Special Sales at 1-866-506-1949 or business@simonandschuster.com.

The Simon & Schuster Speakers Bureau can bring authors to your live event. For more information or to book an event, contact the Simon & Schuster Speakers Bureau at 1-866-248-3049 or visit our website at www.simonspeakers.com.

Interior design by Kyoko Watanabe

Manufactured in the United States of America

1 3 5 7 9 10 8 6 4 2

Library of Congress Cataloging-in-Publication Data

Names: Golbeck, Jennifer, author. | Colino, Stacey, author.
Title: The purest bond : understanding the human–canine connection / by Jen Golbeck, Ph.D., and Stacey Colino, M.S.
Description: New York : Atria Books, 2023. | Includes bibliographical references.
Identifiers: LCCN 2023003065 (print) | LCCN 2023003066 (ebook) | ISBN 9781668007846 (hardcover) | ISBN 9781668007853 (trade paperback) | ISBN 9781668007860 (ebook)
Subjects: LCSH: Dog owners—Psychology. | Dogs. | Human–animal relationships.
Classification: LCC SF422.86 .G635 2023 (print) | LCC SF422.86 (ebook) | DDC 636.7001/9--dc23/eng/20230628
LC record available at https://lccn.loc.gov/2023003065
LC ebook record available at https://lccn.loc.gov/2023003066

ISBN 978-1-6680-0784-6
ISBN 978-1-6680-0786-0 (ebook)

This book is dedicated to all the dogs we've loved before and the ones we have yet to meet.[*]

With a special shout-out to Maggie, Riley, and Hopper (from Jen) and Wolfy, Inky, and Sadie (from Stacey).

CONTENTS

Contents

AUTHORS' NOTE

The stories in this book are from real people who are identified by their first names to protect their privacy. In some instances, people who shared their experiences asked to be identified with a pseudonym; those anecdotes are marked with an asterisk (*).

INTRODUCTION

Dogs have long been considered people's best friends, but never before has the bond between humans and their canine companions been as vitally important as it is now. While dealing with seismic shifts in the world as we once knew it, including social distancing, working from home, and re-evaluating our priorities, people have been turning to their dogs for solace and stability. In the face of having their lives upended, families that didn't have dogs have been welcoming them into their homes at record rates—in recent years, dog adoptions have dramatically increased, and rescue organizations and breeders have amassed waitlists of people seeking a dog to call their own.

On both a national and global scale, we're living through a period of profound distress, not only because of the pandemic but also in response to recent political strife and scandals, international conflicts and wars, increasing awareness of police brutality and other racial injustices, widespread financial hardships, horrific weather and natural disasters, and other harsh, and sometimes catastrophic, circumstances. Human relationships are being strained, and we've been living with high rates of loneliness and social isolation that actually predate the pandemic. Meanwhile, rates of anxiety and depression have been soaring.

But amid these dire realities, something wonderful has taken shape: People have brought furry friends into their lives for the first time or seized the opportunity to deepen the bonds they already had with their dogs. This isn't surprising, given that research from the University of Sydney in Australia has found that acquiring a dog improves mental well-being, dramatically relieving loneliness and playing a significant role in the reduction of depression, anxiety, and irritability. Basically, dogs are comfort animals for all of us. In fact, research shows that people who have dogs are happier than people who have cats or no pets.

Dogs can also serve as a sort of balm to the mental health struggles and ongoing stress that are plaguing people worldwide. Our canine companions help us feel grounded and present-minded, leading by example. Dogs are always focused on what's happening now, whether it's playing with us, being fed, or going for a walk. They continuously remind us of what's important, whether it's showing loved ones how happy we are to see them when they come home or appreciating small pleasures such as the scent of fragrant bushes on a walk. Their loyalty, commitment, and friendship are singular. You can dance badly or sing off-key, and your dog will think that you're great no matter what (as long as you're nice to them).

That's why we are writing *The Purest Bond*—to explore and illuminate the profound impact the human-canine connection can have on our physical, emotional, cognitive, and social health and well-being, often without our realizing it. A bit about us: Jen is a scientist whose research includes studies of personality, psychology, and people's relationships with their pets, as well as a seasoned dog-owner/rescuer and the founder/manager of the social media sensation the Golden Ratio. Through her role as the internet's "dog mom," she frequently shares the joys that dogs bring to our lives and advises dog-owners on training issues, dealing with sickness and loss of beloved pets, and ways to find joy in the everyday care of our pawed friends. Stacey is an award-winning writer, who specializes in health and psychology, as well as a certified health coach and a lifelong dog lover and dog-owner. The two of us are intimately familiar with the physical, emotional, social, and even spiritual gifts that come from this special bond—and the many ways it can have positive, life-altering effects.

The Birth of The Golden Ratio

In December 2016, Jen and her husband, Ingo, took in Maggie and Jasmine, a bonded pair of golden retrievers. They were nine and eight, respectively, and their previous owners had moved away and left them in the backyard where a neighbor found them. Jen and Ingo had already fostered a dozen dogs, but the moment Maggie and Jasmine arrived, it felt like they had always been part of the family. They joined golden retrievers Hopper and Venkman, permanent squad members who were half sisters born a year apart. As Jen watched Maggie and Jasmine chase Hopper and Venkman around the backyard, she was shocked to realize, "Well, now we have four dogs!"

This was also during the aftermath of the 2016 U.S. presidential election, when everyone on social media was angry, regardless of whom they voted for. Being on social media is part of Jen's job, but she really needed a virtual place where she could escape from the negativity and just catch her breath. She couldn't find it, so she decided to create it herself. Now finding she had a squad of four dogs, she thought, "What's more wholesome and uplifting than a pack of golden retrievers?"

Jen started a Twitter account, TheGoldenRatio4,* and began posting group pics. It turned out there was pent-up demand for a fluffy, peaceful corner of the internet. The Golden Ratio quickly grew a following and expanded to include posting a daily Snapchat story that provides glimpses into the dogs' lives.

Since then, Jen and Ingo have fostered more dogs and started to shift their focus to taking in seniors, hospice cases, and dogs with special medical needs. Their followers have joined them on these dogs' journeys, watching them transform as they come into a loving, healthy home, seeing them play, rooting for them when they needed surgeries, sending encouragement when they were sick, and crying with Jen and Ingo when they lost them. Many of their stories appear throughout this book.

---

*Named for the mathematical proportion called the golden ratio to honor Jen's math background, and with a "4" because that's how many dogs were in the original squad.

Jen became a true believer in the human-canine connection in eighth grade when she was seriously depressed, lonely, and bullied. Every day at school in her small town in Illinois, which was surrounded by cornfields, she was mocked and harassed. She felt worthless and hopeless. While she didn't talk to her parents directly about how she felt, it was more than obvious, and they began to worry about her. One day her parents brought home Major, a golden retriever puppy who turned out to be the best friend she could have had. The family had always had a dog, but Major was the first *second* dog in the family. Jen immediately thought of him as *her dog* because his loyalty and playfulness were exactly what she needed in that dark time. After school and on the weekends, she would sit on the floor with her legs splayed out in front of her, and he'd lie between them on his back, with his head on her lap and his tail by her feet. She'd pet his chest and he'd make a happy, rumbly noise. When Jen's mom walked past, she would tell her, "We're bonding!"

That became Jen's mantra with him, as they cuddled or played every chance they got.

Back then, Major brought her everything she needed emotionally. The time she spent with him let her forget all the bad things she couldn't change. But more importantly, he made her believe she had value. He made her feel appreciated and loved for who she was. He was a golden angel with the sweetest eyes and softest ears. He didn't care what Jen wore or how she looked or that she was an awkward preteen. He was always ready to play—and ready to console her when she needed it. When Jen cried, he'd lean against her to comfort her—and it always worked.

The transformation he brought to Jen sparked her intellectual interest in dogs, not just as pets and friends but also as powerful, positive forces in our lives. She knew, as many other dog-owners do, that they are a kind of medicine as well as treasured companions. They have a remarkable sense of empathy and a sixth sense for when we need them to comfort us and bring us calm. And they never hesitate to show us how happy they are to see us, even if we've just returned from getting the mail.

But beyond what they give us directly, our canine companions also serve as models for how we all could be better. They are patient and kind. They don't hold grudges; they forgive freely, easily, and repeatedly. They live in the moment and seek out joy without worrying about judgment. Their well of love and gratitude is bottomless—and we, their people, benefit enormously from this, in every aspect of our lives.

The emotional support and sense of meaningful connection that dogs offer their people are particularly crucial in this ongoing time of uncertainty and instability. This mutually beneficial relationship reminds us of what's right in the world—love, trust, affection, playtime, fresh air, and sunshine—even when so much feels wrong. As researchers found in a large online survey, "Many people reported feeling more bonded with their dog since COVID. Dogs also help increase many people's ability to maintain a regular schedule, feel a sense of purpose and meaning, cope with uncertainty, and have compassion towards oneself."

As you'll see in the chapters that follow, an expanding body of research confirms numerous powerful perks of sharing life with a canine companion. Each section of the book will focus on a different aspect of this sublime connection, while weaving together groundbreaking research, heartwarming stories, and our own personal experiences as dog-owners. In Part One, you will learn how the human-canine bond develops and how it helps people enhance their relationships within their families, friend groups, and communities. Part Two will reveal the unexpected ways dogs can benefit our physical health by reducing our blood pressure, easing chronic pain, alleviating our stress response, helping us get fitter, and even detecting warning signs of diseases. Part Three will explore the science showing how dogs improve our emotional health, mental acuity, and our ability to focus, even as they serve as stabilizing influences throughout our lives. In Part Four, we will address issues related to maturing along with our pets, dealing with health challenges that arise as dogs and their humans get older, and coping with grief and sorrow over the inevitable loss of our furry loved ones.

Besides helping you understand the profound connection you may already be feeling with your pooch, this book will give you a language with which to think and talk about the different parts of your relationship—and offer strategies that will help you maximize these benefits, for your sake and your dog's. *The Purest Bond* is a celebration of this amazing connection, and we hope that it will open your eyes even wider to the transformative power of caring for a creature that is both adorable and adoring. Your dog(s) will benefit, too, because you will become that much more invested in the relationships, even if you hadn't thought it was possible. We hope this book will help you revel in the joy your dog brings to your life and bask in that mutual adoration, or perhaps convince those who are on the fence about getting a dog that it's high time they bring a canine creature into their lives. There's really nothing sweeter or richer than the profound connection behind this reciprocal lovefest. Let the celebration begin!

Part One

CREATING CONNECTIONS

CHAPTER ONE

The Birth of a Bond

Why do we take in new dogs? Because their joy for living renews our own.

—Michael Gerson, a former columnist for the *Washington Post*

Choosing a dog is a bit like speed-dating or an arranged marriage. Even when you know what qualities you're looking for in a pup— perhaps friendliness, playfulness, affection, loyalty, intelligence, a certain energy level, and the like—it's hard to gauge all this when you first meet a dog. And it may or may not be love at first sight. As with human relationships, there's often an element of chemistry at play in the dynamic between you. You may feel an instant connection or have a hunch that you'll hit it off—or not. Or you may end up simply taking a leap of faith that you will eventually forge the bond you want to have with a particular dog. And sometimes you don't even have the chance to meet the dog ahead of time, in which case it's a total crapshoot.

When Stacey's family was looking to adopt a new dog in September 2020, a five-year-old shepherd/chocolate-lab mix named Sadie caught her eye on the website of a dog rescue group that had been highly recommended by a friend. After applying and getting vetted by the group, she drove down with her family to a horse farm in Virginia where one of the rescue organization's foster mother's lived. After they parked, several dogs came to greet them, including Sadie. The five humans immediately started petting and playing with all the dogs as their foster mom told them where they were from, how old they were, and described their personalities. Right away, Stacey was smitten with Sadie, whose warm, intelligent eyes and gorgeous smile lit up the world. Meanwhile, her sons and husband were trying to get her attention, saying, *How about Mocha? Or Champion? Or why don't we get two?*

As the primary dog-parent in the family, it was tacitly acknowledged that the decision was ultimately up to Stacey. She wanted one dog, and after spending an hour playing with all the dogs, she was leaning toward Sadie. While the foster mom got the paperwork together, Stacey went to the car to get a bag of dog treats to give her as a thank-you and inadvertently left one of the back doors open. Before anyone realized it, Sadie had jumped in the back seat, lain down, and turned to look at Stacey as if to say, *Can we go now?!* That's when Stacey realized they had chosen each other. It has proved to be a stellar match.

Alana, twenty-two, a recent college graduate living in Indianapolis, had a similar experience. When she and her family went to adopt a dog from a litter of mini goldendoodles in 2020, she initially had her eye on a particular dog. But then another pup walked over and sat in her lap and "it felt like the storm that had been floating around me calmed down," says Alana who had recently been diagnosed with post-traumatic stress disorder, generalized anxiety, and depression. "I instantly knew she was the one I had to take home." She named the pup Queso and the two have been inseparable ever since. "She listens and loves without judgment and gives me a reason to take care of myself," says Alana. "I only hope to be as good of a friend to her as she is to me."

Sadly, not all dog adoptions are happily-ever-after stories. Before Jen and her husband, Ingo, started working with dogs who had special medical needs, they would foster any golden retrievers who came in through GRREAT,* the golden retriever rescue group they work with in the Washington, D.C., area. They took in lots of dogs who were between nine months and two years old. These were young, healthy dogs that had often been bought as presents, usually for kids. While there's nothing cuter than an eight-week-old golden retriever puppy, they very quickly grow into big, rambunctious dogs and they need a lot of exercise and training. Eventually, that dog's size and energy can overwhelm a family, and many dogs came into a rescue group after the home situation became unmanageable. When Jen and Ingo would pick up the dogs from their surrendered homes, it was easy to see how the dog was making life difficult in the family. These dogs would bark, chew things, knock the kids over, and cause all forms of chaos. In some cases, these families had resorted to keeping the dog crated most of the time to prevent destruction, but the exuberant dog would run wild as soon as it was free.

Every time they took in one of these dogs, they saw a rapid transformation. After a month of daily runs and walks, playing fetch in the yard, playing with the other dogs, and going through basic training for commands like "sit" and "come," the dogs were calm, happy, well-adjusted creatures. It turned out that they were never the problem. It was when people couldn't dedicate the necessary time and attention to training that the poor dogs seemed to get out of control.

---

*For more information about GRREAT (Golden Retriever Rescue, Education, and Training), visit http://grreat.org.

While dogs are almost always happier and better behaved with structure and training, some have an indomitable independent streak. Jen and Ingo's dog Voodoo had epilepsy, and he was the happiest, goofiest, most stubborn dude. He would eat *anything* left on the floor or table below human shoulder height. They even had to raise their toilet-paper holders up the wall because he kept eating the TP rolls. He loved to take walks but would only go halfway down the block before dramatically lying down and refusing to go farther. Jen can't count the number of times she had to call Ingo to bring the car and load Voodoo up because he just wanted a ride home. Even after weeks of training, all Voodoo managed to do was to walk—one time—through a short agility tunnel after receiving a strong push on the butt. After that, he had absolutely no use for anything else the trainer tried to teach him, and Jen and Ingo adored him for it. Sometimes, you fall in love with the dog you have and not the dog you hope he might become.

Great (But Realistic) Expectations

Once you bring a new dog home, there's a process of getting to know each other that involves starting off on the right foot (or paw) and integrating a dog into the family by making them feel comfortable and loved. This isn't something you want to leave to chance because the bond that develops between you depends on your creating a warm, secure, loving environment for your dog. You want to set up your new pet to thrive and grow to trust you, adjust to its new home smoothly, and share with you its boundless love and affection. The adjustment period varies from one dog and family to another, but it's generally relatively short-lived.

In the meantime, it's essential to be realistic about what's involved in the early days after adopting a dog. You're going to need to exercise patience, compassion, tolerance, flexibility, and fortitude when integrating a new dog into your home. If there's one thing new dog-owners can count on, it's that regardless of the dog's age, history, or medical or behavioral issues, that pup is going to disrupt life for a while. The sooner you accept that, the better off you and your pup will be.

Valerie and her husband, Andrew, had lived happily together for ten years without pets before they began discussing the possibility of getting a dog. They spent a year weighing the pros and cons as well as what type of dog might suit their lifestyle (given that they love boating). Eventually they adopted a nine-week-old, tan-and-white terrier with floppy ears that they named Skipper—and after bringing her home, Valerie, an editor in Washington, D.C., was utterly bewildered by their early days together. "The first couple of months I felt more like an ambassador for planet Earth, assigned to wrangle a chaotic extraterrestrial, than anything like a familial bond," she says. "She needed so much guidance and supervision—it was exhausting!"

The living room rug was soon relegated to the basement for its own protection. "Howls, whines, and whimpers from the living room accompanied every meal we ate in the dining room," Valerie recalls. "We started to dread the hour before sunset—Skipper's witching hour—when she would run and bark and bite seemingly nonstop." During those early months, Valerie often sent frantic messages to family members, saying, "We are really overwhelmed right now—what do we do?!" No one's advice really helped, but gradually Valerie and Andrew found their way through this chaotic period and began to build a connection with Skipper. "There was no quick fix or simple solution—it just came down to patience, consistency, and repetition," Valerie says. With the benefit of their love, perseverance, and tutelage, Skipper gradually grew into a confident, friendly, well-adjusted pup (though she hates boating).

While puppies are fresh-eyed and ready to be shown how kind and beautiful the world can be, they will inevitably destroy anything they can with glee—including, at times, their owners' sanity—partly because they have unbridled energy and partly because they just don't know any better. Adult rescue dogs may know better, but they won't be foolproof new arrivals, either. Even well-trained, housebroken dogs are likely to have a few accidents, gastrointestinal troubles, and bouts of misbehavior like chewing or digging, because of the anxiety that comes with the transition to a new family and environment. As happy as the outcome may eventually turn out to be, adjusting to a new home can be stressful for them. But scientific evidence shows that even small acts of kindness (such as bouts of petting or being spoken to kindly) and brief positive interactions (such as playing or walking) can reduce dogs' stress levels and quickly build the bond between new pet parents and adult rescue dogs.

So it's important to commit to making this adjustment period your primary project for a while, in order to make the transition as smooth, calm, and constructive as possible, to lay the foundation for a symbiotic relationship between you. It usually takes two to three weeks for a dog to begin to settle into a new place; this is true of puppies and older dogs from breeders as well as rescue dogs from shelters or foster homes.

To help your dog become a well-adjusted member of the household, it's important to set boundaries and limits from day one—by deciding where the dog is (and isn't) allowed to hang out in your home, where they will eat and sleep, and whether or not they are allowed on furniture. If you're going to use a baby gate to keep a dog in the kitchen or another space, make sure the gates are up and secure before the dog comes home. Give the dog treats, toys, and anything else that will make their special area feel comfortable and rewarding.

When Jen and Ingo take in new dogs, they often do very long walks to get them tired before that first night in the house. It's similar to the toddler-management credo of *Take them out and wear them out*. If they're tired, they're more likely to sleep through the night (or at least most of it). If they're still anxious after the exercise, Jen and Ingo are big fans of better living through chemistry. Their vets have always been willing to prescribe anti-anxiety medications that can help take the edge off and help the dogs sleep. You can also try using the Thunder-Shirt (which is like swaddling an infant), ThunderSpray (an over-the-counter pheromone/aromatherapy preparation that can help a dog relax), or Rescue Remedy Pet (a homeopathic formula). Try to make the passage to sleep gentle and quiet, while soothing the pup as much as you can until they settle down.

And sometimes it just takes time. Jen and Ingo's dog Remi, who was five when he came to them, had lived on a chain in someone's yard for his entire life. He had a bald rectangle between his shoulder blades from where the chain had rubbed away all his fur. When he went blind from unmanaged diabetes, his owners asked for him to be put down, but the vet turned him over to a rescue group instead. He came to the Golden Ratio squad with a laundry list of tick-borne diseases; diabetes; thyroid disease; angry, damaged skin; and a bad attitude. He made big strides in his first few months, but it took almost a year to sort out all of his medical issues and get him the training he needed to become a sweet, snuggly boy who loves to play.

Getting to Know Each Other

When you're bringing any new dog into your home, it's important to consider the situation from their point of view. That pooch has been ripped from the life it knew and is suddenly in a completely unfamiliar place with people they don't know, with no established routine and almost nothing recognizable to rely on. Being in an unfamiliar environment can feel scary and threatening because the poor dog has no idea of what to expect or whom to trust. Your duty to that dog is to reduce its anxiety and do as much as you can to ease its jangled nerves as it settles in. For some dogs, it will be a fast and easy transition, and before you know it, they will seem like they have always been in your home. Others may take longer to feel comfortable and warm up to you. During this adjustment period, you'll need to show compassion for your new canine and give them the space they need.

Shortly after Amy, an ER nurse in Minnesota, split from her wife, she began volunteering with a local dog rescue organization, where she found comfort among canines. When a request for a foster family came through, she couldn't resist saying *yes* to a malnourished golden retriever named Annie, who had sad eyes and six puppies. After the pups were weaned, Amy brought Annie home, where they bonded immediately. Annie forced Amy to get off the couch or out of bed and go for a walk, hike, or run, and she'd cuddle with Amy at night, sometimes even sharing her pillow. Three months after she officially adopted Annie, Amy's divorce was finalized, and she realized she'd found love again—with a furry, four-pawed girlfriend. The level of trust, adoration, and unbridled affection between them was incredibly healing for both of them. "I don't know if angels exist," Amy says, "but if they do, I am pretty sure at least one looks like a golden retriever."

Different dogs have different needs. Some will want lots of attention, while others will want their own space. Some will need a lot of exercise, and others will need a lot of sleep.* Some will want to play with you and your existing dogs, and others will want to be left alone. Nothing they want in these situations is wrong. It's all vital information, and your job is to pay attention, watch closely, learn what the dog wants, and give it to them. The more peaceful your home is for your new dog, the more quickly they will relax, make themselves at home (in a good way), and start to bond with you. Jen and Ingo have found that with their rescue dogs, it typically takes two to three weeks for them to lose that initial anxiety and about six months before they really bond with the whole squad. It doesn't *always* take that long; in some instances, it's much quicker. They have adopted or fostered some dogs that from the day they first arrived acted like they'd lived with them their entire lives! But most dogs do need time to find their place in the home.

At the beginning of 2019, the Golden Ratio had five members, all girls: Hopper, Venkman, Maggie, Jasmine, and Queso. In March of that year, a new foster came along: Riley. He was the first boy to join the squad, and from the moment he walked into the yard, Jen fell in love with him. Unlike most dogs they rescued, Riley had been loved

---

*In general, "dogs need a lot more sleep than humans do—14 hours a day," says Clive Wynne, Ph.D., author of *Dog Is Love: Why and How Your Dog Loves You.*

and cared for. When his owner had died suddenly and no family members wanted to take him in, he made his way to Jen and Ingo through GRREAT, the rescue group they work with. Riley was seven years old, had luxuriously wavy ears, soft brown eyes, and a sugar face. He smiled so much, but when he was annoyed, he would fix his face into an expression with V-shaped "angry eyebrows" until he got what he wanted.

On his first day with the squad, he dove onto the couch to snuggle up with Jen, and after that they were inseparable. Jen started calling him "my boyfren," and he would stare into her eyes as she stroked his head. Ingo is a great guy, but Jen had also harbored a little jealousy that *every dog liked him best*. Even Hopper and Venkman, whom she had raised on her own as puppies, liked Ingo best. But not Riley. He was the first dog who was more interested in Jen than in anything else—sometimes even more than snacks that were being eaten on the couch. It was a bond that formed quickly and easily, like they were two lost puzzle pieces that finally made their way together and found a perfect fit.

When Jen and Ingo take in new fosters, the dogs usually spend the first few nights in a crate. This prevents potential problems, like the new pup getting up and looking for a drink of water during the night and accidentally stepping on one of the other dogs, startling everyone, and it helps prevent accidents or nervous chewing. As the new dogs settle in, Jen and Ingo decide when to give them more space. Some dogs are out of the crate and sleeping in Jen and Ingo's bed on the second night. Others have spent a couple of months sleeping in a crate or in a separate room because they still had some tension with their other dogs.

At first, it's vital to give your pup exactly what they ask for in terms of personal space. Rescue dogs, in particular, may have needs that can range from clinging to their owner and wanting to be at their side all the time (aka Velcro dogs) to retreating to another room and hiding under a table or taking refuge in their crate. Make sure that every member of the family, especially kids, is on the same page about learning what the dog needs and wants and honoring those wishes. This may disappoint kids who expect a new dog to be a certain way or who want to play with a pup who needs space. But it's a good way for kids to learn about consent and empathy—and it's crucial for helping a dog adapt to a new home and new people.

Jen's rescue Queso is a good example. Until her arrival, all the dogs Jen had fostered had immediately blended in. About a year after taking in Maggie and Jasmine and becoming a squad of four, the D.C.-area golden retriever rescue group Jen works with called and asked if she could take in a thirteen-year-old whose owners had decided they didn't want her anymore. Jen asked Ingo what he thought, and he replied, "Sure! What's the difference between four and five?!" Queso had lived her life neglected in a backyard, and she hid in dark corners for weeks after she arrived.

For the first few days, Jen and Ingo couldn't even get her to come out from under the dining room table. Forcing interaction would have done nothing except terrify her more, so they would pet her and give her gentle encouragement while also giving her a lot of space. Eventually, after a few months of settling in, Queso came out of her shell and would play-fight with Venkman, who was just three at the time, as though she had become a puppy again. During the entire time she was part of the Golden Ratio squad, she really seemed to age in reverse. Giving her the space she needed when she arrived was critical to that happy life.

Teaching Kids About Dogs

Whether it's a puppy or a rescue dog, bringing a new pooch into the family is exciting for everyone and often especially for kids. But it's important to help kids temper their exuberance and let the pup acclimate to its new home at its own pace. You might give them messages about not crowding the dog or forcing the pup to interact if it clearly wants to be alone. Similarly, it's smart to tell your kids to leave the dog alone when the dog is eating or sleeping. It's really important for a new dog to learn to like and trust children and not feel harassed or bothered by them. Early on, try not to leave a child and the dog together unsupervised. Err on the side of caution on this matter, and use the dog's crate when you need to.

After all, just as a new dog needs to be trained to behave well in the family, kids need to be taught to behave well around the dog. Learning to respect and honor a pup's body and boundaries is a key part of this. To that end, you'll want to show your children how to pet and stroke the dog in a way that feels gentle and not threatening: Initially, it's wise to encourage kids to let the new pup sniff their hand before petting, then to pet the dog under the chin and neck or on the back, rather than on the top of the head. Make it clear that a dog's tail and ears should never be pulled, and discourage them from hugging the new dog: While kids may perceive hugging the pup as affectionate, the dog may view it as an aggressive or dominant action. Depending on the dog's temperament, they may snap at or bite the child, try to escape from the hold, or display submissive behavior such as urinating on the spot.

Eventually, as the dog relaxes into the new home and bonds with individual family members, it may grow to appreciate hugs and cuddles. As a dog warms up and begins to feel safe and secure, it may start to show greater flexibility in being close to others or more willingness to play. But it's important to let the dog take the lead on this. One of the best lessons you can give your kids is to teach them to respect the dog and not treat it like a stuffed animal or toy. Teach them how to read a dog's body language (see "Understanding Canine Cues") and to behave calmly and gently with the pup. If you'll be working with a dog trainer, depending on the age and maturity of your school-age kids, you may want to involve them in the training process.

A common guideline for rescue dogs settling into a new household is the rule of 3's. For the first three days, the dog will likely be overwhelmed. They may want to hide or they may be extra needy; during this time, the pup may have accidents in the house or startle easily.

This is not necessarily a reflection of your dog's real personality, so temper your reaction and show them that you are someone they can trust and feel safe around. After three weeks, your dog will start to feel more comfortable and settle in; that's when their real personality will emerge, but you may also see behavioral issues, like begging, counter surfing, barking, or trying to bolt out the front door, that were re-pressed during the early days—this is a great time to work on training, which will build your bond. After three months, you should be well on your way to forging a connection.

As you integrate a new dog into your family, keep in mind that the notion of a pack mentality has become a bit archaic. "Wolves form packs—dogs don't," says Clive Wynne, PhD, a professor of psychology and founder of the Canine Science Collaboratory at Arizona State University. "Dogs have a fluid, easy-come, easy-go social structure." And because research has shown that wolf theories regarding pack mentality don't apply to bringing a dog into your home, people should *not* adopt a dominant "alpha" role in their relationship with their dog. It can lead to stress, especially in sensitive dogs, and it does not help build social harmony in the household. Instead, modern training techniques focus on positive reinforcement training, which rewards dogs for good behavior, and relationship-based training, which focuses on building a bond of trust between human and dog. This way you will learn how to ask your dog to do something, and they will be happy to go along with it. After three months, your dog should feel like part of the family; you will see their full personality, they should feel comfortable in their routine, and the bond between you should be growing and deepening.

Joining the Squad

If you already have dogs in your home, it's important to introduce the newcomer properly, as Jen has learned through experience. Just as the U.S. was going into lockdown at the start of COVID in 2020, she and Ingo took in two foster dogs just a week apart. Their dogs Jasmine and

Queso had just died, a week apart. When the rescue group told Jen, "We have a crazy young boy who needs a new foster," she jumped at the chance to take in a healthy dog. Thus arrived Guacamole, a wild, three(ish)-year-old with minimal socialization and no manners. He had been dropped at a shelter and came to the house full of insecurities and uncontrolled emotions. A week later, they took in a dog they named Chief Brody, a nine-year-old who had been terribly neglected. He had bad allergies and was kept in a cone for years with untreated skin infections, which made him smell bad. His previous family had kept him locked away, overfed and under-loved, until they finally got tired of dealing with him and surrendered him to a rescue group.

Ingo drove Chief Brody from Maryland to Florida, arriving after midnight. When they came inside the house, all the other dogs woke up. They were overexcited that Ingo was home and surprised and unsure of the new dog who had just walked in. Everyone was barking, jumping around, and confused. Guacamole, still unsure of his place in the new house, started growling and trying to hump Brody. Brody was profoundly confused and scared, unsure if he should hide or if there was anyone he could trust. To calm the escalating tensions, Jen and Ingo ended up having to lock the dogs in different rooms, with Ingo and Brody sleeping in the guest room to stay isolated from the rest of the squad. Lesson learned. It was the last time Ingo arrived home with a dog in the middle of the night, making proper introductions impossible. (Guac has since matured into a distinguished gentleman with very good manners, and Chief Brody's allergies have entirely resolved with a series of injections and the right food.)

Here is Jen and Ingo's tried-and-true method for safely bringing a new dog into the home: If you have a yard, let the new dog explore the space on its own for as long as it likes—so it has a chance to relax and get the lay of the land. If your yard is fenced, walk the new dog on the leash in the yard, then let it wander freely so it can check out the scene and sniff to its heart's content. If you don't have a yard, find a nice, open space (a parking lot or green area will do), which will prevent a dog from feeling cornered or trapped.

Next, it's time to introduce the resident dogs. Choose a time when you're not rushed or stressed, so you can set the tone for everyone involved to be as calm and collected as possible. If you have multiple pooches, start with one and repeat this process, adding one dog to the group at a time. Put the new dog and your other dog on their own leashes and then let them slowly approach and sniff each other while holding the leashes; if either one gets their hackles up or tries to back away, you can move them away from each other; the goal is to make this as stress-free an introduction as possible. If one dog wants out of the situation, cater to its wishes and try again later. Eventually, they will be interested in sniffing each other. This may take time, and that's okay. Remember, this is worth getting right. Then let them walk around with both dogs still on their respective leashes. (If you don't have a yard, try a short walk up and down the block together.) If things are still going well and you have a fenced space, let the new dog off leash and then let your other dog off leash. Be sure to keep an eye on them so you can pull your older dog back if it's crowding the new dog.

This meet-and-greet situation can go many different ways. Jen and Ingo have had some dogs who meet and within thirty seconds are playing and chasing each other around the backyard as if they were old friends. They've had others who just want to hide because they get very stressed out when the resident dogs approach. Jen and Ingo give those new dogs a private room with a baby gate so they can see and smell the other dogs through it, but they let them take as many days as they need to indicate that they're comfortable coming out and joining the squad. While it can be tempting to force the dogs together, hoping they will just sort things out and become best pals, don't. It's really important to minimize anxiety for everyone—the four-pawed creatures as well as the two-footed ones—so be prepared that some dogs may require more time and space as you embark on the process of merging a new dog into your home.

Keep in mind that sometimes playful battles can look a lot like fighting and sometimes they can cross over into something a bit more aggressive. If one dog is trying to disengage, but the other dog isn't letting them, it's important to interrupt and let the scared dog escape, even if they choose to jump right back in. For dogs, feeling overwhelmed or scared can lead to aggression. As someone dealing with this situation, you might feel scared and worried about what's going to happen, and you may feel like you need to lash out with anger to protect yourself. But if you see one dog getting amped up with their hackles raised, or they're chomping too hard on their companion, you'll want to do something to bring their level of stimulation down rather than scaring them. Sometimes, just momentarily interrupting their play will work. Then, wait for the dogs to shake, as if they are shaking off water when they're wet—dogs use this movement to shake off stress, and it's a good sign to look for when they are play-fighting. Stepping in to interrupt the encounter, then letting them shake off the excitement, will often bring them back to a comfortable level of enthusiasm.

You can also introduce toys as calming or transitional objects. Jen and Ingo's dog Guacamole sometimes has trouble managing his emotions. When he came to them as a foster, Jen gave him an Ikea Blåhaj stuffed shark that he carried everywhere for a week—and even kept *in his mouth* when he was sleeping. He still sleeps with a stuffed toy at night and when he gets overexcited in play (or any other time, like when guests come over), handing him a stuffed toy quickly brings his stimulation level down by about 50 percent. If your dog can self-soothe by carrying a toy or ball around, by chewing a Kong or bone in their crate, or by sleeping on the bed or towel they've taken a liking to, give them those opportunities. The more they learn that your home is a peaceful, safe environment, the more open they will be to forming a bond with you.

In the meantime, it's crucial to establish routines early on—and to keep them consistent. Having a routine helps dogs with learning, housebreaking, and bonding, and enhances your dog's emotional well-being. Research has found that when dogs arrive at a shelter, they have elevated levels of cortisol (a stress hormone), which isn't surprising. However, after a routine is established during their first few days there, their cortisol levels decrease; this suggests that the disruption in routine was partly responsible for their stress. This echoes many other studies in animals that show a change in routine increases stress hormones.

Routines are beneficial for people, too. Peter and his wife rescued their first Bouvier, named Olive, when she was four months old. A letter carrier in Canada, Peter found a kindred spirit in Olive, who was reserved by nature. Not only were they in sync emotionally but Olive helped relieve Peter's anxiety and enjoyed meditating with him. "No matter where Olive was in the house, when the soft music started to play, she would come running to join in," recalls Peter. This was a habit for the two of them until Olive died just after her tenth birthday. Now the couple have Hank, also a Bouvier, who is two years old. "Hank is *all* about his routine—walks, meals, treats, playtime, potty breaks, bedtime," says Peter. "His daily routine has enabled us to maintain a sense of normalcy in these unprecedented times. Hank gives us purpose every single day."

While some people think schedules don't matter because dogs can't really tell time, scientific research has shown this is not the case. The medial entorhinal cortex (MEC) is an area of the brain that's responsible for navigation and the perception of time. It's been known that animals have this area in their brains, but that didn't necessarily mean they could tell time (they might have used it primarily for navigation). However, a study published in a 2018 issue of the journal *Nature Neuroscience* revealed that animals have a set of neurons in the MEC that are activated when an animal is waiting. In the study, researchers had mice run on a treadmill in a virtual-reality environment that led down a hall to a door; after six seconds, the door would open and the mouse could continue down the hallway to receive its reward. This was the routine, and after six weeks of training, the mice learned to stop for the six-second waiting period—because they could tell how much time had passed—before they could collect the reward.

Here's where things get interesting. When the mice later had the opportunity to grab the reward sooner, they continued to wait six seconds, and the MEC in their brains was activated while they waited. Simply put, they knew what was expected of them and they honored it, based on their perception of time. According to study coauthor Daniel Dombeck, PhD, an associate professor of neurobiology at Northwestern University, these findings reflect that dogs know when their routine is disrupted: "This is one of the most convincing experiments to show that animals really do have an explicit representation of time in their brains when they are challenged to measure a time interval."

Other research with dogs has shown that they can tell the difference in time intervals from seconds to minutes. Basically, dogs have the cognitive capacity to monitor time; they can tell how much time has passed, and they can learn patterns in their day. When their routine is disrupted, their stress levels go up, both psychologically and physically.

Given that dogs thrive on steadiness, it's important to make an effort to feed your dog breakfast, snacks, and dinner around the same times every day. Similarly, go on walks, have playtime and snuggle time, and take potty breaks at regular times, during the day and evening. This kind of consistency will reduce your dog's stress level and provide a sense of predictability and stability that will help your pup feel secure. And if you're the person providing this routine, your dog will learn that you are someone to trust and someone who makes them feel better.

Anyone who has had a dog with a well-established routine knows how much it means to them. We have all awakened, on a day we planned to sleep in, to a nose on the edge of the bed, letting us know it's time to get up. We've seen our dogs stand next to their bowl at mealtime waiting for it to be filled. We've seen them go to the door and give us a look that says, *No matter what the weather is, it's time to suit up and go for a walk!* Routine doesn't bore dogs. They're almost grateful for it because it gives them a structure to center their lives around. It makes them feel secure and confident, and it helps them connect with us through all of those activities.

Doing the Locomotion Together

Jen has found that walking properly on a leash is rarely a strong suit for puppies or new rescue dogs. The experience often results in frustration . . . and sometimes in injuries. She has sprained ankles when dogs pulled her off the sidewalk to lunge at other dogs. She has sprained fingers, developed tennis elbow, and aggravated a shoulder injury while trying to contain an exuberant young dog who used their full power to run at anything that caught their eye. Guacamole has caused so many problems that Jen sometimes jokes that he's trying to murder her: He has become startled by big trucks going by and bolted, yanking Jen to the ground, bloodying her knees, and he has wrapped the leash around her legs then run toward another dog more times than she can count. Other dogs have slipped out of their collars and re-quired dramatic chase-downs to get back. Many dogs have endangered their own lives as they wandered into a busy street because they had no concept of what a sidewalk is for.

The good news is that dogs can be trained to walk properly on a leash. Your dog may still pull, but within a range that is safe for them and for you. During walks, be patient with your new pooch. Finding a relatively quiet spot to walk, even if it's around the perimeter of a field, will help. Jen likes to use a body harness instead of a collar so the dog can't easily pull away or choke themselves if they do pull. To protect her arms and hands from a dog that might jerk her around, she also likes to use a waist leash, which has a loop that goes around the waist or hips and the leash clips onto that. This lets you use your full body weight to control the dog instead of just your arm.

On these initial walks, let your dog stop and sniff as much as they want to—it is mentally stimulating and helps tire out their brains, as well. Don't expect perfect behavior on a leash. The purpose of these early walks is to reduce anxiety and help your dog learn that you are a source of love, kindness, and support. Whenever you can, take a beat and check your own stress level because research shows that people can transmit stress through a leash while walking their dogs. If you want to have a calm and happy dog, you will need to learn to train your pup in a calm and happy way—that initial tone will become the foundation of your relationship. Making a dog feel fearful will ratchet up their stress level and ultimately backfire in terms of helping the dog adjust. New research has found, for example, that when dogs are trained using aversive stimuli (as in, punishment for incorrect behavior), they exhibit more stress-related behavior. They also show greater increases in saliva levels of the stress hormone cortisol after negative reinforcement training sessions than dogs who are coached with reward-based approaches, such as treats, verbal praise, or petting. When your pup is good and behaves well, praise them lavishly so that they will come to associate those training sessions or walks with positivity. (If you don't have experience with dog-training, you'll find specific recommendations for books, training videos, and socialization and obedience classes in the "Resources" section of the book's website.)

Learning to Speak Your Dog's Language

As a dog acclimates to your home, stress-related behaviors will start to fade. As you get to know each other, make an effort to read your dog's barks and body language and figure out what they want and need. For example, dogs that are submissive often "lower their posture and lick the mouths of individuals—dog or human—whose preeminence they recognize," according to Clive Wynne, PhD, of the Canine Science Collaboratory at Arizona State University. So if the thought of having a canine tongue on your mouth strikes you as icky—as it initially did for Stacey when she discovered that Sadie is an incorrigible mouth-kisser with people (but not other dogs)—it may help to remember that it's a sign of respect and admiration from a pup. Whether or not you choose to *let* your dog lick you on the mouth is up to you. But recognizing this as a signal that your dog views you as being in a position of authority is not only reassuring but also a reminder that you don't need to go to great lengths to establish your dominance.

Just as good communication is essential for healthy human relationships, the same is true of the human-canine connection. Building trust, respect, and understanding is essential to forging a healthy, joyful bond between you, and learning to communicate well with each other is a cornerstone of that foundation. The reality is, dog-owners often spend a considerable amount of time and energy training their canine companions to understand directions and commands. But humans don't always dedicate the same attention or effort to learning what their pooches are trying to tell *them*.* Interestingly, dogs' facial expressions aren't simply an expression of how they're feeling; they also may have a social communication function. To test this proposition, Juliane Kaminski and colleagues evaluated dogs' changes in facial expression in an experimental situation in which a person was either paying attention to them or turned away from them and either presented an arousing stimulus (food!) or not. They found that dogs produced significantly more facial movements when the person was paying attention to them than when she wasn't; the presence or absence of food had no effect on the dogs' behavior. The researchers' conclusion: Dogs' "facial expressions are not just inflexible and involuntary displays of emotional states, but rather potentially active attempts to communicate with others."

Dogs communicate their wants, needs, feelings, and perceptions in many different ways, including through posture, body language, facial expressions, and verbalizing, such as barks, whines, growls, sighs, and groans. It's generally a mistake to rely on any one signal to interpret how your dog is feeling; it's often the constellation of cues that conveys the message your dog is trying to give you. If you learn what your dog is trying to tell you and your dog knows that you "get it," you'll develop

---

*As American author Edward Hoagland noted: "In order to really enjoy a dog, one doesn't merely try to train him to be semi-human. The point of it is to open oneself to the possibility of becoming partly a dog."

a deeper bond, including greater trust and respect between you—and you'll have a lot more fun together.

Sometimes it's fairly easy to detect how a dog is feeling. Other times it's not. Some of it depends on the dog's personality. When they want to eat, go outside, be petted or played with, some dogs will paw at their owners or nudge them with their noses, while others will whine or bark. Jen's dogs make a habit of taking a big, sloppy drink and then resting their wet jowls on her laptop keyboard, which always gets them immediate attention. In other instances, the meaning behind communication signals may depend on the circumstances. When a dog wags its tail and barks, for example, that may be a sign of wanting to play or being excited—or it could be a sign of aggression or hostility. The truth is, people frequently misinterpret tail-wagging. All it really means is that the dog is emotionally aroused or ramped up, and the faster the wagging, the more emotionally aroused the dog is—in either direction.

A case in point: While walking her dog Inky, an Akita mix, Stacey used to encounter people who wanted their dogs to say *hello* on the sidewalk in their neighborhood, despite the fact that Inky was crouched low to the ground and essentially stalking the other dog. She'd explain that he wasn't friendly toward other dogs, especially when on a leash. The typical response was "But his tail is wagging!" Yes, she'd explain, but that's because he had fear-aggression and he wasn't sure if he wanted to play or fight. And she didn't want to risk finding out.

Interestingly, a study by Angelo Quaranta and colleagues in Italy found that the direction of a dog's tail-wagging may hold clues to how a dog is really feeling. In an experiment, thirty dogs were each placed in their own large, rectangular wooden box that was covered inside with black plastic so the dogs couldn't see outside the box (the box was illuminated inside so the dog wasn't in darkness). One by one, the dogs were brought to a testing box that had a rectangular opening on one of the shorter sides of the box, and a new stimulus (the dog's owner, an unfamiliar person, a dominant unfamiliar dog, or a cat) was introduced for sixty seconds with a ninety-second break in between each one.

During each encounter, the researchers evaluated the dog's wagging behavior. When dogs saw their owners (a positive event), they tended to wag more vigorously to the right side; by contrast, when they saw an unfamiliar dominant dog, their tails wagged more strongly to the left side (suggesting withdrawal tendencies). Interestingly, tail-wagging to the left is tied to activation of the right hemisphere of the brain, which specializes in the expression of intensive emotions.

In another study, Elena Gobbo and Manja Zupan Šemrov investigated physiological responses—namely, changes in facial and body surface temperature and salivary cortisol and serotonin concentrations—in dogs that had showed aggressive or non-aggressive behavior in everyday situations in the past. The aggressive group consisted of sixteen male German and Belgian shepherd police dogs, whereas the non-aggressive group was made up of fifteen male herding dogs that had been trained to behave calmly in new situations. During the ten-minute experiments, the dogs were exposed to potentially challenging situations—such as being approached by a tester and petted with an artificial hand, the sudden appearance of a cat on a sled, the sudden blasting of a horn, being approached quickly and surrounded by three testers, and the like—and their behavior was videotaped and later evaluated. The most interesting findings: It turned out that the aggressive dogs were more likely to engage in left-sided tail-wagging and to have a lower posture with their ears held back—as well as lower serotonin concentrations and increases in their facial temperature during these aggressive moments.

Dogs may bark when they're excited, frightened, irritated, surprised, or experiencing other strong feelings. The meaning can often be detected by the pitch of a dog's bark, how many times it barks consecutively, and how much time there is between barks. During playtime, for example, your dog is likely to release a more high-pitched bark than the one it uses to warn that there's a stranger outside the front door. Paying attention to patterns as your dog barks, including the type of bark that's made and changes in the dog's body language, will help you get better at interpreting these sound effects.

Besides learning how to read a dog's body language and other cues, it's important to consider the following questions: *What makes your dog happy?* (Is it being fed, going on walks, being talked to or pet, getting brushed, playing ball?) *What does your dog simply tolerate?* (Maybe it's having their teeth brushed or being bathed.) *And what activities does your dog try to avoid?* (When you try to give your pup medicine or kiss their face, does the dog turn away?) If you consciously look for your dog's likes and dislikes, you can make a point to give them as many of the desired experiences and as few of the unwanted ones as possible, thereby allowing both of you to thoroughly enjoy your time together. If your dog loves being in the car, for example, take them on errands whenever you can—it'll be a treat for both of you. But if they hate car rides, don't do this. Of course, there will be times when your pup needs a bath, has to go to the vet, or needs to have their teeth brushed, even if they don't like it; you'll want to find ways to make these situations as comfortable as possible for both of you. (Never underestimate the power of peanut butter to improve a challenging situation.)

Learning what stresses out your dog is an important step in fostering a sense of security and helping your pooch recognize you as someone they can rely on to protect them. The early weeks after bringing a dog home are not a good time to try all sorts of exciting new things; simply establishing a routine and getting to know each other is plenty of stimulation. Once your dog seems secure enough to meet new people or try new activities, start small. Invite a few people over, but don't introduce the dog to new people at a big party or café patio. Keep it mellow. Many dogs will be happy to meet a new friend, but some dogs may be scared. We have met many rescues who are afraid of men, for example, or afraid of people wearing a specific type of clothing (like a uniform). A slow, gradual introduction to the rest of the world will let you figure out what scares your pooch and give you the opportunity to immediately take them out of that situation; after that, you can work on helping them overcome that particular fear or learn to live with it.

Understanding Canine Cues

An aggressive or angry dog's posture is upright but may be slightly forward-leaning, with a stiff tail, hackles (the fur along their back) standing up, ears forward and erect, and possibly bared teeth.

An alert dog has a tail that's slightly raised, their ears are forward to pick up sound, and their mouth may be closed or slightly open.

A dog that's curious will perk up their ears, hold their head up with mouth closed, and often cock their head to one side to look at what they're interested in.

A fearful or nervous dog will often pull their ears back or flat against their head. The tail is likely to be low or tucked between their legs, and they may lie down, yawn, or shake as though they're wet, to release tension.

A happy, content dog has a relaxed, casual posture, with their head held high, eyes soft, ears up, and mouth open, often with the tongue hanging out loosely.

A playful dog will have their ears perked up and will look directly at you, usually with an open mouth and tail-wagging. They may do a "play bow" where they place their chest on the ground and their rump in the air.

Also, don't force your expectations about fun places or activities on your dog. It doesn't always work. When Jen spent a winter in Miami near a dog park, she thought it would be great to take her two young dogs (Hopper and Venkman) to play there. They hated it because there were big dogs, including many unneutered males, who humped any dog they could get near and whose owners did nothing to stop it. For a week, the people in the small dogs area invited her goldens to come and play. These dogs were well behaved and Jen's dogs liked this area better. But the overall stress of the dog park made it so that even when she and the pups just walked by, her dogs would try to pull her in the other direction.

Neither Jen nor Stacey has ever had a dog that enjoyed accompanying them to a restaurant for outdoor dining, either—the experience was overstimulating and stressful for the pups. Obviously, plenty of dogs *do* love the dog park and eating with their humans on a patio, but just because it seems fun to you does not mean your dog will agree. You'll have to test the proposition and pay attention to your pup's reaction. Believe your dog when they make it clear that they don't like something; don't force them into it just because you want a dog who will sit with you while you have coffee at a sidewalk café. Your bond depends on you learning and respecting your dog's boundaries; it's not just about having your dog follow *your* rules and respect the boundaries *you* establish. It needs to be reciprocal. You want your dog to trust you, and in order to do that, they have to know that you're acting in their best interest.

By taking these steps to help your dog acclimate to your home and develop routines and rituals that you both enjoy, you and your furry friend will quickly form a meaningful attachment. You'll find a sense of comfort and joy in each other's presence. You'll grow to love and trust each other. And before you know it, you'll both come to feel that the other creature really is *the best thing ever!* As Michael Gerson once wrote, "what other object can you bring into your home that makes you smile every time you see it? [My dog] Jack is a living, yipping, randomly peeing antidepressant."

CHAPTER TWO

Everyone's Best Friend

Finding Companionship and Unconditional Love

As any dog-owner will tell you, having a canine companion is a profoundly life-enriching experience. This isn't surprising, given that they share our homes and yards, our cars and schedules, and sometimes our food, beds, and vacations. Beyond affecting our plans and environments, our dogs change the quality of our lives. Caring for a furry creature who depends on you and showers you with unbridled affection infuses life with a sense of playfulness, comfort, and joy that's meaningful. And on a daily basis, they continue to steal our hearts. Many devoted dog-owners probably accept this kind of love connection at face value without questioning what's really at the heart of this incredibly gratifying relationship. That's a perfectly acceptable way to enjoy having a pooch in the family, but the science and experiences behind why a dog may be their owner's best pal is enthralling.

Victoria has discovered this with her golden retriever Teddy, whom she describes as her "soulmate." Teddy helped her through high school and college and continues to do so as she builds an independent life in her twenties. "She can read my emotions better than anyone else," says Victoria, a color scientist in South Carolina. "In a world of instability, she has become my constant—I know she's always there and I don't care what the day brings as long as I get to see her at the end of it."

Amber, a writer who is single in New York, can relate to these feelings, thanks to her black Lab. "My dog Hook taught me what love is," she says. "Of course I love my family and I have some close friendships, but I never felt what it was like to love someone so much that it makes your heart physically ache." As Amber has been working from home since the pandemic, she says that she and Hook have become even closer. "In this time that has been so horrible, seeing him be so happy to have someone around all the time has been a bit of a silver lining," she says. "I love how he follows me from room to room and how he sleeps in my bed every night. I don't know if I'm ever going to find another soul—dog or human—who I feel this connected to in my life."

Sometimes beloved dogs can even fill a void left by a neglectful or abusive family environment or a romantic relationship that turned sour. At their core, these are more than just subjective experiences. Research into the biological, psychological, and social aspects of this relationship have shed light on the profound love connection we share with our dogs. These findings provide us with a new language to describe our bond and a deeper understanding of why the time we share and our favorite activities deepen that relationship.

The Roots of Attachment

For decades, researchers have devised various techniques to describe, measure, and understand how people connect to each other. It turns out, when you apply their insights to our relationships with our dogs, this works because—on an emotional, psychological, and neurochemical basis—we connect with dogs similarly to the way we do to other humans. The science of connection illustrates how and why our relationships with our canine pals become some of our tightest bonds.

Originally designed to describe the bonds formed by (human) babies to their parents, attachment theory is a psychological construct that describes the bonds between people. Humans' first attachment bonds emerge with our parents when we are infants, and the shape and quality of that attachment influence our relationships for the rest of our lives. Specific patterns of behavior in and around relationships are often referred to as attachment style, which is a combination of how comfortable you are with emotional intimacy and connection (or how much you avoid it) and how anxious you feel in your relationships. The healthiest attachment style is known as "secure attachment," and it's characterized by low avoidance and low anxiety levels in the relationship. Other attachment styles have anxious, avoidant, fearful, or disorganized elements and are less healthy.

While people's attachment styles tend to remain consistent, it's possible to have a different attachment style in different situations. And we form specific attachment bonds with our dogs, too, just as they do with us, their humans. To paraphrase the Bowlby-Ainsworth Attachment Theory, which was developed in the 1950s, our attachment styles can influence how physically close we try to stay to someone we're connected to, how distressed we feel when we're separated from that person, how reliable and consistent the source of our attachment is, and whether the person serves as a safe haven in times of distress. As many dog-lovers can attest to, these patterns apply to the attachment bond that many people have with their dogs.

In the research setting, the concept of attachment has recently been applied to the relationships between people and their pets. In the case of dogs, this is for good reason, given the strength of the attachment or affectional bond between people and their pooches. Because early attachment bonds are an important factor in childhood development, researchers have looked specifically at the connection between kids and dogs—and found that children form strong attachment bonds with their dogs, sometimes stronger than the bonds they form with people. For example, a study by Wendie Bodsworth and G. J. Coleman compared the level of attachment kids had to the family dog in single-parent families and two-parent families and found that in early childhood the bonds are stronger in single-parent homes than in two-parent homes, basically because dogs can supplement the natural limits on the time and attention that are available from one parent.

The attachment is mutual because dogs form attachment bonds with their humans. In research led by Sabrina Karl, dogs were shown videos of their caregiver humans, other familiar people, and strangers, and activity in the dogs' brains was measured with functional magnetic resonance imaging (fMRI). When dogs saw their caregivers, areas of their brain were activated that, in people, are associated with emotion, attachment processing, and reward processing. Basically, when our dogs see us, their brains act like kids' brains do when they see their parents. While the research is relatively new, evidence is mounting to show that dogs form deep connections to their humans that look a lot like the connections we humans have with each other, down to the biological level.

One of the standard ways researchers observe attachment security in young children is with what's called the "Strange Situation" experiment, involving young children between nine and thirty months and their mothers. First, the children and their mothers are brought into a room with toys, and the mother sits in the chair while the child is allowed to explore the room. Then, a friendly stranger enters the room, talks to the mother then gets on the floor and interacts with the child; the mother says goodbye, leaves the room, and the child is left with the stranger. Then, the mother returns and the stranger leaves the playroom; eventually, the mother leaves again and the child is left alone for three minutes. Next, the stranger comes back and interacts with the child. Finally, the mother returns and the stranger leaves the room. Research has found that depending on how children are attached to their parents, they will behave differently in the presence of the parent or the stranger. In a study led by Chiara Mariti, researchers created a variation of this experiment and ran it with dogs: They found that dogs showed distress when their owners were gone, they would seek out attention and physical contact with their owners when they were present, and they were willing to explore and play when their human was present. This led researchers to conclude that dogs see their humans as a secure home base—a critical element of attachment theory.

In a tangentially related study, Lisa Horn and her colleagues explored dogs' willingness to manipulate an apparatus to get food and consume it, depending on whether the owner was absent, present but silent, or encouraging. It turned out that the more engaged the owner was with the dog, the longer the dog spent trying to solve the problem and get the prized food. These findings are similar to how children engage in problem-solving in the presence of their mothers, thus serving as evidence that attentive humans provide the "secure base" element of attachment bonds for dogs just like they do for children.

Back to the human side of the bond: In a study designed to measure the strength of people's attachment to their pet dogs, John Archer, PhD, and Jane Ireland, PhD, at the University of Central Lancashire in the UK, found that dog-owners have a high degree of closeness with their dogs; they have a desire to care for and protect their dog and value its companionship, and they view the dog as a source of emotional comfort and well-being that leads to positive changes in them (the people). Some of the richness behind this relationship has to do with the biology of bonding, while other factors relate to the psychological underpinnings of the relationship. It turns out, there's an invisible matrix of rich connections at play here. It's not just all fun and games and snuggling (though those activities do, of course, contribute).

On the physiological front, there's chemistry between you and your dog, just like there (hopefully!) is between you and your romantic partner. With our canine companions, though, a fundamental part of the bonding experience stems from the release of key hormones. You've probably heard that people get a surge of oxytocin (often called the "love hormone" or the "cuddle hormone") when they hug their partner or kids or breastfeed their babies. This same hormone comes into play in our relationships with our dogs. Human beings can get a surge of oxytocin from petting their dogs or simply gazing into their eyes. Heartwarmingly, researchers have found that our dogs experience it, too. When people cuddle, pet, or play with their dog or look into their eyes, oxytocin is released, causing both species to feel good and experience shared trust and affection. In the study, the pairs who spent the most time looking into each other's eyes experienced the biggest surges in oxytocin and so did their dogs, based on oxytocin concentrations measured in both the human and canine participants.

On a related note, the question of whether dogs are truly capable of love—or simply good at manipulating us for treats—has long been debated. And there isn't a surefire way to get a definitive answer since dogs can't speak. But there is some evidence to suggest that our dogs do indeed love us. The mutual release of oxytocin when we gaze into each other's eyes suggests the answer is *yes*. And there's more proof: In a study by Gregory S. Berns and colleagues, researchers exposed twelve awake, unrestrained dogs, who'd been trained to stay still in an fMRI machine, to five scents: the owner's scent, an unfamiliar person's scent, a familiar dog's scent, an unfamiliar dog's scent, and their own scent. In each instance, the scents activated the olfactory bulb, but only exposure to the owner's scent lit up the caudate nucleus, which helps coordinate the reward response, in the dogs' brains. Cynics might say this is because their owners feed them (thus providing a source of pleasure). But between these physiological responses and the deep, abiding affection most dogs have for their people, there's good reason to believe that dogs are capable of love. Clive Wynne, PhD, founder of the Canine Science Collaboratory at Arizona State University, was once dismissive of the idea that dogs can love their humans, but is no longer. As he wrote in *Dog Is Love*: "I can see no reason to be more skeptical toward our dogs than we are toward anyone else who appears to love us. If anyone loves you, your dog does."

After a positive interaction, you and your dog also experience an increase in feel-good chemicals such as beta-endorphin, prolactin, and dopamine—and humans experience a reduction in levels of the stress hormone cortisol. Besides having a calming, mood-boosting effect on a physiological level, these shared experiences foster trust and deepen affection between you. This is just one factor that sets the stage for the development of a mutual admiration society between you.*

On the Same Wavelength

Another factor that contributes to the depth of this bond relates to shared emotional experiences. It's not only the joy of playing fetch or splashing around in the ocean on a sunny day or sharing a bowl of popcorn and watching Netflix on the couch. It's also the absolute delight you both feel when you see each other again after a few days apart. It might be the shared accomplishment and excitement of training your dog to do a special trick or catch a Frisbee and having them ace it. These mutually enjoyed pleasures and successes help solidify the emotional ties between you.

As far as emotional connections go, there are subtle dynamics at work, as well. It's no secret that dogs can routinely perceive human emotions—being able to read and discriminate between their own-

---

*In case you were wondering, the notion of love languages—acts of service, gifts, words of affirmation, touch, and quality time—also apply to dogs, according to animal behaviorist Kyle Kittleson. For some dogs, touch is the primary love language, and when you pet, groom, or scratch your pup, licking you is often their way of returning that touch and affection.

ers' fear, excitement, and anger, for example—but you may not know that they can "catch" these feelings, too. Just as little kids look to their parents for cues about how to react to the world around them, dogs often look to their people for similar signs. When their owners project feelings of calm and comfort, dogs sense these emotions—and tend to view their environment as safe and secure. But the converse is true, as well, which means that *your* stress or anxiety could become your dog's stress and anxiety through the phenomenon of emotional contagion, which is a building block of empathy. A 2019 study by Ann-Sofie Sundman, PhD, and colleagues found that the long-term stress levels of Shetland sheepdogs and border collies, as measured by cortisol levels in their hair/fur, are in sync with their owners' stress levels. In particular, the presence of human personality traits of neuroticism, conscientiousness, and openness had a significant effect on the dogs' cortisol levels, for better or worse. Based on their findings, the researchers concluded that "dogs, to a great extent, mirror the stress level of their owners."

Between humans, the transmission of emotions happens in a matter of milliseconds, and it can be triggered by unconsciously mimicking another person's facial expressions or body language. Incremental muscle movements that are involved in this mimicry trigger the actual feeling in the brain when mirror neurons fire. These specialized brain cells, which are present in humans and dogs, react both when a particular action is performed (such as smiling or frowning) as well as when it is observed; in the latter instance, this firing conjures the emotion as if the observer were experiencing it naturally and organically. This "rapid mimicry"—an unconscious, congruent response that occurs in less than one second—also occurs in dogs when they interact or play with each other, engage in play bows, or have relaxed, open-mouth facial expressions—play patterns that are typical among dogs. A 2017 study by Elisabetta Palagi, PhD, and colleagues found that the stronger the social bond is between dogs, the higher the level of rapid mimicry there is—and that play sessions that are marked by rapid mimicry tend to last longer.

Emotional contagion also has been shown to occur between species, such as between dogs and humans. Numerous studies have shown that dogs can catch human yawns,* develop lower heart rate variability (a response to stress) or increased cortisol levels when they hear a baby crying, and they respond to the emotional valence of our voices. Dogs also have "affective empathy"—which is defined as the ability to share someone else's feelings—toward people who are important to them. Think about what an angry dog or person looks like: Often their facial muscles are tense, their jaws may be clenched, and their bodies are rigid. So if you're in the presence of an angry dog or you are enraged but your dog isn't, each of you may unconsciously mirror the other's facial expressions or body language and start to feel the same way. "All of empathy has some component of contagious emotions—in order to be able to understand what somebody is feeling, you have to be able to feel it," explains Julia Meyers-Manor, PhD, an associate professor of psychology at Ripon College in Ripon, Wisconsin. "In some ways, recognizing another [creature's] emotion is more complex cognitively speaking, whereas *feeling* what another animal feels is simpler. Because of our close connection with dogs, we have co-evolved to detect each other's [emotional] signals in ways that are different from other species."

What's more, sensory factors can influence emotional contagion between people and their canine companions. For one thing, dogs have a remarkable ability to read people's facial expressions and body postures. A 2018 study by Marcello Siniscalchi, PhD, and colleagues found that dogs respond to human faces that express six basic emotions—anger, fear, happiness, sadness, surprise, and disgust—with changes in

---

*In one particular study, twenty-nine dogs observed a human yawn or controlled mouth movements. When they saw the person yawning, twenty-one of the dogs yawned in response, whereas the controlled mouth movements didn't elicit a single yawn. Not one. The researchers concluded that this yawn contagion may reflect dogs' "capacity for a rudimentary form of empathy. Since yawning is known to modulate the levels of arousal, yawn contagion may help coordinate dog–human interaction and communication." Less is known about whether humans catch dogs' yawns, but we, the authors, frequently catch our dogs' yawns.

their gaze and heart rate that reflect an ability to distinguish between happy faces,* fearful faces, and angry faces. When it comes to sounds, research by Annika Huber and colleagues at the University of Vienna's Clever Dog Lab has found that when dogs hear expressions of distress (such as crying) or expressions of joy or excitement, they respond differently than they do to other vocalizations or non-human sounds. For example, when they are exposed to these emotional human sounds, dogs are more likely to look at or approach their owner than when they hear non-emotional sounds; also, signs of the dogs' arousal (such as lip licking, shaking, and immobility/freezing) increased much more when they heard sounds with a negative valence than those with a positive tone. In addition, dogs have keen olfactory senses and they are very sensitive to body odor, which often changes as people's emotions and moods change.

When they catch or share human emotions, often "dogs use composite signals, which includes information coming in from a cocktail of their senses, including sight, hearing, olfaction, and maybe through touch if someone is nervous," says Marc Bekoff, PhD, professor emeritus of ecology and evolutionary biology at the University of Colorado, Boulder, and author of *A Dog's World: Imagining the Lives of Dogs in a World Without Humans*. All of these abilities are clear signs of emotional and social intelligence in dogs. And taken together, these forms of sensory awareness provide dogs with essential information about how people around them are feeling and clues for how to respond in an empathic way.

Deep down, this ability to share our emotions may serve as a form of social adhesive, helping us forge a mutual sense of connection and understanding and develop strong, enduring bonds. It may be, as some

---

*In particular, looking at your smile has a profound effect on your dog. A study from the University of Helsinki found that dogs love seeing humans smile so much, especially when the dogs are under the influence of oxytocin, that they may ignore threatening cues such as a picture of an angry male stranger's face; they choose to focus on a person's smiling face instead. In other words, the surge of positivity they get from paying attention to a smiling face essentially overrides their protective or survival instincts.

researchers have suggested, that "humans and dogs have a common attachment style," which may explain how and why dogs have adapted so well to being a part of human society. This may explain how and why the roots of this canine-human bond are so deep and enduring.

For many years, it was assumed that it was the domestication of dogs that led to the possibility of emotional contagion as a survival mechanism. More recently, that thinking has shifted. A 2019 study found that the degree of emotional contagion that occurs between humans and their canine companions increases along with the duration of the relationship and the amount of time spent sharing the same environment.

Reciprocal Gifts

Whether you buy and raise a puppy or adopt an older dog, you're really growing up (or older) together and coming to each other's emotional rescue in a sense. The benefits of this bond are in no way one-sided. What dogs want throughout their lives is pretty simple—food, water, exercise, plenty of play, attention, affection, and of course to be with their people. When we give them these things, they're happy, and we feel gratified by their satisfaction. During the pandemic, dogs benefited from more time hanging out, playing, and walking with their family members, as well as from the psychological perks from this connection. What's more, "for dogs, humans seem to represent a social partner that . . . can be a source of emotional fulfilment and attachment," according to researchers at two Australian universities. The attachment bond that dogs develop with people "allows them to interact securely with their environment in the presence of the owner and show less distress in response to threatening events."

On the human side of the equation, our dogs provide us with a highly reliable relationship in our lives, one that can be more authentic, dependable, and consistent than some people's relationships with other humans. Even when our pooches let us down with bad behavior, we forgive them fairly easily because we know that their misdeeds aren't intentional, nor are they personal attacks on us. The reason your pup ate the fresh bread off the table or shredded the newspaper probably had more to do with a momentary lapse in impulse control or a bout of high anxiety. It really did have more to do with your dog than you (and you know that). Fortunately, it doesn't take much—maybe a chagrined look and an extra bout of kisses and wags—for them to atone for their misbehavior and get back into our good graces.

More often than not, with our dogs we get all the good stuff that we derive from positive relationships with people, but without the risks of rejection or emotional abandonment. After all, dogs aren't flighty or fickle the way people can be, and they don't judge us. Unlike our human friends and family members, dogs consistently show us their gratitude, loyalty, and adoration. This doesn't mean your dog should be your only friend or supplant human connection, but your relationship with your dog can add a fulfilling dimension to your life and, in certain instances, even compensate for some of the qualities that may have been lacking in your human relationships. If you had a toxic childhood—if, for example, your boundaries or autonomy were not respected, or you didn't feel loved or valued—the qualities that were missing from those relationships can be present or cultivated with your dog.

Valentina*, a sales rep in New Hampshire, can attest to the power of these emotional perks. When she was in her mid-twenties, she married a man who turned out to have serious anger-management issues. She felt like she was constantly walking on eggshells, worrying that something she said or did would set him off. When her husband said he wanted to get a golden retriever puppy, Valentina agreed, even though she didn't have any experience raising a dog. She hoped the puppy would have a calming effect on her husband. Unfortunately, that didn't happen.

But Valentina quickly grew to love Ben, who served as her "sanity savior" and made her feel safer when her husband flew into violent bouts of rage. After five years of marriage, Valentina eventually took Ben and fled her home in the middle of the night. "The only thing I wanted out of the relationship was my dog," she says. That was many years ago, and since then, Valentina has adopted two more dogs, Brady and Dylan. "I always knew I'd be childless by choice," she explains. "But I had no idea how much I'd thrive by showering my love and attention on dogs. I belonged to them, just as they belonged to me."

DTR: Defining the Relationship

People often assume there's a parent-child relationship between humans and their dogs, but it's often more complex than that. For some, the bond is more of a close friendship or constant companionship, while for others it feels more like a sibling connection. For still others, there's a sense of partnership, mutual reliance, and give and take. To some extent, the nature of the relationship may vary with the age of the people and the dogs, but personality characteristics (including gender), geographic location, caregiving style, the duration of the relationship, and other factors come into play, as well. Interestingly, research has found that dog-owners are more attached to their pets than cat-owners are, perhaps because dogs require more individual care, which can lead to greater affection in the relationship.

One way sociologists describe the closeness of human relationships is with "tie strength," and this idea can give us fitting language to describe our relationships with our dogs, too. Relationships with family members and good friends are typically strong ties, while those with acquaintances are weak ties. The strength of a relationship stems from a combination of the amount of time you spend together and how long your relationship has lasted, the level of emotional intensity and trust between you, intimacy (such as sharing secrets and being vulnerable with each other), and the things you do for each other (formally called "reciprocal services"). While tie strength was developed in the context of human-to-human relationships, a lot of the ideas behind it can help us understand how our bond with our dogs grows. If you think about this concept as it relates to your pooch, you'll swiftly realize that dogs play a very intimate role in your life. We spend a lot of time together, and we both give deeply of ourselves to the other creature. Our dogs are incredibly vulnerable with us, and we allow them into our private lives in ways that it is rare for humans to let other humans in (they may even come to the bathroom with us).* And even as we share strong emotions with them, we see those feelings reciprocated by them.

Tanvi, a lawyer, rescued her dog Felix—a golden/husky/Akita/ German shepherd mix—from a shelter as a puppy. This was during what she calls "the lowest point" in her life, as she was leaving a verbally and emotionally abusive boyfriend. Felix and Tanvi gradually became a lifeline for each other, a connection that has never wavered. "My dog and I are pretty much the same person," she says. "We have the same likes, dislikes, and sense of undying love for each other."

Ardra Cole, PhD, a professor of education at Mount Saint Vincent University in Canada, set out to understand the meaning and significance of people's relationships to their pets. She worked with ten pairs of participants—people and their dogs—and over the course of a year conducted interviews, observed them together, and took photos of them together. What emerged from her research was a set of themes that speak to the deep, loving connection and what Cole calls the "psycho-spiritual nature of those relationships":

> **Beloved attachment:** It's a close, emotional relationship that involves love and attachment, in which you and your dog provide a stabilizing or constant presence for each other. The relationship becomes a source of comfort that both creatures relish and rely on.

---

*The first time Stacey met the Golden Ratio squad, she was charmed by all the pups but especially Guacamole. Before Jen, Stacey, and their husbands headed out to dinner, Stacey used the bathroom and Guac insisted on coming with her, with his tennis ball in his mouth. "It was the first time a dog that wasn't my own ever came to the bathroom with me," Stacey says. Their bond was immediate.

Unconditional love: It's an enduring, uncomplicated form of love that's free of limitations, conditions, or unspoken expectations. This is what leads people to offer diligent attention and care to their dog's needs—and dogs tend to respond in kind with their attention and affection.

Steadfast friendship: Through their loyalty and devotion to their people, dogs help fulfill our needs for companionship, friendship, and affection. This can help buffer us from the loneliness and social isolation that can occur when we have shrinking social networks or lose contact with family members and friends for one reason or another.

Joyful responsibility: Taking care of a dog is often an act of pleasure as well as a welcome form of purpose, stimulation, adventure, and spontaneity. The responsibility is often described as a labor of love or a source of joy. It offers intrinsic rewards such as shared pleasure through play, relaxation, and affection, all of which enhance our quality of life.

In addition to these constructs, some researchers have characterized the dog-human relationship as being in one of the following categories: the dog as possession, the dog as providing benefits (to the people in its life), the dog as companion or child surrogate, and the dog as a respected significant other. In an eye-opening study, Michael Dotson, MBA, and Eva Hyatt, PhD, at Appalachian State University in North Carolina, explored various aspects of the dog-companionship experience among 749 dog-owners and seven dimensions emerged:

• **The Symbiotic Relationship:** With this mutually beneficial bond between people and their dogs, there's a nurturing component to having a dog, as well as psychological benefits to both creatures. People who identify with this dimension report that being with their dog has a calming effect when they feel stressed;

that they feel emotionally attached to their dog; and that their dogs' psychological well-being is important to them.

- **A Dog-Oriented Self-Concept:** With this pattern, the dog is seen as both an extension of the person and the person's best friend. The dog is vitally important to the person's sense of self and social well-being. People who identify with this facet spend less time with other people in general and prefer "dog people" because having people accept their dog is crucial to their relationships with other humans.

- **Anthropomorphism:** With this dimension, people tend to view their dog as more of a person than an animal, perhaps even as a child surrogate or a member of the family. People who score high on this dimension feel like they can communicate well with their dogs and learn a lot from their pooches. They also make a greater effort to understand "where the dog is coming from" in responding to its behavior.

- **Activity/Youth:** Here, the focus is on the increased physical activity and play time someone gets from having a dog, which helps the person feel young(er). The underlying theme is that dogs may serve as the catalyst to overcome people's inertia and inspire them to incorporate more movement in their lives. People who score high on this dimension tend to play with their dogs more and seek opportunities to be physically active with their dogs—by taking them to dog parks or on walking trails, for example.

- **Boundaries:** This is really about a *lack* of boundaries or limits that some dog-owners impose on their pups. Simply put, they have fewer rules for the dog and let the dog sleep on the bed or get on the furniture. They don't see this as a problem because those who score high on this dimension value the closeness they get from sharing their (entire) space with their dogs more than the orderliness of a home that has more limits and boundaries.

- **Pampering Purchases:** The researchers called this "specialty purchases," a category that describes the extent to which people make special efforts to acquire products for their dogs, whether it's online, through catalogs, or in stores. This dimension reflects consumer shopping and spending behaviors for pooch-centric products, patterns that are triggered by a higher level of involvement with their dog.

- **Willingness to Adapt:** This dimension reflects people's readiness and willingness to alter their living patterns (including their choice of living space and vehicle), lifestyle habits, and shopping behaviors to accommodate their dogs. People who score high on this dimension consider their dog when making many household purchasing decisions.

Ultimately, the study found that "dog companionship is a complex, multi-faceted phenomenon, in which various dog-owners might possess varying levels of the different dimensions." With the dogs Jen and Ingo rescue, Willingness to Adapt and Anthropomorphism are key dimensions of their relationships. These dogs have so often been mistreated or neglected, and they deserve to be members of the family. Their medical needs also require adaptation, and that is part of the Golden Ratio mission. That said, some dogs score higher on the Activity and Symbiotic dimensions, especially when they are healthy enough to be Jen's running partner.

Most of us have our own personal mash-up of these dimensions with our dogs, yet some common patterns were found in the study. Women scored higher on all of these dimensions than men did, which isn't entirely surprising given that numerous surveys have found that women are the primary caregivers for dogs in the vast majority—nearly 75 percent—of households. Some of the age-related patterns that were found are more eye-opening. The study found that people under age thirty-five score higher on measures related to having a Symbiotic Relationship or engaging in Anthropomorphism with their dogs, while people over age fifty are more likely to establish boundaries. Those between the ages of twenty-six and thirty-five are more willing to adapt their lifestyles to accommodate their dogs—and make pampering purchases for their pooches. Another interesting tendency: People are more likely to have a Symbiotic Relationship and to engage in Anthropomorphism with their dogs if they've owned their pooches for more than ten years.

This isn't just a fascinating demographic study. It tells us something about the different relationships people have with their dogs. While there are many common denominators—such as treasured companionship, emotional connection, and shared experiences—in people's relationships with their dogs, the nature or tone of these bonds can vary considerably. They can also shift or evolve over time, just as they do with meaningful relationships between human beings.

After all, healthy relationships aren't static; they tend to be dynamic or fluid. They require a give-and-take spirit and TLC to grow and thrive. This is true of relationships between people, and it applies to the bond between people and their pooches, as well. By appreciating the emotional nuances of the human-canine connection and understanding how they may shift over time, you'll be in a better position to establish and nurture a strong, steady bond with your beloved pup. One that you and your canine companion will benefit from for many years to come.

CHAPTER THREE

Family Matters

How Dogs Can Help Us Connect with Loved Ones

In some ways, our dogs really are our *best* family members because they are attentive and nonjudgmental, and they love us unconditionally. Beyond our personal relationships with our dogs, these furry friends can help the entire family function better as a unit and foster closeness between humans in the family. When families are lacking in emotional support or safety, dogs can provide it. They can enhance communication between family members and create ways for the family to have fun together. And when there is tension among family members, regardless of the cause, our dogs can help dissipate that, restoring a sense of calm.

When they were kids, Sophie and her sister Sadie would get into the usual sibling squabbles about annoyances, but they would never bicker about their family dog Ollie, an English cream golden retriever they both adored. The girls could be in the midst of arguing about who got to choose what to watch on TV or who borrowed whose stuff without permission, but they never argued about who was Mom and Dad's favorite; they knew that was Ollie. Whenever he walked into the room, he would immediately become the focus of attention and all resentments would be forgotten (for the moment, anyway), as the girls began playing with him or took him for a walk together. Over the years, "Ollie has helped me get closer with my sister," says Sophie, now a graphic designer in Colorado. "Whenever we visit our parents, my sister and I still text each other photos and videos of Ollie or FaceTime each other to see him."

As a child, Milissa frequently looked for opportunities that would help her grow closer to her father, who was the chief park ranger in Massachusetts. When Milissa was a teenager, her dad wanted to bring his dog Jake, a Lab, to work with him, so he decided to make Jake a member of the search and rescue dog team. "Because I was always looking for ways to bond with my father, I volunteered to help him train the dogs," says Milissa, who's now in her forties and married with two rescue dogs of her own. "Most Saturdays my father and I could be found in the woods at a state forest with the team, training dogs." Milissa often played the role of the "victim," hiding in the woods until she was found by one of "these glorious fluffy friends." She credits these Saturday morning dog-training sessions as playing a key role in helping her develop a close relationship with her dad, one that she maintains to this day.

These days, most of us—85 percent, according to a survey by the American Veterinary Association—consider our dogs bona fide members of the family. In some families, people even celebrate their dogs' birthdays, giving their dogs presents, baking them special treats (like "pupcakes"; see the appendix for the recipe), and signing their names to greeting cards; others give them their own Christmas stocking. In a survey of people with companion animals in the U.S., 57 percent said that if they were stranded on a deserted island and could have only one companion, they'd choose their pet.

Without any conscious effort on their part, these furry companions can become a bonding force, acting as a magnet that brings family members together and sometimes even being "the *glue* in the family—bringing members together and increasing family cohesion," according to Froma Walsh, PhD, codirector of the Chicago Center for Family Health. In addition, our beloved canine companions provide a sense of support and security, sources of pleasure, and ways of defusing tension within the family, as you'll see in this chapter.

Fulfilling Loving Roles

It's not just that dogs are lovable creatures within the family. Kids often describe their dogs as a sibling or best friend, and people of all ages form attachments to their dogs, often viewing their canine companions as reliable, trustworthy, emotional safe havens. Not everyone is fortunate enough to have that kind of support from their human family members, and dogs can help fulfill that need. Dogs also can change the dynamics in a family, as they become a joyful focal point for shared attention and affection. They also teach children responsibility and a respect for life, and they often serve as a catalyst for promoting positive human contact and interaction at any age or stage of life.

Kathy and her husband are in their late seventies, and their golden retriever Angel has senior status as well. In 2019, "we decided that we needed new life in our home," says Kathy, who lives in Minnesota, so right before the pandemic, the couple brought into their family a Bernese mountain dog they named Ella. "At our age, we were confined to our home—Ella added the spirit, humor, energy, and love that saved our mental health," says Kathy. They took her out on daily walks, regardless of the weather, and met up for long, masked walks with Kathy's sister and her dogs. Ella has brought the couple a welcome dose of joy and has enhanced their physical health by forcing them to get regular exercise and fresh air. Though they've had many dogs in their lives, Kathy says, "we have never had a closer bond with a dog than we have with Ella."

In an in-depth study into the power of pets in family relationships, Krista Geller, PhD, an organizational psychologist in Virginia, found that participants portrayed their pets as being "the biggest joy in my life," "almost another child," "better than people," a "younger brother or sister," a "significant relationship," or "another playmate." In each instance, pets enhanced the families' and individuals' lives in many ways. Families function best when all members actively feel loved and supported, Geller notes, and pets in general, and dogs in particular, often serve as role models for how unconditional love can and should be shown within families. In other words, when one family member—in this case, the dog—serves as an aspirational example, it can make the whole family as a unit operate more lovingly and successfully. Indeed, research shows that pet dogs often make families happier and bring family members closer together. A study by Ann Ottney Cain, PhD, found that 70 percent of pet owners reported their family was happier and had more fun after they got a pet, and more than half of the participants said the family spent more time together after they got their pet.

Maureen, an American expat living with her family in London, can attest to this. Many years ago, she was listening to a BBC radio program "with Irish veterinarian Noel Fitzpatrick who said, 'Never underestimate the ability of a dog to transform the love of a family,'" she recalls. At the time, her family didn't have a dog. Eventually they got a black Labrador/cocker spaniel mix named Buddy who has altered their family's life in the best of ways. "When he arrived, our two teenagers wanted to spend most of their time in their rooms, alone," she says. "Once Buddy came on the scene, that all changed. They spent more time with us and we spent more time together as a family."

A dog's impact on the family dynamic can increase the closeness that human family members feel for one another. In a study of ninety-nine tweens, ages nine to eleven, Kathryn Kerns, PhD, and colleagues found that kids who feel close to their family dog are more securely attached to their parents and have more positive relationships with friends, too. The impact of dogs even carries into families who are seeking to create closer connections in difficult situations. For example, in their research, Sam Carr, PhD, and Ben Rockett, PhD, examined how dogs helped children in foster families over a seven-month period. They found that the relationships the kids formed with the dogs fulfilled emotional attachment needs—providing an emotional home base and a safe haven to go to with problems—and the kids wanted to be around the dogs and missed them when they were apart. That's not surprising but this finding is: The benefits extended into the foster families, softening the children's perceptions of the foster parents and creating an opportunity for them to build closer relationships. As the researchers noted, a child's ability to develop a secure attachment with a foster caregiver is a critical element of foster care because it helps the child develop psychological resilience and emotional well-being.

Enhancing Communication

Unbeknownst to them, pet dogs can facilitate communication within a family. Not only do they give people a positive subject to talk about in day-to-day conversation, but they also create opportunities or obligations to talk or interact more in general. It's often better to talk about the dog than to sit in silence or make forced small talk. Ever since Louise's parents got a cocker spaniel they named Jasper a few years ago, she says the dog has "massively improved our relationship, which was always a little awkward." Even though Louise doesn't live with her parents anymore, she lives nearby in London and whenever she goes to visit them, Jasper provides "something else to talk about" and another creature to interact with. This has eased the pressure on interactions with her parents and made it more enjoyable for them to spend time together. That's one of the hidden benefits of having a dog in the family—they provide an ever-ready topic of conversation and a shared interest, as Geller's research found. Even if the details may feel somewhat mundane, this kind of communication creates a collective sense of purpose and responsibility that can bring family members closer.

And sometimes little kids talk to their parents through their dogs, attributing their thoughts and feelings to Rover instead of themselves, because this can feel less daunting or risky. Adults also may use the family dog to try to stop sibling squabbles, perhaps by saying something like, *Stop arguing! It's upsetting Bailey.* In Geller's study, participants also reported that the family pet could unwittingly serve as a sort of intermediary. Some respondents said they would talk to their dogs about a conflict they were having with another family member, loud enough for other family members to hear. This essentially sparked an opportunity for family members to discuss the issue. Granted, this approach is a bit passive-aggressive, but it's better than not talking at all.

In a fascinating study, Deborah Tannen, PhD, a linguistics professor at Georgetown University, had couples audiotape their conversational interactions for a week. Then, she examined how family members mediated their interactions with each other "by speaking as, to, or about pet dogs who are present." Tannen found that in their interactions family members often use their dogs as resources to insert humor into the situation, soften criticism, deliver praise, teach values to children, and "create a family identity that includes the dogs as family members."

For a glimpse of how this plays out, consider this example: In one situation, a man was annoyed when he discovered, as he was getting ready to take the family dog with him on his daily run, that his wife didn't tell him she had already taken the pup out for a walk. Rather than venting his frustration directly to his wife, he turned to the dog and asked why the dog didn't tell him, thereby injecting a note of humor into the situation.

As these examples illustrate, not only can a dog's presence in the home facilitate clear communication within the family, but it also can encourage people to soften the tone of their messages or use humor. Bringing the dog into the conversation can take the edge off a complaint or criticism while still getting the point across, as Tannen's findings show. This gentle approach is beneficial for family members' relationships with one another, and by involving the dog—by speaking to or through the pup, for instance—family members reinforce their bonds with their dog. Because even if the dog doesn't understand exactly what's being said, hearing their name and the playful tone of voice and/or receiving eye contact from the person speaking is bound to elicit a smile or wag from the pup.

Interestingly, when people talk directly to their dogs, their speech often has a high-pitched, singsongy quality that's a bit like baby talk. This actually may be beneficial. In a study in a 2018 issue of the journal *Animal Cognition*, researchers conducted an experiment in which they had pet dogs come into a room where two people held speakers on their laps that played recordings of their own voices: One was in a normal, conversational tone; the other was in what's called "dog-directed speech" which is like the dog version of baby talk. The researchers measured how much time the dog spent looking at each person while the recordings were playing and with each person after being let off leash. The dogs spent more time looking toward the person with dog-directed speech and chose to spend more time with that person. The researchers concluded that use of dog-directed speech "improves dogs' attention and may strengthen the affiliative bond between humans and their pets."

 Family Support from Service Dogs

When families are dealing with serious health issues, the whole household can feel the strain, and service dogs can provide support for the entire group, in addition to the afflicted person. Psychologists know, for example, that post-traumatic stress disorder (PTSD) can have serious, negative impacts on a person's family relationships and general functioning. Research has found that service dogs can be of great help to military veterans dealing with psychiatric issues, as well as to their families.

A preliminary study of military veterans with PTSD compared the family relationships among those who had psychiatric service dogs and those who did not. Partners of the veterans reported that their own quality of life and the functioning of their family was improved with the presence of a service dog. Veterans also seemed to have less anger, isolation, and work impairment, which, in turn, would ease the stress on other family members.

Similar effects have been seen when pet dogs are brought into families with kids who have autism spectrum disorder (ASD). In a study of seventy families that have kids with ASD, Hannah Wright, PhD, and colleagues found that the kids with pet dogs experienced reduced social anxiety, separation anxiety, and obsessive compulsive symptoms. The researchers also compared survey results about family stress from before the families adopted the dogs and from six to nine months later and found significant improvements in family functioning as a result of the dogs' presence. Further research is needed to tease out exactly what's going on, but this could be because dogs help families establish routines and perform household tasks together (like feeding the dog); plus, family dogs generally provide opportunities for family members to have fun together, talk about a common beloved topic, and share love.

A separate study by Hannah Wright's team suggests that parents of kids with ASD experience a significant reduction in their own stress level after getting a pet dog for the family. At first blush, it may seem like adding a dog to an already challenging home environment might increase stress for parents, but that's not necessarily the case. The theory is that dogs provide immediate and enduring stress-buffering effects within these challenging environments—by offering comforting interactions, a sense of unconditional love and social support, and the need to spend time outside and engaged in physical activity.

These benefits are common among families, regardless of the health challenges they're facing. In a study of 126 families where one person in the family had a service dog, Jessica Bibbo, PhD, and colleagues found that the dog improved family functioning and the psychosocial health of the family members. While the extent to which service dogs help the people they are partnered with has long been recognized, there is now consistent evidence that their presence helps the family, too. As the researchers noted, "The impact of a service dog may extend beyond the recipient and have positive impacts on family members' psychosocial functioning as well."

Setting the Stage for Fun

Another major benefit that dogs bring to family bonds is they create a reason for the family to play or exercise together. If everyone in the household loves and wants to be with the dog, then having fun with the dog can also mean having fun with other family members. It can be a group experience. Indeed, research by Carri Westgarth, PhD, and colleagues supports these perks. While studying the impact of dog-walking among thirty-eight dog-owners in the UK, they found that one of the benefits of recreational dog-walking was that it was a time for family bonding. When family members had the time, they would go out together to walk the dog, and it became an opportunity for them to reconnect.

In 2020, when the COVID-19 pandemic hit, Zachary picked up his first full-time foster dog, Davy, a female papillon. "Davy got us out, exploring new parks on walks every day and helped my family and me bond," says Zachary, who is in his early twenties and lives at home with his mother and sister in Kentucky. Since then, Davy has moved on after finding her forever family as a service dog. Meanwhile, Zachary and his family have fostered three more papillon service dogs in training, and he adopted Callie, "a fabulous flunky in the program."

A pilot study by Katie Potter, PhD, and colleagues examined the impact that acquiring a dog had on twelve families who agreed to foster a rescue dog. After six weeks, the families were more physically active and they all reported that the dogs had improved their lives in various ways, often by bringing joy, happiness, fun, companionship, and family bonding into their life. When asked about the best part of fostering a dog, one participant said, "The best thing about fostering X has been our family working together to care for him." Another said: "My pup is a continuous source of happiness in my life—coming home is much more enjoyable than it ever has been. To know she is always at home waiting for me gives me a sense of joy and comfort."

Promoting a More Peaceable Household

Perhaps one of the most critical roles dogs play in family dynamics is defusing tension. Geller's study found that when interactions between human family members grew tense, dogs would make people laugh or at least distract them in a way that could relieve the stress of the situation. Even if the dog couldn't calm down everyone in the family, they provided a source of comfort when people were upset. As we've seen, taking a moment to hug or pet a dog can be soothing and people may then carry that gentler state into the family dynamics.

Research also has found that a family dog can help with "relational anxiety"—meaning anxiety or tension family members may feel between each other, such as between a mother and a father, between a particular child and a parent, or between siblings, which can lead them to distance themselves from each other. In her research, Ann Ottney Cain, PhD, found that dogs can act as peacemakers, doing cute things or requesting attention in times of family stress that would divert people's attention from the issue at hand. In other words, dogs could sense stress within the family and they would try to do playful things to defuse it. This helped family members feel "a sense of balance again" and that they could regain control of their feelings in the time-out that dogs offered with their behavior. In times of intense family conflict, dogs may react by moving close to the vulnerable family member, whether it's to protect them or comfort them.

Sebastian grew up in what he describes as a "very stressful and competitive environment." Even the family dog, Alex, a Jack Russell terrier, sometimes seemed to feel the tension and would come to Sebastian shaking during a four-alarm family fight. Throughout his childhood, Sebastian found comfort in Alex's presence. "He was that sliver of happiness and hope that I needed to maintain my sanity," says Sebastian, now a tutor who lives in Pennsylvania. "He would put a smile on my face when everything seemed to be going wrong."

Over time, Alex became the family's emotional guardian angel. "It wasn't anything specific that he would do—it was his general aura of love that he shared with everyone that made everything feel better," recalls Sebastian. "His sense of family was heartwarming." During the day, Alex would keep tabs on everyone's whereabouts in the home, and he refused to settle down for the night until everyone was in bed. "His kindness and love for the family sticks with me to this day," Sebastian says.

A study by Jennifer Applebaum and Barbara Zsembik, PhD, examined the role of pets in adverse or tumultuous family circumstances. They interviewed 1,421 parents in families that owned pets and found that as family conflict increased, so did people's attachment to their pets. Essentially, the pets became more important in people's lives as the stress in their family environment grew. As Sebastian found, having a loving, affectionate dog can help mitigate the impact of long-term strain in a family.

Whether they're energetic or relaxed, large or small, long-haired or short-, dogs can play a significant role in easing family challenges and even serve as a surrogate for someone in a difficult or unhealthy relationship within a family. That's not to say that they don't contribute just as much to loving, close families—they absolutely do! In any family, pet dogs essentially serve as a bridge between different family members and a source of common ground and connection.

Dogs unwittingly serve as a cohesive factor, helping family members find their way toward one another and strengthening the bonds between them. There's a very good reason why kids often include their dog in genogram drawings of their most significant family relationships. Through one way and another, dogs really do earn their place in the family. As John Grogan, author of *Marley & Me*, put it: "It is amazing how much love and laughter they bring into our lives and even how much closer we become with each other because of them."

CHAPTER FOUR

Social Creatures

How Dogs Can Improve Our Lives in the Community

It's not just in movies like *Must Love Dogs* or *Dog Days* that our canine companions bring people together. It happens in real life, too. That's because dogs make it easier to connect to people outside your home—simply put, they're social facilitators. People can overcome shyness and social anxieties and better relate to others when they have a furry friend to help them along. Serving as icebreakers, dogs also provide a readily accessible, positive subject to talk about, which helps eliminate awkwardness with new people and deflect attention and pressure away from you. Plus, a dog's presence helps their human family members relax physiologically and mentally, which makes just about any social interaction go more smoothly.

It's been dubbed "the pet factor" by Lisa Wood, PhD, and colleagues, who found that companion animals can serve as a conduit or catalyst for various human social relationships, ranging from incidental interactions in neighborhoods, to getting to know people who live nearby, to the formation of new friendships and the widening of social support networks. Interestingly, having a dog has been found to increase "social capital" among people in the U.S. and Australia. Social capital is variously defined as the connections among people and social networks and the sense of trustworthiness and reciprocity that come from them; as the "glue" that holds communities together; and as "the raw material of civil society that is created from everyday interactions between people." In the U.S., people who walk their dogs are much more likely to report befriending someone they met through a dog-related encounter. In other words, your beloved pooch can serve as the antidote to social isolation. It's true for kids and adults alike.

Kathryn, who lives in Trinidad and Tobago, had always been an introvert, but she became less so after adopting two mixed-breed puppies a few years ago. "One of my dogs is also a major introvert, but the other is quite the opposite and loves to say hello to every human—and makes sure we do as well," says Kathryn, who takes care of people's boats for a living. She enjoys her walks in the park with the dogs and even chatting with people she meets on these walks. "I'm learning that strangers aren't bad," she says. "We've even made some friends who say hello outside of the parks."

Kelsey, an only child whose parents had her when they were older, says she was a shy, lonely kid who had trouble making friends. When she was ten, her parents brought home a friendly goldendoodle puppy she named Emma—and their mutual affection was immediate. When Kelsey would take Emma on walks, the pup would pull her toward other kids who were playing in her neighborhood. The kids loved playing with Emma, and Emma loved being the center of attention. In the past, Kelsey had found it difficult to walk up to people she didn't know and start conversations. It didn't take long for Emma to make it clear that Kelsey no longer had a choice, because the friendly pup was a people magnet, drawing other kids toward her and Kelsey. "At first, I would have short conversations with the other kids while they were petting Emma—then, after a while I started opening up and being more confident," recalls Kelsey.

Gradually, Kelsey became good friends with the other kids on her street—they'd hang out together after school and on the weekends, go to movies and parties together, and play games together—and thirteen years later, they remain close. "My friendly puppy taught me people skills and won me friends," says Kelsey, now a university student majoring in mathematics and cybersecurity in Northern Virginia. "Even now, I still use her as an opener when meeting new people."

Stories like hers aren't unusual, and research sheds light on why this is. For starters, dogs encourage people to spend more time outside, and they make people recognizable within their neighborhood. Even when they don't know one another's name, neighbors often know the dogs' names, and sometimes dogs actively solicit the attention of strangers by making eye contact, approaching them, wagging their tails, and occasionally seeking a bout of petting. But even when they don't, dogs can serve as a social magnet, bringing people together. For example, a pair of studies by June McNicholas, PhD, and Glyn M. Collis, PhD, from the University of Warwick in the UK had people walk a dog that was highly trained to ignore attention from passersby. The researchers found that even the presence of a standoffish dog increased the frequency of social interactions, especially with strangers. This may be partly because dogs themselves provide common ground among dog-owners or dog-appreciators, so a stranger's desire to offer a friendly greeting or strike up a casual conversation with a fellow dog lover can be stirred upon seeing the dog. But it's more than that, too.

It may also be because people perceive others to be more likable and attractive when they're with a dog—in real life and in photos. Kelly Ann Rossbach and John P. Wilson, from Cleveland State University, conducted a study in which they showed thirty-four participants photos of people alone, with dogs, or with flowers, and asked them to rate the person in each photo in terms of approachability, looking happy, and looking relaxed. The people with dogs in the photo were rated more highly in all dimensions than people pictured without dogs. People simply appear more relaxed and happier when they're sitting or standing with a dog.

This effect plays out similarly in the physical world. In a study by Deborah L. Wells, PhD, a woman from the research team sat in a park alone or with either a dog, a potted plant, or a teddy bear. When she was with a Labrador retriever puppy or an adult Labrador, the woman got more smiles and had more conversations with strangers than when she was with a teddy bear or potted plant. (This is surprising, in our opinion, because seeing a woman sitting in a park with a potted plant kind of begs for a humorous comment.) The dog-as-social-catalyst effect is so strong that it happens even with dogs that are shy or standoffish, as occurred in a study by June McNicholas, PhD, and Glyn M. Collis, PhD. In every variation of the study, the experimenter had more social interactions with passersby when the dog was with them than when they were alone.

Given that having a dog can help us talk to strangers and connect to neighbors, it's not surprising that dogs can also inadvertently foster romantic connections. Having a dog can create certain impressions that may be relevant to a romantic relationship. Research led by Sigal Tifferet, PhD, found that when women read vignettes about men who have dogs as well as men who don't, the women perceive the guys with dogs as more attractive and nurturing and having the potential to be in more committed relationships, which may increase their attractiveness quotient. The real surprise: This perception was sparked without the women even meeting the men!

When people do meet in real life, our dogs, as you've seen, can make us seem more attractive and approachable. Dogs can make it easier to meet potential partners and talk with them for all the same reasons they help us talk to strangers and neighbors—they serve as social lubricants, asking for attention, creating an easy topic of conversation, and allowing us to relax. They can help love blossom in other ways, as well.

During the summer of 2020, Thomas, twenty-eight, rescued a two-year-old dog—a black Lab/Australian cattle dog mix—named Mia whom he credits with leading him to the love of his life. Mia is a frequent barker on their walks, and the two of them would run into lots of dogs in their suburban Chicago neighborhood. Usually, Mia would bark and Thomas would apologize to the other dog's owner or cross the street to avoid conflict. One day in 2020, Mia insistently pulled Thomas toward a young woman and her dog, who happened to look just like Mia. Despite the social distancing mandated by the pandemic, he asked the woman if their dogs could say hello because clearly Mia wanted to—and they did. Meanwhile, Thomas and the woman, Jenny, ended up talking for forty-five minutes. They hit it off immediately, and Thomas says he felt as if he'd been struck by Cupid's arrow. Within sixteen months, they were engaged to be married. (Funny coincidence: At the shelter where Thomas adopted Mia, her name was actually Cupid.)

Breaking Down Social Barriers

To put all this in the proper context, it's important to remember that striking up a conversation with a stranger on the street is not only awkward, but generally considered impolite or even creepy. Sociologist Erving Goffman, PhD, coined the term "civil inattention" to describe the ways in which people briefly acknowledge the presence of strangers while respecting personal space and privacy when they're in close proximity; this can be done with a flash of eye contact and a fleeting smile before quickly looking away, minimizing the chance for conversation. This social etiquette helps us set boundaries with other people, but it can also make it difficult to connect with those we come across in public spaces. Having a dog with you helps you break down this invisible barrier. Dogs will often demand the attention of strangers, giving them looks that insist they be pet or just running right up to them with their tail wagging. But even perfectly trained dogs who ignore people on the street sometimes invite conversation and connection. (Fortunately, they also provide a ready excuse for breaking off conversations that feel awkward; all you have to say is *Well, I'll see you later. Rover needs to keep moving!*)

The social-facilitation effect can influence us, as dog-owners, in surprising ways, too. Dogs can often sense when someone is "a dog person," whether it's through a sixth sense, the person's body language and behavior, or the dog's ability to pick up friendly, relaxed pheromones with their powerful sense of smell. Dogs are amazingly intuitive creatures. They can even suss out when people are lying—to them, that is. In a series of experiments designed to gauge how dogs respond to unreliable people, a team of researchers led by Akiko Takaoka used the "point and fetch" technique. In the first round, the person truthfully pointed to a container that held treats and toys; in the second, dogs were shown what was in two containers—the treat-containing one and an empty one—then the tester pointed to the empty one; in the third, the protocol from the first round was repeated. Most dogs followed the pointing in the first phase, but after being fooled in the second round, fewer dogs went to fetch what was in the treat container in the third round. The researchers concluded that dogs "make inferences about the reliability of a human who presents cues and consequently modify their behavior flexibly depending on the inference." In other words, the dogs unwittingly subscribed to the saying *Fool me once, shame on you; fool me twice, shame on me.* They weren't going to let that happen.

That said, dogs aren't infallible. Dogs often learn about someone's character from experience and adjust their behavior accordingly; they can't always size up someone's trustworthiness based purely on instinct or intuition. This is important to remember because when our dog takes an immediate liking to a particular person, this can improve our impressions of them and even encourage us to let down our guards and be more immediately comfortable with them. After all, our beloved pooch has given the person their seal of approval. But the person could turn out to be lovely and gentle with our canine companions and with humans or they could be lovely with dogs but controlling, critical, or otherwise disagreeable with people. Stacey will never forget the way her old dog Wolfy, an Australian shepherd, would make a beeline to a particular friend's husband whenever they came over. Wolfy was normally aloof or cranky with people, so this was unusual behavior for him. He adored this guy and would end up groveling at his feet every time her friend and her husband were at Stacey's house. Naturally, this made her like her friend's husband more than ever—until he began lying to and cheating on his wife, and eventually they split up.

The point is, just because our dog likes someone, that doesn't mean we should put our blind trust in that person. On some level, we all know this, but it's easy to have your opinion of someone you've just met swayed when your dog is absolutely gaga about them. That might increase the chances that you'll be charmed by that person, too, which may or not be in your best interest. The reality is, dogs sometimes like jerks, too. They may or may not always be the best judges of character, so don't check *your* judgment at the door.

Connecting with People in the Community

Our dogs make us recognizable to neighbors, even if it's just as "Spot's Mom." From the lightest weight interactions with strangers, to making our casual neighborhood friendships more pleasant, our connections to dogs help us better connect with one another and build a sense of community. In one research project, led by John Rogers, casual conversations among elderly people were recorded as they walked their dogs through a mobile home community. Not surprisingly, dog-owners talked to each other on their walks, mostly about their dogs, but they also talked *to* the dogs, asked each other *about* their dogs, and told stories about them. What's more, passersby talked to the owners about their dogs, regardless of whether or not the dogs were present.

When Stacey separated from her first husband in 2013, she kept their dog Inky, which meant she had a lot more dog-walking to do than ever before. As a result, she often ran into a neighbor from around the corner named John, while he was walking his two dogs. Over the years, John and Stacey had struck up occasional conversations whenever they saw each other, usually about their dogs or their kids, and while Stacey had always thought he was a cool guy and a great conversationalist, she didn't know him well. As they got to know each other better during that sweltering 2013 summer of dog walks, Stacey learned that he and his wife had split up two years earlier, and gradually she and John began to talk more personally.

As they strolled with their dogs and chatted, albeit from a distance of at least fifteen feet because their dogs didn't get along, getting to know each other and finding common ground was effortless. One night while John began sharing his misadventures with dating, Stacey was becoming hoarse as she asked questions. John told her she sounded terrible and should go home and go to bed, but she didn't want the conversation to end. "It would help if we could have a normal conversation over coffee instead of from across the street!" she blurted out. There was a long pause until John said, "That's a good idea."

Then, nothing happened until a few weeks later when John suggested they go out for a drink one Friday night. After that, they began seeing each other regularly. A few weeks later, when Stacey told her sons, then ten and fifteen, that she had started dating a neighbor they knew, John's name didn't ring a bell. When she explained that he lived around the corner, across the street from the tennis court, in a house where Stacey's older son Nate's preschool crush had once lived, he said, "*Who?* . . . You mean Bagel and Abby's owner?" That was their frame of reference for John. One of their first questions was "Does Inky like him?" The answer was a definite *yes*, which helped the boys feel inclined to give John a chance. Two years later, he became their stepfather.

Besides getting us out of our homes and encouraging us to spend more time outside, our dogs help us form connections in the community. Without doing anything special, they make us more recognizable in the neighborhood. This idea of a "familiar stranger"—someone we recognize from repeatedly seeing them in our daily lives, even without talking to each other—helps break down barriers to future communication. In Chapter Two, you read about the sociological concept of "tie strength" as it relates to our relationships. Well, our dogs also can help us build "weak ties" through casual interactions with acquaintances in our community. People generally value the benefits of strong ties more than weak ties, but both have an important place. Interestingly, research led by Gillian Sandstrom, PhD, found that people who have more frequent interactions with weak-tie people are generally happier.

Dogs facilitate these casual social connections in our communities, partly because they approach people and solicit attention from strangers, and partly because they become a natural and neutral conversation point. Malintzin, who works as a nanny for a special-needs child in Dallas, can attest to this: Daily visits to the dog park with Willow, her Great Dane mix, helped her meet other people and their dogs. Many of the twenty- and thirty-something members of the dog-park group came from other states and didn't have family members nearby. What began as casual interactions between the dog-owners gradually brought the group closer together until they began to feel like "a family," she says. "The dogs got us out into the world and created something beautiful that none of us can now live without. We all support each other emotionally and take care of the dogs when someone can't." They also help each other through household disasters, personal crises, and more, through their group on Snapchat.*

Her experience is hardly unusual. Research led by Max Bulsara,

*For many people, looking at pictures of cute dogs on social media provides an enjoyable, wholesome break from the daily grind. Have you ever wondered whether social media could help you grow closer with your dog? Jen did, so she conducted a study in her lab at the University of Maryland and found that the answer is *yes*. In a survey of more than thirteen hundred dog-owners on Twitter, the vast majority said that interacting with dog-oriented social media helped them find more emotional connection to their own dog and enhanced the sense of companionship between them. It also helped them cope with difficult health news regarding their pup, discover new toys and treats, and feel like they were part of a community and not an isolated "crazy dog person." So next time you find yourself scrolling through other people's dog photos online, don't feel guilty—you're finding ways to deepen your bond!

PhD, found that dog ownership in an Australian suburban community enabled neighbors to have more social interactions, do more favors for one another (an important aspect of developing closer ties), feel their neighborhoods are friendly, and develop a stronger sense of community. Amazingly, these perceptions and benefits were found to extend to community members who did not own pets, as well.

Dogs' community-strengthening impacts may even help make neighborhoods safer. Often neighborhood residents collectively deter crime by keeping an eye on what's happening on the street and building trusted relationships with one another. Research by Nicolo Pinchak and colleagues investigated if neighborhoods with more dogs, and hence more people out walking those dogs, would increase the "eyes on the street" and thus lead to less neighborhood crime. Controlling for factors like income, education, race, and age, they found that neighborhoods with more dogs had less property crime, and when neighbors had built trusted relationships with one another, the presence of more dogs was also tied to lower rates of assault, robbery, and homicide. By getting us out into our communities, our dogs help us build safer neighborhoods for everyone.

 The Perks of Bring-Your-Dog-to-Work Settings

It's not just that the presence of furry friends adds a note of levity and cheerfulness to a workplace. Dogs can affect the way coworkers interact, as well, by fostering pro-social behavior. In a series of studies by Stephen Colarelli, PhD, and colleagues, groups of people who worked on an interactive problem-solving task displayed more verbal cohesion and cooperation when a dog was present. In another study that required less interaction between colleagues, participants who worked in the presence of a dog gave higher ratings of trustworthiness to other group members. In short, groups who performed tasks with dogs present were "more cooperative, comfortable, friendly, active, enthusiastic, and attentive."

In another study, led by Randolph Barker, PhD, from Virginia Commonwealth University, when people brought their dogs to work, they reported experiencing lower stress levels throughout the day and they felt like their jobs were more satisfying than their pet-less colleagues did. When speaking to the American Animal Hospital Association, Steven Feldman, executive director of the Human Animal Bond Research Initiative (HABRI) Foundation, explained that, overall, "pets in the workplace contribute to . . . employee teamwork and satisfaction."

Fortunately, pet-friendly policies are becoming more common in the workplace, as more companies try to increase employee well-being. As researchers from the University of Southern California noted, "While pets have been seen as an employee-only benefit in the past, factors that positively affect employees correlate with improved office morale, absenteeism, and a healthy work-life balance." That's a situation where everybody wins.

The Power of Service Dogs

Perhaps there's no greater example of the power of dogs to integrate people into our communities than service dogs. Research shows that for a range of disabilities, service dogs help people forge social connections. A study led by Lynette A. Hart, PhD, examined how service dogs affect the way people in wheelchairs interact with strangers in public. After getting a service dog, those who used wheelchairs reported they received more greetings when they went out shopping, that they were approached more often by adults and children, and that this made them more likely to go out in public in the evening than they had been before obtaining a service dog.

Similarly, research has found that when they're accompanied by a guide dog, blind people experience fewer stresses being out in public, including with communication and social interaction, and deaf people with hearing dogs report improved interactions with neighbors and the general public. Thanks to the presence of a service dog, the participants said things like "people know me now" and "people notice and are nicer." Essentially, all types of service dogs bring similar experiences and social benefits to their people, regardless of their owners' disability or the dogs' breed, and many of these perks are in line with what the rest of us get from our companion dogs. But the effects on people with disabilities can be more profound and meaningful because they often face barriers to socializing when moving through the world.

All of these perks make perfect sense, given the common denominators behind the many ways dogs help improve our social interactions. For one thing, people tend to be more relaxed, physiologically and mentally, when they're with their dogs. Our canine companions help us stay focused on the present moment, which is beneficial for our mental health; social interactions involving our dogs naturally focus on the here and now. And as mentioned before, the presence of a dog in an encounter with a neighbor or acquaintance often provides a conversational icebreaker, enabling humans to connect with each other more effectively.

Whether it's because our dogs boost our confidence and our moods or make us more open to other people, our furry friends often spark and enrich our friendships, romantic relationships, and our connections in the community. Best of all, both species—the creatures with paws as well as those of us with hands and feet—benefit from the boost in attention, as well as the sense of camaraderie and social cohesion, that ensue. These are the kinds of ties that many of us are more than happy to let bind us together.

Part Two

ENHANCING OUR HEALTH

CHAPTER FIVE

Getting Out and About

How Dogs Encourage Us to Go Outside and Move

Modern life is hectic and complicated, and many people feel like their plate of responsibilities is overflowing or like they're being pulled in multiple directions simultaneously. Plus, many people face health-related or environmental obstacles that may prevent them from getting outside and moving regularly. Only 53 percent of adults ages eighteen and older in the U.S. meet the recommended physical activity guidelines for aerobic exercise, according to the Centers for Disease Control and Prevention. This is another reason why having a dog is so beneficial to human health and well-being. Dogs crave time outside and movement— and they provide us, their humans, with a super-compelling reason to get off the couch or the computer and move more often. This is an instance where what's good for the pooch is good for the person, too.

Dog ownership has been referred to in the medical literature as a "public health interest" because it has the potential to promote health-boosting physical activity. And there's no mystery as to why. Dogs unknowingly inspire their owners to be more physically active, help them get in better shape, and manage their weight, all of which can reduce their risk of developing chronic health conditions like diabetes and heart disease.

According to a 2019 study by Carri Westgarth, PhD, and colleagues in the UK, people who own dogs are fourteen times more likely to report walking for recreation and four times more likely to meet the physical activity guidelines of 150 minutes of aerobic exercise per week than non-dog-owners are. The simple act of walking regularly confers numerous benefits for human health, from lowering the risk of developing high blood pressure, diabetes, and heart disease to strengthening bones and muscles, from easing stress and tension to boosting mood, energy, and cognitive function. And it's convenient. You can simply walk out your front door, put one foot in front of the other, and do the locomotion.

Beneficial Domino Effects

It's not just that dog-owners are likely to get more physical activity by walking their pooches—there's a positive ripple effect because they're also more likely to walk for recreation and transportation. In a survey of more than eighteen hundred adults in Perth, Australia, Hayley Cutt and a team of researchers found that less than 25 percent of dog-owners walked their dogs five or more times per week—but they *still* got significantly more exercise than non-dog-owners did. They simply spent more time walking in the neighborhood or for recreation and accumulated fifty-five more minutes of total physical activity per week, including forty more minutes of walking, than non-dog-owners did. The upshot: Dogs get people to walk more, even if it's not through "formal" dog walks.

That said, having a dog as a walking companion usually increases the enjoyment factor and may encourage people to walk longer, farther, or more often. In fact, walking or playing ball with your dog may not even feel like exercise because it's pleasant or playful, a form of fun, and a chance to spend quality time together. Research by Yue Liao, PhD, and colleagues found that exercising with a dog amplifies the mood-boosting effects of physical activity more than exercising alone. When people walk or jog with a furry friend, it doesn't feel like *work*; it feels like enjoyable time together, which makes us want to do it more often.

In a 2017 study by Carri Westgarth and her UK colleagues, researchers investigated dog-owners' reasons for walking their pups. They found that while the activity was usually framed as being "for the dog" and a responsibility that comes with dog ownership, the dog-owners reported deriving feelings of happiness from the activity, as long as they perceived that their dogs were enjoying the experience. There was an element of vicarious pleasure, in which dog-owners derived pleasure from witnessing their dogs' enjoyment of these outings, which created intrinsic motivation* to make walking their dogs a habit. The desire for physical activity and social interaction were secondary bonuses but not the driving factors. It was really the participants' interactions with their canine buddies—which the researchers referred to as the "significant other" of their dogs—that motivated their commitment to walking their pups regularly. And their desire to do "what's best for the dog" stemmed from their strong bond with their dogs.

Amy, who runs a nonprofit organization in Maryland, discovered this firsthand after she got her poodles Auggie and Billie in 2008 and

---

*"Intrinsic motivation" refers to doing something for the inherent enjoyment or satisfaction it brings, rather than for the attainment of a particular reward or outcome such as losing weight (which is a form of extrinsic motivation). While both forms of motivation can be useful in life, intrinsic motivation, in particular, is associated with sustained changes in behavior and improved well-being.

2011, respectively. Though she had always been active, doing yoga and going to the gym a few times per week, Amy's daily walking increased exponentially thanks to her pups. The dog walks quickly became essential, three times per day for ten to thirty minutes each during the week, with longer hikes in the woods on weekends and holidays. Auggie passed away in 2018, so now it's just Amy and Billie on these outings, and it's hard to discern whether the four-legged creature or the one with two legs enjoys them more. When Billie sees Amy reaching for the harness and leash, she spins around in circles like a circus dog. On weekdays, sometimes Amy resents the midday interruptions from her work, but the feeling quickly dissipates. "Once we're outside, I always realize how important the break is for me," says Amy, who has two adult children. "It gives me perspective on my day and forces me to slow down and think a bit, rather than just *doing*."

It turns out that pet dogs serve as a catalyst for increased physical activity for people of all ages, young and old alike. Research has found that kids, ages ten to twelve, who live in a household with a dog spend 29 more minutes walking and 142 more minutes doing physical activity per week than those who live without a dog. And a study by Philippa Margaret Dall, PhD, and colleagues found that older adults who have dogs and live on their own in a community take an average of 2,760 additional steps per day at a moderate intensity pace and spend less time sitting than their peers who don't have dogs.

Holistic Health Effects

In addition to the movement, spending time outside and connecting with nature, even if it's just by walking among the trees in your neighborhood or in a nearby park, can be profoundly therapeutic—for both species. Interestingly, research by Wilma L. Zijlema and colleagues found that people who have dogs not only have higher rates of leisure-time walking, but they also spend more time in natural settings that contain green or blue elements (think trees, forests, parks, or bodies of water) than non-dog-owners do. This is beneficial in its own right because being in natural outdoor settings has profoundly restorative effects on people, calming us down and easing our anxiety, improving our memory and cognitive function, reducing our blood pressure, improving our immune function, and increasing vitality and energy. If our beloved pups inspire us to get outside and get a healthy dose of sunlight (hello, vitamin D!), fresh air, phytoncides (aromatic, airborne particles with antimicrobial properties that are emitted by plants and trees), sounds from nature, and other health-promoting stimuli, we owe them a debt of gratitude for that, too.

Emma, who recently finished her university education in veterinary nursing in Scotland, can attest to this. She has had depression since she was fourteen, and it's her dog Murphy, an English springer spaniel, that inspires her to go outside regularly and get some movement. This has helped her control her mood disorder and cemented their bond. "When I walk with my dog alone outside or when he's running free off lead, I tend to sort out any pressing thoughts in my head or even tune them out completely and feel much better," she says. "I love him so much and have no clue where I'd be without him."

 Eating and Exercising for Two

During the pandemic, many people and their pooches put on extra pounds, especially early on when we were hunkered down inside and we fell into bad health habits. While your dog can't prevent you from stress-eating cookies or ice cream at night, they can help you move more, which can help you and your dog lose weight if you need or want to. By itself, walking with a dog isn't necessarily enough to help dog-owners regain healthy habits, but it's certainly a step in the right direction. And it turns out that the connection between you and your dog can amplify these benefits because these changes can be maintained for the long run.

In an intriguing pair of studies by J. Rebecca Niese and colleagues in the

Netherlands, researchers examined the effects of a human-centered versus a canine-centered approach to losing weight—meaning, the primary focus of the intervention was either on people or their pets—using diet- and exercise-related programs. Diet and exercise advice for weight loss were given to four different groups: humans only, primarily humans with extra advice for dog weight loss, dogs only (the advice was given to their human caretakers), and primarily dogs with extra advice for human weight loss. In all four conditions, both the people and their dogs lost weight. It didn't matter if the focus of the program was on helping the person or the dog lose weight; when they did either program together both creatures slimmed down. But when the advice was given for both humans and dogs, the weight loss for both was significantly greater than when the focus was on only one species. People's sense of responsibility for taking charge of their own and their dogs' body weight increased significantly, and unhealthy feeding and exercise practices in relation to the dogs decreased. In other words, there was a powerful synergistic effect between eating well and exercising and losing weight among people and their pups.

Similarly, a weight-loss program at the Wellness Institute at Northwestern Memorial Hospital in Chicago sought to capitalize on "the human-companion animal bond." In a one-year study called "People and Pets Exercising Together" (PPET, for short), thirty-six pairs of overweight or obese people with an obese dog and fifty-six overweight or obese people without a dog participated in a weight-loss program. In both cases, the people received dietary and physical activity advice as a group; meanwhile, the dogs were given a calorie-controlled prescription diet. At the one-year mark, the people's weight loss was comparable in both groups (around 5 percent, which is known to be beneficial for human health and leads to a reduction in cardiovascular risk) and the obese dogs lost an average of 15 percent of their weight. Both groups increased their weekly physical activity level, but the dog-owners did even more and there was better adherence to the program with this group.

Among the most interesting findings was that the people who did the program with their pets identified key themes that were uniquely helpful to them: that their dog served as a motivator and consistent initiator of physical activity, that they thoroughly enjoyed walking their dogs, and that they felt parental pride in their newly svelte dogs. Simply put, the dogs served as a powerful form of social support and motivation during the weight-loss period, largely because they inspired their human partners to move more—and the creatures on both ends of the leash ended up benefiting.

Even outside of a formal weight-loss program, dogs can help their owners lose excess weight. Katie, who is in her early thirties and lives in Colorado, says that after spending most of her life on the heavier end of the weight spectrum, her dog Addie, a Lab/chow chow mix, helped her slim down. After finishing her master's degree in meteorology, Katie was struggling with depression, for which she began taking medication. Fed up with feeling sluggish, miserable, and uncomfortable with her body and state of mind, she decided to take steps to improve her physical health. As a starting point, she upgraded her diet and began consuming more veggies and whole grains and fewer burgers and less junk food. She also kicked a stress-eating habit (often involving chocolate). She started taking Addie on several walks a day, which they both loved. That inspired Katie to embark on a regular exercise program and train for a 5K. Having Addie's joyful company and smiling face at her side motivated her to stick with these new healthy habits. "I have lost almost twenty-five pounds and I have never felt better," says Katie. "I can't thank my dog enough."

Feeding the Love Between You

Jen is a dedicated runner with a long list of tricks to use on a cold, rainy, gray day when she just doesn't feel like getting off the couch and out the door. First, she'll put on her running clothes. Then, she'll put on her running shoes and stand up. If that isn't enough, and Jen is looking for excuses to linger on the couch and maybe send another work email, there is always a fail-safe way to get herself moving: Hopper. The most senior member of the Golden Ratio squad was Jen's #1 running pal for six years (until arthritis made slow walks easier). All Jen had to do was put Hopper's outside collar on her and the excitement would kick in. Hopps would wag her tail, spin in circles, and stand with her nose against the door, absolutely ready to go regardless of the time or the weather. No one with a heart could say no to that, and soon enough, both of them would be out running through the woods, happy for the physical activity and each other. These days, Jen needs to muster her own motivation to run on dreary days.

While the perks of spending more time outside are undeniable, perhaps the biggest benefit of being physically active with our dogs is that it deepens the bond between us. A study by Kate Campbell and colleagues at the University of Otago in New Zealand explored the effects of dog-walking on adult dog-owners and identified three common themes: The participants had an "emotional connection" with their dog, walking their dog led to "healthy interactions" with other people and nature, and the participants valued dog-walking for its contributions to their own "psychological wellbeing" because it allowed them to do something that brings their dog pleasure. All of these elements improved the lives of humans and dogs alike, and the walks helped the dog-owners feel better. As the researchers reported, "Participants explained that dog-walking generated feelings of relaxation, calmness, and stress-relief."

It's hard to stay tense or in a bad mood when you're strolling along with your beloved pooch, soaking up the fresh air and occasionally looking into each other's smiling eyes. More often than not, we're happy when our dogs are happy—and they tend to be happy on their walks. As soon as you grab the leash, your dog's tail may start wagging, or they may do a happy dance with squeals of excitement—these are expressions of joy, which can be contagious. And when you're actually outside on a walk, the mutual enjoyment you're experiencing may serve as a form of positive reinforcement for the emotional bond between you.

Participants in the New Zealand study explained that there are several ways their dog walks brought them closer to their pooches. The dog walks gave the people a sense of purpose and personal satisfaction, especially when they saw how excited their dogs got for the walks and how happy they were while walking. The walks also helped people understand their dogs better. By having focused time for just them and their dogs, dog-owners learned how to read their dogs' expressions, glances, and body language better. The regular exercise also helped some dogs behave better—something any trainer will tell you is true—and that, in turn, brought more peace into the home. Reducing anxiety surrounding bad dog behavior also allows people to feel a more positive connection with their dogs.

Interestingly, the influence of dog-walking and bond enhancement may go in both directions. Regularly walking your dog can make you feel closer to each other, and having a close bond with your pup may make you more inclined to walk your dog regularly and often. In a study by Angela L. Curl, PhD, and colleagues, researchers examined the associations between dog ownership, bonding, walking behavior, and physical health among older adults in the U.S. It turned out that people who had stronger bonds with their dogs were more likely to walk them and spend more time walking their dog each time.

After moving in with her boyfriend in 2020, Sarah, who works in marketing, quickly became attached to his pug, named Tiberius. Sarah has fibromyalgia—a disorder that causes widespread musculoskeletal pain that can be quite debilitating—and she noticed that Tiberius was "getting a bit too chonky." Because she needs regular exercise to try to control her pain level, she recruited him as her fitness buddy, and they began going on regular walks together. Since then, Tiberius, now seven years old, has lost weight, and the frequency and intensity of Sarah's pain flare-ups have improved considerably. "He has been such a benefit for my mental health," says Sarah, who lives in the UK, "and he enjoys walks as much as I do now."

In a study by Joan Wharf Higgins, PhD, and colleagues, researchers conducted focus groups and interviewed dog-owners about their walking practices and their relationships with their dogs, in order to try to better understand how and why dog-walking enhances physical activity levels. Four prevailing themes emerged, two of which were familiar—that dogs serve as social conduits and that they help us move more—and two of which were novel—that dog-walking transcends the human-animal distinction and that dogs serve as "walking sole mates." The dog-owners in the study described their pups as family members, with whom they have a strong emotional connection, and they empathetically felt their dogs' happiness at walk time, which reinforced their desire to walk their dogs. As the researchers noted, "an empathetic stance benefits dog guardians because, as valued family members whose health and happiness they are responsible for, their canine companions serve to motivate, enable, and sustain walking behaviors."

In other instances, beloved canine companions may help their people dig deep and find the inner strength to cope with or overcome incredible physical challenges by moving more often. In 2015, Charlie*, a paramedic in the UK, was in a serious car accident that she was lucky to survive. Even so, she was left with significant injuries, including a shattered arm, fractured kneecap, and nerve damage. When she got home from the hospital, she spent time with her dog Diesel, a German shepherd/rottweiler/Staffordshire bull terrier mix, curled up under her legs at the end of the recliner. Gradually, Charlie recovered enough to start taking Diesel on short walks that slowly became longer. Through these, "I was able to build my strength back up, and I eventually returned to work as a paramedic," says Charlie, who is now in her late twenties.

Unfortunately, in 2017, an older shoulder condition that was aggravated by the car accident forced her to take a break from work. Hardship didn't stop there for Charlie because she became extremely weak due to severe anemia and developed a large stomach ulcer from all the anti-inflammatory medications she'd been taking, under her doctors' orders, for her joint pain. In 2019, her stomach became perforated and she had to undergo emergency surgery.

When she finally went home from the hospital, Diesel was over the moon with excitement. "I felt more loved than I thought possible," Charlie recalls. The recovery process began anew, this time at a slower rate. Slowly but surely, Charlie began to regain her strength, and "more than a year on, I'm back to being able to walk him," she says. "Really, without him, there's no way I would have regained physical fitness as quickly as I did if I didn't have him." Because they've spent so much time together in recent years, their bond has become unbreakable. Diesel is now approaching his senior years (approximately nine years old) but he's still an eighty-eight-pound hunk of "ginger love." "That dog is my heart animal through and through and I genuinely don't know how I would have managed without him," says Charlie, who is now a social media manager. "He, and he alone, is the reason I coped mentally with everything that's happened."

As Charlie discovered, the comfort and support that can come from someone's bond with their dog can enhance their motivation to take their beloved pooch for walks, as a form of loving payback. In a small study of adults with long-term health conditions such as multiple sclerosis, osteoarthritis, asthma, or anxiety and depression, researchers accompanied them on their usual dog walks, captured conversations about their health and well-being through audio recordings, then interviewed the participants about how walking their dog contributes to their health and well-being. They found that the participants with long-term health conditions had close relationships with their dogs and felt an "obligation of love" that brought them into the dog-walking space "where gentle encounters and pleasant sensations" enhanced their sense of well-being.

Even when some of us may not feel like going outside because it's freezing cold or raining or we're feeling wiped out, we'll take our dogs for a walk because we're willing to do things for our pups that we're not inclined to do for ourselves. It's an expression of love, a gesture of goodwill. We see it as our duty or responsibility—"an obligation of love"—and we don't want to let our pooches down. They undoubtedly appreciate it.

And over time, a positive self-perpetuating cycle may develop in which the physical benefits and emotional connection that come from being physically active with your dog enhance the bond between you; this in turn is likely to motivate you to continue walking, jogging, biking, Rollerblading, or doing other physical activities alongside your pup, which will strengthen your bond even more . . . and so on. To change things up and expand your mutual comfort zone, you could go swimming or train for a race together. Or you could go hiking and camping, which would maximize the benefits for both of you by extending the amount of time you spend together in the great outdoors. Whatever physical activity you choose to do, you and your furry fitness buddy can spur each other on every step of the way and bask in the sheer enjoyment of your shared outing. You're likely to return home feeling closer than ever.

CHAPTER SIX

Strong Always

How Dogs Can Support Our Physical Wellbeing

Doctors don't usually write prescriptions advising patients to get a dog—but perhaps they should. After all, dogs can have amazing effects on people's physical health and their ability to handle various medical challenges. Canine companions can protect people from developing allergies, reduce blood pressure and heart rates (especially in response to stressful situations), and ease chronic pain (from chronic migraines and low back pain, for instance). Research has also found that dog-owners fall asleep more easily than non-dog-owners do. The beneficial effects on our physical wellbeing are wide-ranging and have various underpinnings, as you'll see.

For starters, when people are entrusted with taking care of another creature, that can make them more willing to take good care of themselves, so that they'll be around for the long haul. Dogs also help promote a consistent sleep routine, based on when they go out to pee before bedtime and when they get up in the morning. In the long term, more restful sleep can help people maintain a healthy weight, strengthen their immune function, preserve their memory, reduce stress, and lower their risk of developing serious health problems like heart disease and diabetes.

For Amy, who has several health challenges, including chronic pain and depression, Leia, her nine-year-old cattle dog, keeps her going. Amy's husband is in the Navy and has been deployed for much of the last few years, so it's just Amy, Leia, and their two cats at home. "Having Leia to push me to get outside and be more active has been invaluable," says Amy, who's in her early forties and lives in Washington State. Besides going for walks, they do a lot of gardening together, and seeing Leia's delight about getting out and chasing squirrels makes Amy feel better. "I know some days I would just stay in bed, but because I have her and have to take care of her, I press on," she says.

As it happens, dogs generally seem to make us healthier than we would be without them, and this seems to be true across cultures. Bruce Headey, PhD, conducted a survey of Australian dog-owners and found they take fewer trips to the doctor and sleep better than non-dog-owners do. They are also less likely to be on heart medications. It's not that dog-owners are naturally healthier; bringing a dog into your life somehow brings these benefits along. James Serpell, PhD, conducted a study in the UK that followed pet owners through the ten months after they adopted their pet. Among dog and cat owners, there was a significant reduction in minor health problems such as headaches, difficulty sleeping, indigestion, and sinus trouble in the first month, and this was sustained for dog-owners throughout the study's duration; their scores on measures of general health also improved, and dog-owners increased their physical activity considerably. In China, a study by Headey and colleagues, published in the journal

Social Indicators Research, also found that dog-owners "exercised more frequently, slept better, had higher self-reported fitness and health, took fewer days off sick from work and were seen less by doctors."

These effects are hardly a coincidence. Sharing your life with a dog can affect your health profoundly from head to toe, from your state of mind to your movement habits, and even some of the inner workings of your body and its response to environmental influences. American thriller writer Dean Koontz had it right when he said, "Petting, scratching, and cuddling a dog could be as soothing to the mind and heart as deep meditation and almost as good for the soul as prayer."

Changing Our Biology

Some of the health benefits that stem from living with a canine companion are invisible to the naked eye and can't be felt because they occur deep down inside us. As you'll see, sharing life with a dog can influence the human microbiome, the community of bacteria, fungi, and other microorganisms that live inside us and on our skin. These microbes are a major part of who we are—our bodies contain as many microbial cells as human cells, according to the latest research. This may sound problematic, but the majority of these bacteria are actually beneficial. The bacteria in our microbiome aid with digestion, produce vitamins our bodies need, regulate our immune systems, and help protect us from harmful bacteria that can cause diseases.

Of course, humans are not the only species with microbiomes. Our dogs have them, too, and as we live together, we swap microbes with our furry companions, who roll in mud, sniff all kinds of things on walks, and bring microbes into our homes on their fur and skin. Research by Rob Knight, PhD, at the University of Colorado, Boulder, and colleagues found that people who have one or more dogs in their homes have many of the same microorganisms on their skin as their dogs do. Essentially, people and their dogs end up having similar populations of microbes on their skin and fur, and to a lesser extent in their guts, due to frequent direct contact with each other. Which makes sense if you consider how much fur-to-skin (and vice versa) transfer there is of microbes when we pet, play, or cuddle with our dogs.

Bringing a dog into our homes even alters what's in our household dust. A study by Albert Barberán and colleagues examined the contents of household dust in approximately twelve hundred homes throughout the U.S. and found that while bacterial and fungal communities varied according to climate and geographical region, the presence of pets, especially dogs, had a "significant influence on the types of bacteria found inside our homes, highlighting that who you live with determines what bacteria are found inside your home." No matter how tidy your home may be, there's some dust in the air, on the floor, and on surfaces. In a study by Alexandra Sitarik and her colleagues, researchers collected dust samples from fifty-four family homes—half of which had a dog and half of which didn't—when the dog was initially brought into the home and a year later. By the one-year mark, the presence of a dog in the home was associated with "a higher percentage of variation in bacterial dust composition," including traces of *Moraxella, Porphyromonas, Capnocytophaga, Fusobacterium, Streptococcus*, and *Treponema* bacteria. The real surprise: This isn't a bad thing.

On the contrary, what's come to be called the "Microbiota Hypothesis" suggests that dust from homes with dogs may influence the development and response of the human immune system by changing the composition of the gut microbiome in ways that reduce someone's risk for allergies and asthma. A considerable body of research has found that young children who grow up with dogs in their households are less likely to develop allergies, eczema, or asthma, which often occur together as part of what's called the allergic triad. The theory, according to allergists, is that early exposure to dog dander could induce a high-dose tolerance to allergens and that living with a dog could provide a "mini farm" environment that modifies development of a child's immune system. By stimulating their immune system *not* to react to dog dander and other microbes carried by pups, growing up with a dog helps kids develop a greater tolerance to dogs, certain germs, and airborne allergens, thus preventing potential allergies from developing.

Scientists believe this may be why kids raised with dogs have fewer allergies than those from pet-free homes. Research by Bill Hesselmar, MD, PhD, from the University of Gothenburg in Sweden, and a team of researchers examined data from more than one thousand seven- to eight-year-old children and found that among those who grew up without pets, 49 percent went on to develop allergies, while the rate dropped to 43 percent for kids with one pet and to 24 percent for kids with three pets. They concluded that the prevalence of allergic conditions in children was reduced in a dose-dependent fashion, based on the number of household pets living with the child during the first year of life. This is an example of the "mini-farm" effect in action. Another study by Dennis R. Ownby, MD, and his colleagues at the Medical College of Georgia found that living with two or more dogs or cats in the first year of life cut a child's risk of developing future allergies significantly. The upshot: Living with more animals means exposure to more types of microbes—and potentially more protection from allergic diseases.

A Natural Form of Pain Relief

In recent years, Risa has developed ulcerative colitis and psoriatic arthritis, a painful double whammy that has put her on disability leave from her job. Since she adopted her maltipoo Penny in the summer of 2017, the pup has been a great source of comfort. "She likes to lick the swollen joints on my hands and tuck herself into me at night," says Risa, who is in her mid-thirties and lives in New York. "She can sense when I'm not feeling well and will not leave my side if I'm having a particularly bad day." Having a dog has greatly improved Risa's mental health and helped her physically, inspiring her to go outside and move more often—because Penny "relies on me day in and day out. We have grown rather dependent on each other, but I'm okay with that."

Having a dog doesn't make you impervious to pain, but it can make the discomfort more bearable. This is partly because having a canine companion provides a continuous source of meaning, connection, and support in your life, which can indirectly help with pain. Research led by Mary Janevic, PhD, from the University of Michigan School of Public Health, examined how older adults with chronic pain felt their pets affected them. Some of their responses were illuminating. The participants reported that their dogs motivated them to get up and get moving, which helped alleviate their pain. The pets distracted people from their pain and generally improved their moods. They facilitated socializing, allowing these people to connect more with others and receive social support. And these canine companions brought pleasure and laughter, which also helped distract people from their pain. In analyzing the themes to these responses, the researchers found that they align with cognitive-behavioral self-management strategies that are recommended for people with chronic pain conditions such as migraine, back pain, arthritis, and fibromyalgia. These strategies include managing moods, relaxing, distracting your mind from how your body feels, participating in everyday activities and socializing, and engaging in physical activities (such as walking your dog). As Janevic noted in an interview, "Engaging in pet care can give a sense of daily purpose and routine that keeps a person going, even when they are having a pain flare-up. In this way, pets can be thought of as a *natural* resource for chronic pain self-management."

These findings were echoed in a study by April DuCasse and colleagues at Florida A&M University, which found that people with chronic pain reported that their pets improved their mood, their sense of hope, their activity levels, their comfort, and their functionality. In another study, led by Eloise Carr, PhD, at the University of Calgary in Canada, researchers interviewed a dozen people with chronic pain who lived with a dog, and identified four common themes: that dogs give life meaning, they serve as caregivers, dogs give emotional support, and they provide companionship. Besides having a positive impact on their human's quality of life, the research found that canine companions provided some of the participants with "a reason to live and focus on the future" and "support that mitigates their suffering and enables them to live a more meaningful life."

Perri, thirty, a fourth-grade teacher in Florida who has chronic migraines, as well as anxiety and depression, can relate to these findings. Whenever Perri has a migraine flare-up, her dog Maya, a shepherd/terrier/sheltie mix, refuses to leave Perri's side until she feels better. It's as if Maya has a sixth sense for when Perri is in pain and serves as her canine guardian angel. Maya isn't a trained service dog, Perri says, "but she's very in tune with how I'm feeling and knows just what to do to make me feel better, which is usually lying close to me."

Getting to the Heart of the Matter

When it comes to the cardiovascular system, research suggests that having a dog is associated with lower blood pressure and cholesterol levels, a reduced risk of having type 2 diabetes, and reduced physiological responses to stress. These effects may partly explain why dog ownership is associated with a 31 percent decreased risk of death from cardiovascular disease. This isn't entirely surprising given that being in the presence of a dog has a calming effect on most of us. But when you're with your *own* dog, the perks are even more pronounced because of the trust, affection, and connection that exists between you.

Across various age groups, multiple studies have found that people's heart rate, blood pressure, and stress levels are lower when there's a dog around. In a study by Erika Friedmann, PhD, and her colleagues, researchers examined the impact of a dog's presence while kids, ages nine to sixteen, were asked to read aloud. The kids' heart rate and blood pressure readings were lower when the dog was present, which the researchers interpreted to mean that the pup's presence led the participants to modify their perceptions of the situation, making it feel less threatening and more friendly. Similarly, in a study by Julia K. Vormbrock and John M. Grossberg, male and female undergraduate students

interacted with dogs tactually, verbally, and visually while the participants' blood pressure and heart rate were recorded. It turned out that
the participants' blood pressure levels were lowest while petting the dog
and their heart rates were lower while touching or talking to the dog.

It's not just that when people are thrust into stressful experimental
situations, the presence of *any* friendly creature provides support and
eases their stress. Research shows that the presence of other people,
for example, doesn't always have the same beneficial effects as the presence of pooches. In a study by Karen Allen, PhD, and her colleagues,
adults were placed in mentally and physically stressful situations, in
which they were asked to perform mental arithmetic and endure a
"cold pressor" test in which their hand was immersed in ice water (this
test induces a physiological stress response). The participants endured
these tests alone, with their spouse present, with their dog or cat present (if they had a pet), with a friend (if they didn't have a pet) present,
or with their spouse *and* a pet or friend present. In all of the scenarios,
the people who had their pets present had lower baseline heart rates
and blood pressure levels; what's more, their blood pressure and heart
rate increases during the stressful situations were smaller and they
recovered faster when their pets were present.

What this likely means is that when these dog-owners are faced
with the stresses and strains that are ubiquitous in modern life, their
bodies tend to be less physiologically reactive to the situation at hand;
even as they cope with the challenge mentally, their cardiovascular
response remains relatively calm. Given the vicissitudes of our world,
this is a potentially significant asset in the health department. If having
a dog can help you avoid getting ratcheted up physically when dealing
with stress, there will be less strain on your cardiovascular system,
which is beneficial over time.

Even if you develop a heart-related problem, having a dog may help
mitigate some of the effects on you. A case in point: A study by Karen
Allen, Barbara Shykoff, and Joseph Izzo, Jr., found that, when people
were faced with mental stress, pets effectively limited their blood
pressure increases, but medication did not. In the study, patients with

hypertension were given a difficult mental problem to solve. All had similar baseline responses to doing the difficult math test. Then, the participants were given a blood pressure–lowering medication. While this uniformly lowered resting blood pressure, the impact under mental stress varied. Pet-owners who took the medication had significantly lower physiological responses—such as blood pressure spikes—to mental stress than people without pets did. This led the researchers to conclude that the social support provided by pets plays a major role in reducing their owners' physiological response to mental stress.

Of course, having a dog isn't enough to prevent people from developing cardiovascular diseases, but when serious problems do arise, dogs can help us recover better. Among people who have heart attacks, research by Mary Herrald, PhD, and colleagues found that those who have dogs are significantly more likely to complete cardiac rehab—which typically involves physical therapy and education about how to manage risk factors and avoid everyday sources of stress—than those who don't have canine companions. What's more, research by Mwenya Mubanga, PhD, and colleagues found that people who have dogs survive longer after having heart attacks or ischemic strokes. Many other studies support these findings regarding dog ownership and survival after cardiovascular events.

One of the early explorations into this subject came in a study by Erika Friedmann and Sue Thomas in 1995. They followed 369 patients for a year after they had a heart attack and found that dog-owners were significantly less likely to die within a year of having a major heart attack than non-dog-owners were. While the explanation for these positive effects isn't immediately apparent, one logical theory could be that because dog-owners need to take their dogs for walks on a regular basis, they get more physical activity, which in turn leads to better cardiovascular health. But it's not the driving force behind the results. Among the pet-owning patients who did *not* have dogs, none had died within a year of having a heart attack. The protection was there even for people with pets that don't require exercise.

So there has to be more to the story, and a big part of it probably has to do with the emotional and social support these furry creatures give us. Social support—a theme that recurs throughout this book—is the foundation for the many ways our dogs improve our lives. In the realm of psychology, "social support" describes the feeling that we are cared for, supported, and as though we are part of a community. Two important pillars of social support are emotional support, which includes intimacy, love, affection, trust, and acceptance, and companionship, where we feel accepted and as though we belong with the supportive person or community.* During the COVID-19 pandemic, a study led by Jonathan Bowen investigated how dog-owners in Spain characterized the social support they obtained from their dogs and found that the human participants "got comfort from physical contact with their dogs, shared activities with them and treated them as confidants in a similar way to friends and family." The researchers noted that in many instances "dogs offer the advantage of being more available than human sources of support."

Having social support doesn't just feel good—it is actually a significant factor in people's mental and physical health, contributing to our being physically healthier and reducing our risk of premature mortality. In fact, a meta-analysis by Hsiu-Hung Wang, PhD, and colleagues found that people's level of social support significantly predicted every one of sixteen different health-outcome variables, including their overall health status, physical and psychological symptoms, coping behavior, depression, and stress level. When human beings don't have access to robust social support—whether it's because they are generally socially isolated, estranged from their family, living in unsupportive situations, or elderly and have seen much of their social network move or pass away—their health can suffer. Under these circumstances dogs can provide increased feelings of social support and bring all the associated health benefits.

Besides providing us with many daily activities that foster a bonding

---

*The other two pillars are financial support and informational support, which, unfortunately, our dogs usually can't provide.

experience, such as feeding, walking, grooming, and petting our canine companions, their needs and their attention lend a welcome sense of order, structure, purpose, and responsibility to our lives. In addition, researchers speculate that dogs may provide us with a subtle form of support that goes above and beyond what people can do for us.

Beyond the studies and statistics, many people have experienced these benefits firsthand. After Michelle's husband Clint had a stroke in 2018, he was left with memory and cognitive challenges as well as speech problems that required him to go on disability leave from his job with the county government. He was always their hound dog Allie's favorite in the family, and ever since Clint came home from the stroke rehabilitation center, Allie has been Clint's stalwart companion. "She has been by his side every day—he'll talk to her, which has helped him with his speech problems, and she'll box him in on the couch when he's doing too much or his blood pressure increases," says Michelle, who works part-time at their local library in Arizona. Having Allie to watch over Clint while she's at work gives her great comfort.

Having support and attention from a canine caregiver can be particularly valuable as someone is grappling with a chronic health condition or recovering from a serious illness. As Erika Friedmann and colleagues wrote in *Public Health Reports*, "Pets are also a constantly available source of and direction for [our] attention. The unambivalent nature of the exchange of affection between people and animals differs from exchanges with close family members and other relatives." While family relationships are often "charged with ambivalence and negative emotional states," our feelings toward our dogs are often unequivocal. Not only do we love and adore them unconditionally, but we choose to bask in the unbridled affection and comfort our dogs provide us, without any strings attached. "Pets are a source of comfort that can be scheduled on demand of the owner, in almost any quantity, without bargaining or supplication," as the researchers noted. That's powerful medicine, indeed, and it changes us, both physiologically and psychologically.

Besides having specific effects on various parameters of your health, your relationship with your dog may unwittingly alter your attitude and approach toward your health and your life. Because you probably want to be around as long as possible to take care of your beloved canine companion, you may feel inspired to improve *your* lifestyle and stress-management habits. You may feel motivated to take better overall care of yourself, whether that means taking your medication as directed, exercising regularly, or going to bed earlier. If you're not inclined to do it for your own well-being, you may be for the sake of your beloved pooch. When you love a dog with all your heart and soul, you want to maximize and enjoy the time you have together.

CHAPTER SEVEN

To Serve and Protect

How Dogs Can Detect Diseases and Danger

A few years ago, John, a thin, athletic-looking guy in his early sixties, had a persistent case of indigestion that lasted for ten days. He tried to ignore it and power through his daily routine, working in marine construction in the Florida Keys, even though he felt weak. While he didn't plan to go to the doctor, his dog Chomp—a Brug (a Brussels griffon/pug mix) with wiry blond hair and an unforgettable underbite—had other ideas. Three times during that ten-day span, John woke up to Chomp standing on his chest, furiously licking his face with his sandpaper-like tongue. For John, these weren't like normal middle-of-the-night awakenings to a strange sound, his wife's movements in bed, or another disturbance; each time, he felt like he had to drag himself back into consciousness. Once he did, John would push Chomp off him and roll over to go back to sleep. Meanwhile, Chomp, who was usually funny and playful, would stand guard, resting his head on the side of the bed and staring at John while he slept. "I could feel his breath on my face, and every time I opened my eyes, he was sitting there with his little coal-black eyes staring back at me," recalls John.

John knew that Chomp was trying to tell him something, so he finally went to see a cardiologist. During a stress test, John's heart literally stopped—he essentially died in the doctor's office—and they had to resuscitate him. Within a few hours, he was airlifted to a hospital in Miami where it was discovered that he had a 98 percent blockage in his left anterior descending artery, the main artery that supplies blood to the left side of the heart. Heart attacks that happen when this artery is blocked are called "widow-makers" because they're so deadly. John was lucky to be alive.

While he had been sleeping, apparently he would stop breathing periodically, which Chomp sensed; it was why he would jump on John's chest, doing what John called "doggy CPR." At the hospital, doctors put in a stent and John immediately felt better when he woke up. While Chomp is no longer with us, he continues to live large in John's heart. When John relayed this story, the love and appreciation for Chomp were palpable in his voice. "I would not be here without him—I am absolutely certain I owe Chomp my life," says John.

Dogs have a powerful ability to sense when their humans are experiencing medical problems. They can detect the onset of low blood sugar in someone with diabetes, a seizure in someone with epilepsy, or the presence of airborne allergens in those with life-threatening allergies. These trained canine companions make it easier for people with certain illnesses or medical conditions to go about the business of daily living with a greater sense of security. Even dogs that aren't trained as service dogs can detect signs of certain cancers, diabetes, allergies, and other medical conditions through their incredibly keen sense of smell.

The Power of a Dog's Nose

Medical-alert dogs rely on their acute sense of smell to sniff out bio-chemical changes in the human body. Before taking a deep dive into the science behind these abilities, let's consider some amazing facts about dogs' noses. A dog's sense of smell is far superior to a human's because canines have 200 million to 1 billion olfactory receptors in their nasal cavities, depending on the breed, compared to approximately 6 million in people; plus, the olfactory lobe of the brain, which analyzes scents, is roughly forty times larger in a dog than in a human. Dogs also have a unique olfactory organ called Jacobson's organ, which is located at the bottom of their nasal passages and detects pheromones and other body chemicals. Scientists estimate that dogs can smell ten thousand to one hundred thousand times better than people can. That's why dogs can tell with a quick sniff if a new furry friend is male or female, friendly or aggressive, healthy or sick.* While humans mostly perceive our environment visually while also noticing smells, the reverse is true for dogs, who rely primarily on scent augmented by vision.

Dogs' sense of smell is incredibly vital to their functionality and sur-vival. Jen has seen this with her own dogs. In her older years Jen's dog K developed uveitis, inflammation in the middle layer of the eye that can impair vision; it often runs in golden retrievers, and the flare-ups are incredibly painful. Jen spent months trying to control it, but K eventu-ally needed surgical ablations in both eyes; these stopped the pain but left her blind. For the first week at home, she would bonk into furniture and doorways, even though she knew the layout of her small house very well. Then Jen got the idea to buy a set of essential oils to mark the house. Using a cotton swab, she put a tiny dab of oil at the height of K's

---

*When dogs sniff other dogs, as they often do, males tend to go for the tail area first (skin glands around the anus secrete odors), while female dogs more frequently start by sniffing other dogs' faces (where saliva smells are plentiful), according to Alexandra Horowitz, author of *Being a Dog: Following the Dog into a World of Smell*.

head around all the door frames, the staircase, and on some furniture that she was prone to walking into. Jen used a different oil for each area so the doorway to the kitchen smelled different from the threshold of the stairs. The amount was so small that humans couldn't smell anything, but it was enough that K was instantly able to navigate the house with almost no collisions. Those tiny dabs of scent essentially gave her back her ability to "see" the house.

Dogs can also see into the past with their noses. The scents we leave behind provide clues that our dogs pick up on. Just like people can tell if someone snuck into their home and smoked a cigarette, dogs know who has been nearby, how long ago they were there, and what was going on with them, by the scents that linger after they're gone. Of course, we have all seen this in action—at least on TV—with scent-tracking dogs who take a couple of whiffs of a sock and run off into the woods to hunt down a missing person. Their bodies have evolved to support this. In fact, many hounds and other tracking breeds have long ears because they help direct and concentrate smells toward their sensitive noses. Take bloodhounds, for example. When their noses are pointing down toward the ground, their long ears sweep up odors from the ground and fan scents from the environment toward the nose to maximize smelling opportunities, according to Alexandra Horowitz, author of *Being a Dog: Following the Dog into a World of Smell.*

Detecting a Whiff of Disease

With such finely tuned olfactory abilities, dogs can notice subtle changes in the chemicals our bodies produce, changes that would escape human sensory detection or that occur so early in the course of a disease that the affected person doesn't feel much different. Human beings don't have an olfactory system that's strong enough or sensitive

---

*For humans and dogs alike, sneezes are reflexive ways of ridding the nose of something that's ticklish, irritating, or foreign. But for dogs, there may be a secondary purpose: to clear the nose of a scent that's been detected, in order to get ready for the next one, according to Horowitz.

enough to detect any of these chemicals. "Dogs are preternaturally sensitive to changes in their people," explains Horowitz, head of the Dog Cognition Lab at Barnard College in New York City. "If a person is infected with a virus or bacteria, they will smell different." It has to do with illness-related changes in their body chemistry.

This is why dogs are increasingly being used experimentally to detect diseases in humans—such as cancer, diabetes, tuberculosis, narcolepsy, malaria, and even COVID-19—by sniffing their blood, sweat, skin, or urine samples or their exhaled breath in order to identify changes in the scent of these substances. In the fall of 2020, it became clear that dogs were able to detect COVID-19 infections by scent. Working sniffer dogs were trained to smell COVID in sweat samples, and in early trials, they were able to detect COVID even before a PCR test would come back positive. A recent study by Edward H. Maa, MD, and colleagues found that trained canines can detect the scent of menthone, a volatile organic compound, in human sweat before and during epileptic seizures as well as in fear-scented sweat. Similarly, dogs can be trained to detect isoprene, a common chemical in human breath that rises significantly when people with type 1 diabetes are experiencing dangerously low blood sugar.

These super-sniffers can also detect the scent of hypoglycemia (low blood sugar) and hyperglycemia (high blood sugar). When blood sugar levels go outside the target range in people with diabetes, it can be dangerous, leading to blurred vision, confusion, slurred speech, seizures, coma, and other life-threatening events, if they're left untreated. Pet dogs can sometimes sense when this is happening, and studies have found that dog-owners with diabetes report changes in their dogs' behavior when their blood sugar swings in a dangerous direction. Researchers suspect that changes in smell are what help dogs detect this worrisome drop in blood sugar, given that dogs have alerted their (human) family members to changes in their blood sugar while they were sleeping or in another room behind closed doors (so dogs couldn't have picked up on changes in their humans' behavior).

Lauren, who has type 1 diabetes and is in her late twenties, says that her yellow Lab Ricki, who was trained to be a diabetes-alert dog, signals her about worrisome changes in her blood sugar levels. Ricki can detect the blood sugar changes through shifts in Lauren's body odor. While Ricki was initially trained to alert Lauren to blood sugar levels above 200 mg/dL and under 100 mg/dL, in recent years the canine guardian has honed her detection skills to a narrower range, which has helped Lauren with her blood sugar regulation. Once, when Lauren had a bad cold and was sleeping in the afternoon, she heard a snorting sound that kept getting louder and "tippy tap nails" that kept circling her bed. Eventually, Ricki pawed Lauren to wake her up. "My blood sugar was around thirty-five and judging by the amount of drool on the floor, she'd been trying to get me up for quite some time," says Lauren, a communications specialist in Southern California. "I know she saved my life that day—I was in such a deep sleep and my blood sugar was so low." Since then Ricki has woken her up numerous times, usually when her blood sugar is at a less dangerous level.

The theory is that the components of volatile organic compounds that are emitted by the human body through breath, sweat, skin, urine, feces, and vaginal secretions reflect the metabolic condition of that individual. Chemical analyses have found 1,840 volatile chemicals that may serve as markers for cancer and other diseases in humans. When a medical condition changes the concentration of these chemicals or introduces a new one, a person's body odor changes. Untrained dogs may notice that their human family member simply smells differently, and trained dogs may recognize specific scents that are tied to specific diseases. In each instance, a dog's sense of smell is the common denominator in these illness-detection abilities.

CLUES ABOUT CANCER

Scientists first hypothesized that dogs could detect the scent of cancer back in 1989. Melanoma was one of the first cancers studied with respect to canine detection. Dogs that were trained to recognize the scent of melanoma were able the vast majority of the time to identify it in melanoma tissue samples that were hidden on the skin of healthy volunteers, with no false positives, meaning the dogs never indicated there was cancer when there was not. Since then, dozens of studies have provided evidence that this cancer-detection phenomenon is real, and it could have major impacts on healthcare. In a study by Gianluigi Taverna, MD, and colleagues at the Humanitas Clinical and Research Center in Milan, Italy, two bomb-detection German shepherds were trained to recognize prostate cancer–specific volatile organic compounds in urine samples and detect the difference between cancerous and noncancerous samples. One dog found 100 percent of the cancer in the 362 samples and the other was 98.6 percent accurate.

In a study by Hideto Sonoda, MD, and colleagues at Kyushu University in Japan, standard breath samples and watery stool samples were obtained from patients with colorectal cancer and healthy participants before undergoing colonoscopy. Then, a Labrador retriever that was specially trained in the scent detection of cancer was brought in to smell the samples, and the dog sat down in front of the samples in which the scent of cancer was found. Amazingly, the sensitivity of the dog's ability to detect the scent in breath samples was 91 percent accurate, and the canine's sensitivity to detecting it in stool samples was 97 percent accurate. This was true even for early cancers. These findings are just the tip of the iceberg. In their review of the literature, Federica Pirrone, PhD, and Mariangela Albertini, DVM, PhD, wrote, "Several lines of evidence suggest that dogs may play a critical role in cancer research and diagnosis, [and] eventually be major contributors to a reduction in mortality for certain cancers."

Dogs can also alert people to acute medical emergencies stemming from common infections or illnesses, as Chelsea and her husband discovered. From the moment they brought their baby girl home from the hospital, their dog Striker kept a watchful eye on her. One week in August of 2021, the little girl came down with hand-foot-and-mouth disease, a viral infection that she'd caught at preschool. Chelsea stayed home with their daughter while her husband went out of town for his best friend's wedding. Aside from discomfort from the mouth sores and the rash, their daughter didn't seem particularly sick. But at 5 a.m. one day, Striker, a golden retriever/husky/Australian shepherd mix, jumped out of bed and ran to the door of the little girl's room, growling and whining.

When Chelsea opened the door, she found her daughter on all fours, gagging, her face turning purple. "She was choking on mucus and couldn't breathe," Chelsea recalls. "I immediately bent her over my knee and smacked her back repeatedly to clear her airway." When her daughter started breathing normally again, her mother called 911 and an ambulance rushed them to the hospital, where her daughter was diagnosed with croup on top of hand-foot-and-mouth disease and given epinephrine and other treatments to make it easier for her to breathe. "She would have suffocated if our dog didn't alert me when he did," Chelsea explains. After they returned home, Striker stayed by the little girl's side until she had recovered fully. "I don't know that our daughter would be alive today if it weren't for Striker," Chelsea says.

On social media people have provided a mind-boggling array of stories about how dogs have alerted their owners to various health problems. In one family, the family dog kept sniffing a particular part of the grandmother's foot, prompting her to see a doctor, who diagnosed a suspicious growth as skin cancer. A couple in Australia got a service dog—a boxer mix—for their son's autism and sensory needs, and the dog detected the child's absence seizures—which were causing him to blank out or stare into space for a few seconds—without any seizure-alert training.

A little background: Seizures typically have three phases: the aural or prodromal phase, the seizure itself (the ictal phase), and the recovery period after the seizure (the post-ictal phase). During the prodromal phase, some people can tell that a seizure may be coming because they experience mood changes, difficulty sleeping or staying focused, dizziness, a sense of déjà vu, headache, or tingling in parts of the body. Knowing when a seizure is coming is valuable, especially if the person is in a dangerous situation such as driving. Even if the person is at home, seizures can cause them to fall to the floor, which can lead to serious injuries.

Having even a few seconds of warning can be enough to create a safer environment when a seizure happens, which is why having a trained seizure-alert dog can be especially beneficial for people with poorly controlled epilepsy. A study by Edward Maa, MD, and colleagues at the Comprehensive Epilepsy Center at Denver Health, found that trained service dogs were not only able to identify a unique seizure scent in the sweat of people who have seizures, but they also could detect the scent's presence *before* 79 percent of the seizures that occurred among the sixty study participants. In this study, the average duration of the warning (or prodromal) phase of the scent was 68.2 minutes—which is ample time for someone to initiate "many therapeutic or logistical safety interventions."

In a review of research on seizure-alert/response dogs for people with epilepsy, Amélie Catala and colleagues at Normandie University in France found that the reported times of dogs' attention-getting, alerting behaviors before seizures varied widely—from ten seconds to five hours—but were 70 to 85 percent reliable, according to their owners. Previously, research by Val Strong and colleagues in the UK found that dogs could be specifically trained to detect oncoming seizures and send overt signals to their owners (such as barking or jumping up and pawing the person) fifteen to forty-five minutes before the seizures occurred. Not only did this make the people feel more assured and engaged in life because they felt confident they could manage a seizure situation, but it actually led to a reduction in seizures. Knowing a seizure may be coming gives some people with epilepsy an opportunity to take medications that are known to help control seizures.

Real-world experiences among people with epilepsy can attest to these benefits. For example, D, a college student in Arkansas, has had epilepsy for most of their life. When they were fifteen, D had a tonic-clonic (aka a "grand mal") seizure at home, in which they stopped breathing and their pulse slowed dangerously; afterward, D was partially paralyzed on the right side of their body for several hours. The post-ictal phase can cause considerable exhaustion, and D slept for sixteen hours that night. When they woke up the next day, their dog River, an eighty-pound Labrador/border collie mix, was resting his head on D's hands. River wasn't trained as a service dog, but he wouldn't leave D's side for days. "He stood guard by me all night and day," D recalls. "I was shaky and weak for several days afterward, and my dog always took the stairs with me. When I'd stop, he'd stop and wait for me to keep going." Having River's company helped D feel safe and gave them the confidence to carry on with their regularly scheduled life.

This is a common response, especially among people who have trained seizure-alert dogs.

In another study of seizure-alert dogs by Val Strong's team, a quality-of-life survey found many benefits for people with tonic-clonic seizures. "Patients reported benefits arising from the ownership of a trained alert dog in areas that included improved interpersonal relationships, greater self-confidence, ability to work, feelings of safety/security, decreases in poor mood or depression, decreased anxiety, and greater independence."

In other instances, medical-alert and service dogs help their owners simply by being highly observant. Dogs are incredibly perceptive creatures, and our canine companions keep an eye on us, often watching our body language and behavior. When they see a worrisome or mystifying change, even a subtle one, these canine guardians may come to our rescue if we're on the verge of fainting, or they may prop themselves against us if we're feeling physically shaky, or jump on our chests if we're breathing abnormally, as happened to John.

A dog's keen sense of smell can often tip them off that their beloved human is sick or unwell. And because they can read our facial expressions, they may be able to sense if we're experiencing pain or another form of physical discomfort. This dynamic duo of sensory perception skills explains why a canine companion, whether or not they're trained to detect flare-ups of chronic or life-threatening diseases, may help you ward off or avert danger. It also means that if Rover suddenly starts obsessing about a particular spot on your body, it might be a good idea to get it checked out by a doctor. It could make a difference to your health and longevity.

Even in one-off situations where a dog alerts you to a possible medical danger, it can strengthen the bond between you. When you have a dog who knows you so well that they can sense even the tiniest shift in your body's signs, you're likely to feel incredibly grateful that your well-being is in such safe paws.

CHAPTER EIGHT

Supporting Mental Health

How Dogs Can Help with Psychiatric Issues

Marian*, who has an anxiety disorder and a panic disorder, says that her dog Rusty has come to her emotional rescue numerous times. "In high school, before I was being formally treated, my dog was my only source of anxiety-relief when I would be up at ridiculous hours having panic attacks over homework and classes," says Marian, who is now in college in Boston. Until she went to bed, Rusty would stay with Marian and try to distract or comfort her whenever she'd start to panic, which was fairly often especially when she had papers due or a test on the horizon.

There were times when Marian felt so overwhelmed and hopeless that thoughts of suicide would come to mind. "Without Rusty I would have been in a much worse place and would have likely gone through with my suicidal ideations," she says. Fortunately, she didn't act on them, and she got the psychiatric treatment she needed for these disorders, which put an end to her suicidal ideations but not her emotional vicissitudes. When her mother died from cancer in 2020 and Marian was overwhelmed with grief, Rusty helped her then, too. "Taking care of my dog kept me going," she says. "He has saved my life more times than I'd like to admit just by existing and being there for me during the lowest points in my life."

Above and beyond being able to buoy our spirits when we're feeling blue, our canine companions can help ease some of the emotional turmoil that stems from a serious mental health disorder, as you'll see in this chapter. And in the aftermath of emotional tumult, people can harness the power of the human-canine connection to help themselves thrive. Of course, dogs are no substitute for therapy or other essential medical treatments for those with psychiatric conditions, but they can provide an additional layer of support. And they give meaning and purpose to our lives, and that, in turn, can make us want to live for them if for no other reason.

Mental health disorders are increasingly common in the U.S. and throughout the world. Anxiety disorders affect 48 million adults in the U.S., while 21 million people have had a major depressive episode in the past year and 9 million have experienced post-traumatic stress disorder (PTSD). Meanwhile, it's estimated that nearly 9 million kids, ages three to seventeen, were diagnosed with anxiety and/or depression in recent years, and these were often accompanied by behavioral or conduct problems. These figures add up to a whole lot of emotional suffering.

In recent years, research has shown that being with a dog can help people with clinical depression and anxiety, improve symptoms of PTSD, help reduce acute distress from trauma, facilitate recovery from addictions or eating disorders, and more. The presence of a dog can even reduce people's fear before they undergo electroconvulsive therapy to treat severe depression, research has found. And therapy sessions in which a trained dog is an active participant can reduce anhedonia, the inability to experience pleasure from normally enjoyable activities, which often accompanies schizophrenia.

These mental health benefits may stem from the fact that their canine companions force people to get out of their comfort zones and carry on, to go outside and get fresh air and exercise, and/or to realize that they're actually more adaptable than they thought they were. And some of these soothing perks stem from our neurochemical responses to interacting with a precious pooch. Being with a friendly or beloved dog increases the level of serotonin, oxytocin, and other feel-good chemicals in the human brain while leading to a decline in the stress hormone cortisol—a combination of effects that cultivates a sense of calm.

Our dogs have an uncanny ability to tune into and ease our physiological and psychological stress. In a study in a 2022 issue of the journal *PLOS One*, Clara Wilson and colleagues collected breath and sweat samples from thirty-six people before and after they participated in a stress-inducing mental arithmetic task. Then the samples were presented in containers, in a specially built apparatus, along with blank samples or baseline samples, to four trained dogs during thirty-six sessions, and they performed "alert behavior"—standing in front of the target port, with their nose close to or touching the port for five seconds—to indicate the samples that were taken when the people were under stress. Amazingly, the dogs were able to accurately identify the "stress sample" 94 percent of the time.

Samantha, an occupational therapist who has anxiety and obsessive-compulsive disorder, was on the verge of being hospitalized when she got her dog Clara, a Lab, who has since been an emotional lifesaver for her again and again. "She has always seemed to understand when I am in emotional or physical distress and her behavior changes—she will come and lie near me and rest her head in my lap," Samantha says. "She makes me feel more myself than I ever had before."

Having a dog also provides a daily sense of purpose and routine, which helps foster a meaningful connection between people who are struggling emotionally and their canine companions. Perhaps one of the biggest benefits is that people feel free to be whoever they are and to feel however they feel in the presence of their pooches; they don't feel the pressure to put on a happy or brave face if they're feeling depressed or fearful, the way they might with other people. By way of example, consider Kimberly, a military veteran who served in Afghanistan and has PTSD and seizures. She says that Cooper, her golden retriever/border collie mix, "has taught me that it is okay to be who you are and that life is so much more than the things that are wrong with me."

A study by Cheryl Krause-Parello, PhD, and Kristie Morales investigated the impact of service dogs on twenty-one military veterans, many of whom had depression, anxiety, or PTSD, and found that service dogs provide relief from social isolation. Speaking of his service dog, one participant said, "He gave me something to love and he shows me unconditional love and because of that it brought me out of a deep depression, gave me a reason to live and to love again and to be a whole person. If it wasn't for him, I honestly believe I would have killed myself."

In addition to benefiting from their stellar canine company, people often feel supported and understood by their dogs on an emotional level, which can be tremendously beneficial for those who feel isolated by psychiatric issues. This feeling isn't a figment of their imagination. Research by Attila Andics, PhD, and colleagues found, using functional magnetic resonance imaging (fMRI), that dogs' brains possess the same sound-decoding regions that human brains do. This allows dogs to process vocal intonations and pick up on the emotional valence of what's being said. Even if they don't understand the exact words, dogs get the gist of the message, and they are often sensitive to humans' body language. For these reasons and because our dogs provide us with unconditional love and unwavering support, people with mental health challenges may feel more inclined to seek the company of their affectionate, nonjudgmental pups when they're struggling emotionally than to risk a less predictable response from people in their inner circles.

In 2015, Lily's* "mental health took a complete nosedive" while she was working full-time and completing a university degree in Australia. She was hospitalized in a psychiatric ward and spent more than eight months in the hospital, battling PTSD and major depression. After being discharged, she went to live with her parents while she tried to figure out what to do with her life. One day, her mother took her to "just look" at puppies and she came home with Baxter. "He brought me meaning when life was so bleak, and he taught me how to care for him, which led me to learning it was okay to care for myself," says Lily, who's now married with a two-year-old daughter. "The connection we have is indescribable. He is without a doubt the reason I am still alive today." Their lovefest has been so magical that the family has since added another dog to their household.

Deriving Strength from Your Dog's Support

It's widely recognized that having strong social support—feeling that there are people who care about you and whom you can turn to when you need assistance—helps improve symptoms and recovery in a variety of conditions, including PTSD, bipolar disorder, and major depression. But living with a psychiatric illness can be isolating, and for people with serious mental health issues, it can be difficult to maintain healthy relationships. Dogs, on the other hand, are so easy to connect with, and they don't care if you're having a bad day, need to cancel plans (even better so we can stay home!), or if you process the world differently than most humans. As long as you treat your dog well, they won't judge you; they'll simply be happy to serve as a reliable, supportive companion.

That's why dogs can play an essential role in providing social support for people with chronic mental health issues, the value of which should not be underestimated. In a fascinating study by Helen Brooks, PhD, and colleagues at the University of Manchester and University of Southampton in the UK, researchers conducted twenty- to ninety-minute in-person interviews with fifty-four adults who had long-standing mental health problems such as schizophrenia or bipolar disorder. The goal was to explore the sense of security and connectivity the participants' social networks provided them. When asked to draw target-shaped diagrams of their networks to represent the roles that pets, activities, and various people played in their lives, 60 percent of the participants placed their pets in the central, most important circle of support. The majority of the participants reported having difficult relationships with friends and family members in their social sphere, a "gulf of understanding" between themselves and other people, or limited support beyond their companion animals. Some participants described having strained or fractured relationships with friends and family members as a result of their own past behavior that was related to their mental illness. This wasn't an issue with their pets. Instead, they noted that their dogs or cats were there for them no matter what, which engendered a sense of enduring trust and security in the bond.

The results of this study are not unusual. In a meta-analysis of twenty-one studies, Javier Virués-Ortega, PhD, and colleagues examined the social support impacts of animal-assisted therapy—which almost always involves therapy with dogs—in elderly patients, as well as those with depression or schizophrenia, and found similar results. In particular, the participants' social functioning, behavioral disturbances, depression, and anxiety were all significantly improved when they had the social support of dogs through therapy.

Sometimes this bond can be an absolute lifeline for those who are stuck in the depths of despair, as Brittany, a program specialist at a government agency in Texas who has bipolar II disorder, found. Besides experiencing long episodes of depression and suicidal ideation, she occasionally engages in self-injury, such as cutting or burning her skin, in an attempt to relieve her emotional pain. Brittany credits her goldendoodle Jefferson with saving her life on multiple occasions. Without being trained as an emotional support dog, "he's sensitive to my emotions, and anytime I cry, he jumps up and licks my face and it helps," she says. "When I start self-injuring, he usually snaps me out of it by barking, jumping on my lap, and lying on top of me" with all seventy pounds of his weight.

And when Brittany felt suicidal, Jefferson would lie next to her and comfort her. Other times, the very thought of Jefferson being left alone without understanding what had happened to her has stopped Brittany from following through on her suicidal thoughts. At one point before the pandemic, her parents were visiting from another state and she tried to convince them to take Jefferson home with them for a while. "That made my mom realize things were bad again without me actually saying I was suicidal," Brittany says. This helped Brittany ask for the extra support she needed from her mother and her therapist. "I honestly don't think I'd be alive now without my dog," Brittany says.

Loneliness is often a factor in various mental illnesses, whether it's because people who have serious psychiatric conditions often have trouble forging supportive relationships, because they retreat from the outside world when they're suffering, or another reason.* Unfortunately, loneliness can exacerbate some mental health conditions. For example, a study by Jonathan Prince, PhD, and colleagues found that people with severe mental illness who identified as most lonely were 2.7 times more likely to be hospitalized for their psychiatric problems than those who were less lonely. If dogs can mediate loneliness, they can potentially improve outcomes for people with psychiatric illnesses.

In fact, research by Janet Hoy-Gerlach, PhD, and colleagues at the University of Toledo explored the effects of emotional service animals

---

*A similar phenomenon can happen with people who have dementia, and dogs can help in these instances, too. A study by Carol Opdebeeck, PhD, and colleagues examined the impact of dog ownership on people with dementia and found that those with a dog who were involved in its care were less likely to be lonely than those who didn't have a dog. In addition, research by Nancy Richeson, PhD, examined the impact that therapy dogs had on older adults receiving inpatient treatment for dementia: For three weeks, the dogs were brought in five times a week so that patients could pet them, feed them treats, brush them, and talk to the dogs and their handlers; after the sessions, the staff measured how often the patients interacted with each other and found significant increases in their level of social interaction, as well as decreases in their disruptive or agitated behavior, after the three weeks of dog visits.

on adults with serious mental illnesses who participated in a pilot program that paired patients with shelter dogs (or cats). The program provided free vet care and would also care for the dogs if the patients were hospitalized. Patients were dealing primarily with major depression, bipolar disorder, or schizoaffective disorder, and they completed surveys, including one that measured loneliness, at the start of the program and one year later. During that time, the results showed that participants experienced a significant reduction in loneliness, anxiety, and depression, and they attributed the improvements in their mental health and well-being to their emotional service animal.

The Element of Touch

When people with severe mental illnesses isolate themselves from other people or receive inpatient treatment for their condition, one of the valuable aspects of social support that's disrupted is being able to receive affectionate touch. We're talking about getting hugs from friends or cuddling with a parent or partner. The sense of touch is incredibly valuable not only for allowing us to experience the world in all its richness but also for our physical and emotional well-being. After all, touch decreases people's anxiety and blood pressure, while increasing the release of feel-good brain chemicals like oxytocin and serotonin. Touch deprivation, on the other hand, is associated with greater anxiety, depression, feelings of loneliness, and decreased well-being.

Since Olivia adopted Kona, a German shepherd/golden retriever mix, from Rescue Ranch in 2018, she says that he has changed her life. She needed a service dog for her PTSD and anxiety, and Kona proved to be a natural. "Kona has exceeded my expectations—he has learned how to mitigate my PTSD and anxiety and help with my ADHD," says Olivia, who also has fibromyalgia and works for a public affairs firm in Sacramento. Not only does Kona ground her or provide deep pressure therapy with his body when she needs it, but he also offers a source of tactile stimulation that helps with her ADHD.

Of course, there are times when it's simply not possible to receive human touch—as many single people discovered during the early COVID-19 lockdown, for example. Touch deprivation also happens in institutional settings, such as when someone with a serious psychiatric illness is hospitalized for in-patient care. Research has found that in these situations pets can step in and provide what's called affective touch—which is often a sign of affection or intended to soothe or show support to someone. In other words, petting or snuggling with a friendly dog can bring the same benefits you might get from hugs or snuggling with your favorite humans.

Green Chimneys is a residential therapeutic school in New York that specializes in animal-assisted therapy for kids with behavioral issues that make it difficult for them to thrive in their home school districts. In a study there, researchers examined the importance of dogs in the kids' treatment by interviewing and surveying students and staff, and even reviewing poetry that students wrote about the dogs who lived in the dorms. They found overwhelmingly that dogs were treasured, affectionate companions for children living in the dorms, and the role of touch was emphasized. One student said of Lambert, the dog who lived in their dorm, "Lambert in the dorm is to have someone to snuggle on and hug and kiss, and he kisses you back, too!" The children also reported they loved having the dorm dogs spend a few minutes sleeping in their bed with them. It was a valued source of solace and comfort.

Having a dog present in the therapeutic setting isn't just beneficial for the patients; it helps the therapists, too. In the study of dogs in the dorms at the Green Chimneys school, staff members reported that the dogs offered unconditional love, both to the students and the staff, and they appreciated it.

John, who works in healthcare administration at a high-volume outpatient addiction treatment facility, has three dogs and says that he doesn't know how he could have gotten through 2020 without them. During the chaos and challenges of the early part of the pandemic, he found himself barely making it through the day. At home, he increasingly turned to his dogs to ground him, and spending time with them became part of his own mental health regimen. "Before anything else, upon arriving home, I immediately head to the yard for playtime and fresh air for an hour or more if the weather isn't too awful," says John, who is married and lives in Minnesota. The dogs have come to love this ritual, but John says he thinks he does even more. "As a therapist myself, I have begun to more clearly grasp the need I have each day for the changes [spending time with them] can make in my brain. I have become more ritualized with how I seek them out and spend time with each, in order to fill my own cup each day."

Furry Facilitation of Social Connection and Anxiety Relief

Another way dogs can increase the social support available to people dealing with mental illness is by putting them in a situation that improves their ability to connect with other people. As you've read, dogs can serve as easy conversation starters, helping people who don't know each other overcome shyness, social anxiety, or awkward moments and connect. After all, a dog's presence deflects attention away from you, helps you relax physiologically and emotionally, and provides something easy to talk about. Not surprisingly, the study by Krause-Parello and Morales found that service dogs improved the functioning of the veterans' human family units by providing a central connection around which the family could revolve. The service dogs seemed to serve as a social lubricant or social facilitator within the family or as a catalyst for engagement with other family members. One participant told the researchers, "I wouldn't have as close of a relationship with my family as I do," without the service dog.

As you've read, being with a dog can decrease people's anxiety levels and improve their moods, for various reasons. This is true when people are at home, when they're out and about in everyday life, when they're in school settings—and even in therapeutic situations. The latter is particularly noteworthy because for people who are receiving mental health treatment, the process itself can sometimes spark greater anxiety. Here, too, dogs can come to the rescue, because researchers have found that having dogs present can reduce people's fears in therapeutic situations and potentially improve their long-term outcomes.

In a study of 107 undergraduates at the University of Pennsylvania, Melissa Hunt, PhD, and a colleague asked some students to write about a traumatic memory or, as a control, to write about the objects in a furnished room. Those groups were then broken down into subgroups, some of which had a dog present for the writing exercise and some of which didn't have a dog with them. Not surprisingly, the researchers found that writing about trauma led to more anxiety than describing a furnished room, but when a dog was present, the increase in anxiety was significantly lower. Both groups that wrote about traumatic events crafted comparable essays, so it's not that anxiety was lower because the participants were writing about less traumatic events—it was simply the presence of the dog that seemed to make a difference. Furthermore, depressive symptoms were significantly lower at the end of the study among the participants who wrote about trauma while in the presence of a dog, compared to other groups.

In hospital settings, dogs also can quell people's anxiety. For example, in one study, Sandra Barker, PhD, and Kathryn Dawson, PhD, evaluated the impact of a single session of group therapy with therapy dogs present, on anxiety levels among 230 hospitalized psychiatric patients. The participants could pet and interact with the dog and its handler during the session; meanwhile, a control group participated in a dog-free recreation session. The researchers measured the participants' anxiety levels before and after the session. In both the dog-present and the control group, anxiety levels decreased for patients with mood disorders—but only the dog-assisted therapy reduced anxiety among people with other disorders, including psychotic disorders. The researchers' theories: "Perhaps the therapy dog provides some sense of safety and comfort not found in more traditional inpatient therapies. Alternatively, the dog may provide a nonthreatening diversion from anxiety-producing situations. Or perhaps it is the physical touching of the dog that reduces patients' anxiety, as has been reported for other populations."

Among those who are scheduled to have more extreme or invasive treatments, the presence of a dog can help reduce fear and anxiety. Another study, conducted by Sandra Barker, PhD, and colleagues at Virginia Commonwealth University, examined the impact of animal-assisted therapy on anxiety, fear, and depression in psychiatric patients who were scheduled to undergo electroconvulsive therapy (ECT), which is most commonly used for treatment-resistant major depression or bipolar disorder. In the study, thirty-five patients were divided into two groups and assigned on alternate days to spend fifteen minutes with a dog before treatment or fifteen minutes with magazines in a waiting room. When patients spent time with a dog, their fear was reduced by 37 percent and their anxiety by 18 percent, suggesting that dogs may be helpful in medical therapies that are inherently fear-inducing.

Providing Reasons to Recover

Outside of hospital settings, dogs can be helpful allies in therapy, as well. For example, behavioral activation is a skill that's sometimes incorporated into cognitive behavioral therapy (CBT) for depression and PTSD. In a nutshell, the idea behind behavioral activation is for people to identify activities they enjoy and that make them happy, then schedule those activities with the goal of improving their mood. Ideally, the positive feelings that come from doing the activity will make people more likely to do it in the future, and this in turn makes them more likely to feel better for the long haul. But sometimes it's hard for people to get started with behavioral activation. Dogs can help.

After all, dogs have needs that they require humans to take care of, which creates a routine. Most pet-owners feel responsible for giving their dogs what they need, whether it's food, walks, playtime, or affection. Research by Mary Janevic, PhD, and colleagues found that having a dog motivates people with chronic pain to go outside or for walks even when they, the humans, are in pain or fatigued—this is an example of behavioral activation in action. A similar effect can occur with mental health conditions.

In a study involving 119 adults who had been diagnosed with a mental health condition or who were struggling with their mental health, Roxanne Hawkins, PhD, and colleagues explored how companion animals, primarily dogs, can impact people's mental health and well-being. They found six common themes related to their pets: increased hedonic tone (which underlies the ability to experience pleasure), increased motivation and behavioral activation, reductions in anxiety symptoms and panic attacks, increased social connections and reduced loneliness, a reduction in risky behaviors (such as self-harm), and aid in the recovery process. As one participant noted, "Having to walk my dog when I didn't want to go out made me get out and see the beauty of the world, get some fresh air, see her joy at running about and playing and made me exercise. All of that helps you . . . when you aren't in a good place." As another put it: "I do not think that pets can fix mental health problems, but [they can provide] a source of coping. I still experience anxiety but believe that my dog can help to relieve these emotions."

While it's essential to get the right medical treatment for mental health disorders, people also need to take steps in their own lives to regulate their moods, gain support from others, and help themselves cope with adversity. After all, stress is unavoidable in the modern world—and it can exacerbate various mental health conditions. Dogs can help with all of these challenges by providing a sense of comfort and affection, giving you a reason to get fresh air and exercise, and serving as a stabilizing force in your life and a consistent source of support.

Your canine companion also can provide you with a sense of meaning and purpose to your life. As Jaimie, a graduate student in Missouri who has anxiety and depression, puts it: "A lot of times being *alive* is hard. My dog makes me *want* to be alive. I need her as much as she needs me."

Part Three

SUPPORTING US EMOTIONALLY

CHAPTER NINE

They're All Emotional Support Animals

As any dog-owner will tell you, our pooches can bolster our spirits when we're feeling upset, cranky, or otherwise out of sorts. Whether we realize it or not, our dogs serve as everyday emotional support animals for us, their humans. Personally, Jen counts on her dogs in this way on a regular basis. When she feels down or overwhelmed by the stressful state of the world, she often lies down on the rug in her living room and within moments is enveloped in a cloud of golden retrievers. Even if they're not watching, the dogs seem to have a sixth sense that lets them know she is within reach, and they'll swarm her, battling for position to get in some face licks or lie on top of her, then circling around to share more affection. These encounters don't last more than a few minutes—they can quickly feel overwhelming—but the dogs'

exuberance and sheer love for Jen makes her let go of whatever was upsetting her. It's a simple way of hitting the emotional reset button. After enjoying this group hug, she can practically feel her blood pressure and stress levels coming down and her endorphin levels going up. Their cuddle sessions never fail to make her feel happier and more relaxed.

It turns out this isn't just a quirky thing she enjoys. Research shows that spending even a little time with a dog makes us feel better in myriad ways, and our canine companions can help us through many different emotional challenges and forms of frustration, heartache, and distress. For one thing, interacting with dogs takes people out of their heads and into the present moment, as they attend to their dogs' needs and bask in the positive feedback they provide, making it a mindful, stress-relieving experience; at times dogs may even insist on having their owners' undivided attention, continually nudging them until they get it. What's more, being in the presence of an upbeat dog for even a short amount of time can lower people's blood pressure, improve their mood, decrease their anxiety, and boost their overall well-being.

A study by Molly K. Crossman and colleagues at Yale University evaluated the effects of a single, brief interaction with a dog on people's mood and anxiety. Before the experiment, the researchers measured the participants' moods then let them have unstructured time with a dog (a seventy-pound, gray, mixed-breed dog whose name was not given, but who had a sweet disposition). They could pet or play with the dog, or just hang out with the dog. Meanwhile, other participants served as controls, either by spending time in the waiting area or looking at dog videos and photos online. After seven minutes, researchers re-administered the mood surveys to all the participants and found that interacting with a dog improved people's moods and reduced anxiety compared with people in both control groups.

Another study, by Dasha Grajfoner, PhD, and colleagues at Heriot Watt University in Edinburgh, found similar results. After administering a set of mood-based surveys to 132 university students, the participants spent twenty minutes interacting with just a dog, interacting with the dog *and* its handler, or interacting with just the handler. Afterward, they completed another survey to measure the impact of the experimental condition. The researchers found that spending twenty minutes with a dog significantly improved the people's well-being, anxiety, and mood more than any other condition. The effect was greatest when the interaction was with the dog alone, without the handler present.

Seven to twenty minutes—that's all it took for people's moods and mindsets to improve, thanks to the comfort that comes from being with a canine companion. In these studies, the dogs weren't familiar to the participants—they were essentially strangers—and they still worked their magic. So imagine what happens when people spend time with a dog they feel emotionally connected to. The possibilities are endless.

In Dogs We Trust

When these mood-transforming effects happen with your own dog, they may stem at least in part from the unconditional love and affection between you and the deep sense of faith you have in each other. When it comes to soothing anxiety, there can be a two-way street between dogs and their people, as Stacey discovered. From the time her family adopted Inky, an Akita mix, at four months old, he was shy, sensitive, and utterly terrified of everything, from thunderstorms and the sound of fireworks to car rides and trips to the vet. To try to soothe his frayed nerves, she would often talk or sing to him in a calming voice. She'd also have him wear a snugly fitting ThunderShirt during storms and give him Rescue Remedy, a vet-recommended homeopathic formula, during especially anxious times. After settling down, Inky would show his appreciation with snuggles and kisses, which would in turn have an uplifting effect on her.

That level of trust is just as strong on the human side of the equation. Research shows that people tell their dogs things they wouldn't dare tell other people. In particular, dog-owners are more willing to talk to their pets (than to their friends or romantic partners) about feelings of depression, jealousy, anxiety, apathy, and fear. We trust our dogs implicitly, and we know they won't judge us, so there's no risk involved in letting them become our canine confidants. Generally, dogs just want to love and adore us and be with us—and on some level most dog-owners know this. Our expectations of each other are pretty basic—to share love and to take care of each other physically and emotionally—a simplicity that naturally sets us up to experience emotional solace and satisfaction from our interactions.

A study by Lawrence Kurdek, PhD, found that people were more likely to turn to their dogs as confidants in times of emotional distress than to turn to their parents, siblings, friends, or children. People who were uncomfortable with self-disclosure were even more likely to turn to their dogs, perhaps because many of us form "attachment bonds" with them. We feel those bonds not only when we're with our dog but also when we're away from them and we miss them. They are a dependable source of comfort, and we know that we can turn to them in distressing times.

Further research, conducted by Aislinn S. Evans-Wilday and colleagues at the University of Lincoln in the UK found similar results. People were more likely to confide in their dogs about difficult emotional issues—such as depression, jealousy, anxiety, apathy, and fear-related emotions—than they were in romantic partners or friends who act as confidants. While these researchers didn't explore why this is the case, they did note that dog-owners often consider their pooches as "safe havens" who act as a "secure base," allowing them to explore difficult issues and take risks more comfortably and confidently.

One way or another, these comforting canine companions consistently come through for us; they rarely let us down emotionally the way people sometimes do. Whereas human friends might criticize us or gossip about something we told them in confidence, we can always count on our dogs to keep our secrets and listen to us when we need to vent our frustrations. Sure, they may misbehave once in a while—by tearing something up, getting into the trash, or eating something they shouldn't have—but they don't let us down emotionally the way people sometimes do.

Sam, a graduate student in New Jersey, says that Zoey, her seven-year-old Terrier mix, makes her laugh with her weird antics. Zoey also helps Sam break out of a depressed mood by looking up with her *Can-we-please-go-on-a-walk?* eyes. During their hour-long walks, Sam often talks to Zoey because "she won't tell anyone and won't judge." Having this safe space and trusted confidant with whom she can vent feelings has been invaluable, Sam says, adding that during the pandemic, "it has become evident that my dog is better than any human friend."

For the most part, our dogs also make us feel socially supported—we feel cared for, encouraged, loved, and championed by our beloved canines. Research consistently shows that having ample social support is a critical component for our mental and physical health. While we traditionally think of social support as coming from other people, dogs can serve as naturally supportive figures in our lives and give us many of the same benefits. Even a short session of petting a dog in a time of stress can make us feel that this dog is focused on us, feels affection toward us, and supports us—and this improves our mood. Plus, hanging out with an affectionate dog can temporarily distract us from what's bothering us. That alone can provide some relief from stress and anxiety.

Carrie, a recent law school graduate who lives with her husband in Austin, Texas, gained tremendous comfort from her golden retriever Layla in recent years. As if law school, studying for the bar, and the anxiety and social isolation of the pandemic weren't stressful enough, Carrie's father died, following a difficult battle with cancer, at their family home in the UK. Carrie was able to take a short trip home to say goodbye, but she wasn't able to mourn with her mother, which magnified her own grief. Fortunately, Layla has always had a remarkable way of sensing how Carrie is feeling—"sometimes even before I realize that I'm feeling that way!" she says—and the six-year-old pup kept a watchful eye on her during this time.

"Often I found it really hard to put my emotions into words and express how I was feeling and what I needed, even to my husband," Carrie says. With Layla, "I didn't have to explain. Somehow she understood when I was overwhelmed by emotions, and she'd respond in a way that would fit what I needed in that moment." If Carrie was feeling sad and crying, Layla would put her paws on her chest and lick her face or rest her head on Carrie's shoulder. "When I'm stressed out, she brings a toy and sets it on my knee so I can play with her and take a break from thinking about whatever is worrying me," Carrie says. "It was truly such a relief to feel supported and loved and not alone without having to express how much I needed it in that moment. Just the feeling of being close to her soothes my anxiety. I feel like she grounds me, like our bond has a way of reminding me about the things I truly care about and what really matters to me."

Besides offering a welcome source of distraction and a reminder of what's most important, having a dog can motivate people to do things—such as taking a break from work, going outside, or exercising—to improve their mood, even when they don't feel like engaging in that activity. In other words, the dog-human bond can stimulate people to use behavioral activation—a treatment approach that involves considering how you can change your behavior in order to help yourself feel better—a skill that's an important part of cognitive behavioral therapy (CBT). As Carrie found, that might mean taking a break from dwelling on her problems to play with Layla, an activity she finds not only pleasantly distracting but also emotionally uplifting.

Below the Surface of Emotional Support

For people who feel deep connections with their dogs, there's no doubt that the emotional support their canine companions provide is real. Scientists have sought to understand what's at the root of this, and while researchers don't (yet) have a full understanding of what's going on, Andrea Beetz, PhD, has studied the scientific literature on human–animal interactions and offers a set of theories to explain what is undoubtedly a complex process. On a physiological level, when we interact with dogs, especially when physical touch is involved, it activates the oxytocin system in our brains *and* in the dogs' brains. Oxytocin, as you may remember, is a chemical that's widely connected with feelings of love and bonding and leads both species to feel good and experience shared trust and affection.

Another theory relates to the biophilia hypothesis, the idea that humans have evolved to want to be close to other living things, including animals and plants in the natural world, partly because this engenders positive feelings and partly because it instills a sense of safety. This is something that comes naturally to people—it's an innate desire for humans to want to connect with canines and other creatures, rather than a conscious one. There's also the possibility that people anthropomorphize animals, especially when their own social needs are unmet and they're lonely, for example.

Indeed, a study by Lauren Powell and colleagues in Australia found that getting a pet dog can relieve loneliness and improve people's moods in a variety of ways within just three months. Besides providing companionship, the pups provided support and increased the owners' interactions with other people through dog-walking. As the researchers noted, "Dogs may act as catalysts for social interaction."

And even when things don't go well socially, dogs can help us feel better simply by being there. Research by Ilona Papousek, PhD, and colleagues found that after an incident involving messages of social exclusion, having an unfamiliar dog present in the room bolstered people's moods. The effects dogs have on our emotions are so strong that even thinking about them can make us feel better. In an experiment by Christina M. Brown, PhD, and colleagues, people were asked to reflect on a time when they had been socially rejected. Afterward, those participants who came into the study believing that dogs have human-like emotions and characteristics (examples of anthropomorphism) found that simply looking at pictures of dogs or spending time thinking about them resulted in an improved sense of well-being.

A self-described "loner," Maggie, who is single and in her mid-twenties, can relate to these findings. While she has generally felt fine about being alone and far away from her family, a couple of years ago she realized she had reached her limit for spending time by herself without feeling lonely and bored. To the rescue: her dog Maya, a Chihuahua/chow chow/Mexican street dog mix she adopted in January 2021. Since then, "I have felt so much less alone. It's so nice to have someone to talk to even if she can't understand or talk back," says Maggie, who works in cybersecurity in Florida. "She has helped me get out of an emotional rut."

Having a beloved dog as an emotional partner is *not* a one-way phenomenon in which people lean on their dogs for support and reap all the benefits. There's a feedback loop of positivity that enables us to feel even more closely connected to our dogs as a result. As you've seen, research has shown that positive interactions between humans and their dogs lead to the release of many feel-good brain chemicals in humans *and* in dogs. In other words, emotions aren't purely a reflection of a psychological state; they are experienced through the release of specific brain chemicals and hormones.

There is also a neurological component to the deepening of this bond from our positive interactions. A study by Johannes Odendaal and Roy Meintjes examined the physiological effects of positive interactions between humans and dogs and found that the benefits go both ways—from dogs to humans and humans to dogs. In other words, there is a neurological component to the deepening of our bond from our positive interactions. The researchers found that after a session of playing with a dog, there was a decrease in blood pressure from the baseline in both the people and their pooches. There were also increases in various feel-good brain chemicals, including beta-endorphin (which is tied to euphoric states and lowered stress), oxytocin and prolactin (both of which promote bonding), and beta-phenylethylamine and dopamine (which are associated with pleasurable experiences). For all of these, both dogs and humans showed increased levels after their positive interactions—it was a mutual effect. Given that humans and dogs are social creatures, and we fulfill these needs for each other, the researchers concluded that the shared physiological benefits that stem from the positive interactions between us play a significant role in deepening and perpetuating our bonds.

Coming to Our Emotional Rescue

As spontaneous as their consoling behaviors might seem in some instances, dogs can actually detect, respond to, and help alleviate our emotional pain and stress in significant, and often surprising, ways. On some level, they understand that we are in a relationship with them, that there's an attachment and a deep abiding trust between us. And for those reasons, when we get upset, our dogs want to comfort us.

Scientists have shown that dogs are able to recognize emotional states in other dogs and in humans. In a study by Natalia Albuquerque and colleagues, researchers showed dogs images of human faces that were either happy or angry and paired them with a human voice speaking in an unfamiliar language (basically, sounds a dog wouldn't recognize as words) that were also either happy or angry. They also showed the dogs images of dog faces that were playful or aggressive, paired with barks that were playful or aggressive. When the emotional valence of the sound matched the facial expression (an angry bark and an angry face, for example, or a happy human sound with a happy human face), dogs spent more time looking at the face than when they didn't match. This shows that dogs were able to extract emotional meaning from the faces and the sounds, an ability that was previously known only to exist in humans. The theory is that because they're armed with the ability to integrate different forms of emotional expression, dogs are willing and able to comfort us when they sense we are upset.

Brittany rescued her dog Cooper, a Great Dane/black Lab mix, as a puppy and more than eight years later he is her best friend. When Brittany got divorced, Cooper consoled her as she cried. "When I got home from crappy dates, he would be there keeping my bed warm," says Brittany, who is in her early thirties and works in marketing in the Chicago area. "Knowing I was coming home to someone who was always excited to see me and loved me made even the worst day bearable." Cooper helped her pull through downbeat and anxious days because he was there for her without "judgment, just love."

A study by Emily Sanford and colleagues evaluated how dogs responded to their owners' sounds of distress. In the experiment, thirty-four dogs and their owners came into the lab; the dogs were in a room and the humans sat in an adjacent space with a glass door between them that was lightly held closed by a few magnets. The dogs could see and hear their humans through the door, and they could even push it open if they wanted to. In the experimental group, the humans would say "help" in a distressed-sounding voice every fifteen seconds, and they would make crying sounds in between. In the control group, the people would say "help" in a flat, unemotional tone of voice every fifteen seconds and hum "Twinkle, Twinkle Little Star" in between. While about half of the dogs went through the door to their owners under both conditions (basically, because our dogs just want to be with us), when owners were crying the dogs went forty seconds sooner, on average. As the researchers noted, this suggests "that human distress commanded the dog's attention and perhaps even conferred urgency to the dog's actions, leading them to open [the door] more quickly" in order to help or comfort their human companions.

Another study, by Joshua Van Bourg and colleagues, tested if dogs would rescue their humans, without being trained to do so, if they were trapped. In a room in the research lab, the people climbed into a big cardboard box and either pretended to be trapped, calling out in distress, or they sat and read out loud. Researchers added a third condition where treats were placed in the box. Then, they observed the dogs' behavior and found the dogs acted more stressed when their owners seemed trapped than when they were reading out loud. As with the previous study, some dogs went to their owners no matter what; however, dogs were significantly more likely to liberate the box contents if they heard a human in distress or there was a snack present compared with hearing a human calmly reading out loud. Dogs also appeared to be more stressed when their humans seemed stressed—a sign of empathy on the pups' part.

Essentially, dogs can read what we, their people, are feeling and if we are upset, they often respond by trying to help us feel better. They really do feel our emotional pain, either because they empathize with us or because they catch our feelings through the phenomenon of emotional contagion. As psychologist Stanley Coren, PhD, author of *How Dogs Think*, noted, "In the same manner that young humans show empathy and understanding of the emotions of others, so do dogs. Furthermore, we appear to have bred our dogs so that they not only show empathy, but also show sympathy, which is a desire to comfort others who might be in emotional distress." In some ways, the ability to share emotions serves as a form of adhesive that helps us develop and maintain strong, enduring bonds with our dogs.

By now, you may have gained a newfound appreciation for the many ways in which your canine companion comforts you emotionally, provides you with valuable support, and even helps you cultivate a more mindful approach to life. Whether or not we feel like talking about what's bothering us, basking in the presence of a loyal, affectionate pup can make us feel at least a little bit calmer, steadier, and stronger. Having a dog's unwavering love and support has always been a treasured asset, but it may be more than ever as we collectively navigate times of uncertainty and instability in our ever-changing world. This mutually beneficial relationship reminds us, the humans, of what's good in the world—love, trust, affection, humor, fun, and the like—even when so much feels amiss. To paraphrase American poet Mary Oliver, who wrote *Dog Songs*, a dog's enthusiasm and joyfulness elevate our own, and that's a significant gift in this life.

CHAPTER TEN

Star Teachers

How Dogs Help Children Learn and Grow

Hopper, a champagne-blond golden retriever with long fur on her ears that looks like it was crimped eighties-style, is trained as a therapy dog. From the time she was two, Jen has taken her to a local library, where they would sit cross-legged on the carpet in the children's section for reading time with kids. When Jen was growing up, the mother of one of her friends did this with her black Lab Kalani, and Jen always thought it was incredible how dogs could help reticent readers become comfortable with reading. Inspired by her experience, she decided that to help kindergartners and first-graders who were struggling in school, she would bring Hopper, whose favorite activity is to lie on her side and drape herself across the lap of whomever she is meeting. She is silky soft and fluffy like a cloud and has always been great with children. Research and real-life experience show that students who refuse to read in class are much more willing to do so if they're reading to a dog, even when an adult is there. In a way, this is counterintuitive; some might assume that having a dog there would be distracting. Instead, the pup encourages kids to dig in and persevere.

Dogs enrich kids' lives in so many ways. From a child's vantage point, dogs are fluffy friends or siblings and nonjudgmental confidants. Through no conscious effort on their part, dogs teach kids responsibility, empathy, and caring, and they create relaxed environments where kids can learn and grow, both academically and outside of school. These effects are in keeping with the biophilia hypothesis, which suggests that humans have evolved to want to be close to other living things, including animals and plants in the natural world, partly because this brings about positive feelings and partly because it lends a sense of safety and security.

Because kids are less jaded and more trusting than adults are, they have the potential to form instant friendships with animals, which sets them at ease around them. This is more than a feel-good, touchy-feely proposition. Kids may see dogs as allies, as creatures they can nurture or teach, or as supportive friends who can cheer them on. In academic settings that involve dogs, a child's status is elevated from having to be completely deferential and compliant to teachers, to having a more comfortable footing by serving as a peer or even as a mentor to their canine companions. Outside the classroom, dogs also help kids learn valuable life lessons. Let's take a deeper look into the school setting first.

Dogs as Teachers' Aides

A significant body of research has found that reading to a dog can improve kids' reading performance, and a comprehensive review of the literature on human–animal interactions in educational settings by Sophie Hall, PhD, and colleagues concluded that dogs have beneficial effects on children's motivation, behavior, and the environment in which reading is practiced. This influence may be especially important for kids who have reading anxiety or difficulties with reading, which can create a form of negative "classical conditioning" in classroom settings. Simply put, the more anxious kids feel about reading, the more reluctant they are to do it, which in turn fuels their anxiety and development as readers. Reading to a dog seems to remove these obstacles by helping kids relax and work at their own pace in the presence of a dog, without worrying about being criticized. Kids also report feeling more supported while reading to a dog, an experience that improves their mood and cultivates a positive association with reading. All of these factors help kids build confidence in their reading ability and feel motivated to read more often, which creates an upward spiral effect toward greater literacy.

The effects of dogs on kids aren't limited to elementary school. Rebecca, a former high school English teacher in Michigan, loved her dogs Kippy (a chow/Lab mix) and Henry (a chow/collie mix) with all her heart. But what amazed her even more was the effect that talking about her dogs had on her students. "As a teacher in alternative high school settings, I worked with students who were often disillusioned, disengaged, and disappointed by the educational system," she says. "One of the ways I was able to form connections and find common ground was through our mutual love for animals. The students opened up and wanted to know my dogs, through pictures and stories, and wanted to share their own stories." This became a bonding experience between Rebecca and her students. Though Kippy and Henry passed away long ago, Rebecca, who's now in her early sixties and works as a tutor, says, "Dogs bring a purity to all they encounter. We don't deserve dogs, and yet they continue to bring their magic to our lives and make us better versions of ourselves."

 The Canine Gift for Language

Learning a language isn't just for humans. Researchers have found that some dogs are "gifted" in their ability to learn language. Scientists measure dogs' ability to learn words by teaching them unique names for toys and then checking if they can pick out the right toy by name. Some border collies can learn a dozen new words every week that they remember for months. Claudia Fugazza, PhD, and colleagues investigated whether dogs that are gifted this way have different personalities than their peers: In their research, they found that gifted dogs were more playful; however, their study couldn't determine if playfulness helps dogs learn more words or if the dogs learn more words (which, remember, are all words for toys) because their owners play with them more. Either way, this is a scientific experiment you can do at home: Name some toys and see if you can teach your dog to remember them by name. No matter what, you'll get in some bonus playtime, and you may discover your dog is secretly a genius!

On a related note, the cocktail party effect is a phenomenon where we are able to focus our attention on listening to something specific (like a conversation) while there is a lot of noise (like background chatter at a party). Human adults are good at this, but human babies are not. What about dogs? In the Canine Language Perception Lab at the University of Maryland, Jen's dogs participated in a study to test this. The dogs sat in a room with pegboard walls that disguised speakers. First, the researchers played the dog's name or a random word. Because dogs know their names, they would usually turn their attention to the speaker when their name was said, but not for the random word. Then this protocol was repeated with steadily increasing background noise. Researchers learned that dogs are quite good at hearing their name through the noise, surpassing the attention ability of one-year-old human babies. A little personal surprise for Jen came while her dogs were participating in the study; she learned that her dog Venkman does not actually know her own name: Venk got just as excited when the word "sage" came out of the speakers as her own name, so she wasn't allowed to proceed with the study.

Stacey's Australian shepherd Wolfy played an integral role in helping her son Nate develop a love of reading from an early age. From the time Nate was a baby, Stacey would read to him every night before bed. Story time quickly became a cherished bedtime ritual for both of them, and Wolfy often joined in, curling up on the rug next to Nate's bed. By the time Nate began learning how to read at age five, he had a baby brother, Nicky. While Stacey was tending to Nicky in the late afternoons and evenings, Nate would often snuggle up on the living room floor with a blanket and Wolfy for their own story time. Not only was this adorable to watch, but Stacey is convinced that reading to the dog reinforced Nate's association of reading with relaxation and comfort. Having his beloved dog at his side took all the pressure away and made reading an exercise in pure enjoyment. Now a young adult, Nate remains a voracious reader (though he no longer reads to a dog).

The learning-related benefits that come with the presence of a canine companion extend well beyond reading. In a series of controlled lab-based investigations, Nancy Gee, PhD, and colleagues from the State University of New York explored how dogs affected young children's performance on various cognitive and motor tasks. In a 2007 study, they found that preschoolers performed a series of gross motor tasks, such as long jumps and high jumps, faster in the presence of a dog, without sacrificing accuracy—compared to when they performed the same challenges without a dog there. In other studies, the kids required fewer instructional prompts to complete memory and imitation tasks in the presence of a dog, and they made fewer errors in an object-recognition task, compared to when they performed the same challenges without a dog. The theory: The presence of a dog may improve kids' motivation to fully engage with and accurately complete tasks.

Similar effects occur for kids in elementary school. To see how kids would behave with a dog present in the classroom, Kurt Kotrschal, PhD, and Brita Ortbauer videotaped twenty-four children, with their parents' permission, for two hours each week during "open teaching situations." After a one-month control period without a dog in the classroom, three dogs were alternately introduced into the class. The researchers found that while the kids did pay a lot of attention to the dog, they also paid more attention to their teacher; what's more, the group became more socially cohesive, with decreases in aggressive and hyperactive behaviors and a greater integration of previously withdrawn students. The cumulative result: better learning conditions for all.

After reviewing thirty articles published between 2001 and 2017 about the benefits of therapy dogs in classrooms, Jerri J. Kropp, PhD, and Mikaela M. Shupp, from Georgia Southern University, concluded that among kids, from preschool to high school age, the use of dogs in classrooms was associated with three broad categories of benefits: increased reading and language skills; social, emotional, and humane skills (such as kindness and empathy); and improved gross motor skills. They also found that the presence of therapy dogs can "provide stability and comfort to children who are living in poverty or abusive homes." This is relevant to learning because, as the researchers noted, children living in poverty or in abusive households experience high levels of stress that can hinder their success in school. Other research has found some evidence that the presence of a therapy dog in schools is linked to improvements in school attendance, student confidence levels, and motivation to participate in various learning activities, as well as in children's emotional, physical, academic, and social well-being.

Dogs in the classroom can even help kids with attention-deficit/hyperactivity disorder (ADHD) improve their focus. In a study by Sabrina Schuck, PhD, and colleagues, twenty-four children with ADHD were placed in cognitive-behavioral group therapy classes. One group read to dogs once a week for thirty minutes, while the control group read to puppets that looked like dogs. After twelve weeks, the kids who read to real dogs had greater reductions in their ADHD symptoms, as well as improvements in social skills such as cooperation, good sportsmanship, and appropriate assertiveness, than the kids who read to puppets.

One possible explanation for some of these benefits, according to Ann Berger, MD, a physician and researcher at the National Institutes of Health Clinical Center in Bethesda, Maryland, is that "dogs are very present. If someone is struggling with something, [dogs] know how to sit there and be loving." This support helps the person receiving that loving attention be more present-minded and focused. "The foundations of mindfulness include attention, intention, compassion, and awareness—all of those are things that animals bring to the table," Dr. Berger says. "People have to learn it. Animals do this innately."

Positive Ripple Effects in Real Life

In any setting, a child's relationship with their pet dog can be an important component of their cognitive and language development, according to Megan Mueller, PhD, a developmental scientist at the Tufts University Cummings School of Veterinary Medicine in Massachusetts. For example, kids may integrate their dog into language practice by talking about the dog or to the dog. Learning about a dog's needs can help with a child's cognitive development, and "experiencing the tactile nature of interacting with an animal" helps with self-regulation, she notes. There's also some evidence that positive interactions with a dog are associated with improved executive function—a set of important cognitive processes such as working memory, mental flexibility, planning abilities, and self-control—in children.[*]

---

[*]Some of the cognitive benefits of spending time with dogs may not be unique to kids. Research has even found that older adults who own dogs have better cognitive function—especially in the areas of verbal learning/memory, visual perception, and overall recall—than those who have cats or no pets.

Krista Geller, PhD, a researcher who has studied supportive relationships with a focus on people's relationships with their pets, highlights two major areas where dogs can help kids build important skills for life: communication and learning to care for someone before caring for themselves. Even when dogs are helping kids learn to read by creating a relaxed environment in the classroom or at home, she says, "they are also teaching that child socialization [skills], being able to communicate to people, and the ability to delay gratification."

Because dogs are nonjudgmental and attentive listeners, most children with dogs turn to them as their confidants. Researchers found that preadolescents regularly have intimate talks with their dogs and more than 70 percent of adolescents reported that they confide in their pets. Children also may find it easier to share difficult emotions with their pet dogs than with people, because they feel safer with and have unwavering trust in their dogs. So talking to the dog becomes a way of processing uncomfortable feelings and gaining insight into them.

While some people may worry that talking to a dog is not as useful or healthy as talking to people in terms of processing emotions, Geller believes this relationship means that kids will ultimately talk *more* about their feelings. "Children will share their deepest secrets with an animal," she says. "Even though they're not sharing with people, the fact that they are sharing it at all allows them to come to terms with it." And by learning to put into words what's concerning them, kids may become more emotionally expressive with other people over time.

After begging her parents for a dog for many years, Miriam came home from a field trip on her last day of elementary school to find that her wish had come true: a Tibetan terrier had joined the family. As a young child, Miriam had struggled with anxiety, frustration, and loneliness, and Merlin changed everything: He was always waiting for her and ready to play after school, and he listened patiently when she needed to vent her frustrations or anxieties. Merlin "flipped my whole world upside down—he made me feel understood and loved no matter what was going on or if I failed something," says Miriam, who recently graduated from university in Germany. The look in Merlin's eyes and his comforting behavior "encouraged me to try again every time," she says. "I couldn't have done it without him."

Dogs also help kids learn the very important lesson of delaying gratification and putting others first. Delaying gratification means resisting an immediate impulse or pleasurable temptation in the hope of obtaining a more valuable outcome in the long run. "As a child, if you're willing to step forward and take care of a pet and put your needs second, as you grow that makes you an actively caring person," Geller notes. "It makes you a person who can take a step back and not need immediate gratification." Research suggests that children with the ability to delay gratification may have better long-term outcomes in life, such as finishing college and earning more money. Caring for a pet dog also teaches kids empathy. Multiple studies have found that developing empathy for animals in childhood leads to greater empathy for people as those children grow up. There's a positive transfer effect. This is a critical lesson for many situations in life where someone else's needs take priority over our own, such as letting your dog out in the morning before you make coffee, or going to a concert you know you won't like so that you can make your partner happy. Kids who were integrated in taking care of pet dogs have that understanding and know-how, Geller says.

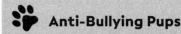

Anti-Bullying Pups

Roughly one in five students experiences bullying, and kids who deal with it have more depression, anxiety, sadness, health complaints, and negative impacts on their academic achievement. Dogs can help in a variety of ways. When kids come home to a nonjudgmental, adoring creature such as a dog, this helps counteract some of the social stress they experience at school. After all, when kids talk to their pets, as they often do, it's a healthy way of helping them work through their feelings and cope with them. Besides offering unconditional love, a pet dog may serve as an emotional safe haven, a source of consistent support, and an ever-ready listener.

Ashley's family got their dog Muugen, a black Labrador retriever, when Ashley was ten and struggling with school and bullying issues. The timing couldn't have been better. "Muugen was my savior—the one thing that always helped was coming home and being with him," says Ashley, now a graphic designer in Rhode Island. "When I would cry, he was always there and he would bring me toys. He would have a sixth sense and know what to do and where to be whenever I had anxiety. He still does. He is the goodest boy you could ever ask for."

Kathleen, who is on the autism spectrum, got her dog Cuddles, a Staffordshire bull terrier/rottweiler/lurcher mix, when she was ten. "To be autistic means that you are most likely alone," says Kathleen, who was bullied in school and miserable day and night, while growing up in Scotland—that is, until Cuddles arrived. "She would be waiting for me to come home from school, and for someone to need and love me that much was the best thing ever," says Kathleen, now in her early thirties and a data analyst for a global bank. "Even when I started work, following high school, and things improved for me, Cuddles was still the one soul I told everything to."

Dogs can also teach anti-bullying lessons in school. One study looked at a program called Healing Species, designed to use rescue dogs in a school to help students learn skills to disrupt the cognitive-emotional circuits that can lead to violence. The dogs are incorporated into lessons on empathy, compassion, responsibility, and forgiveness. In a pilot study with 201 fifth- and sixth-grade students, researchers found that participants in the program had significantly fewer disciplinary referrals, as well as reductions in aggressive behavior.

As they grow up, sometimes dogs and kids learn and thrive together. When Stacey was seven, she was often bored and lonely after school. Few of her friends lived within walking distance and those who did often had after-school activities. Left to her own devices, she became an avid reader, but she also craved some kind of interaction and challenge. A friend had given her a Hula-Hoop for her birthday that year, and she was terrible at it, so she decided to train her dog Roscoe, a medium-sized black poodle who looked more like a shaggy sheep-dog, to jump through it. Stacey knew nothing about dog-training, but Roscoe was smart, and he already obeyed commands to *sit*, *stay*, and *come*, so she was optimistic.

They started their training in the basement. First, she got him to walk through the hoop when one side was placed against the floor, then gradually she lifted it off the ground an inch at a time every few days. (Of course, there were lots of treats involved.) Within weeks, Roscoe was able to jump through the hoop when it was nearly two feet off the ground. Stacey was super-proud of him, and her family was appropri-ately impressed when she showed off Roscoe's new skills.*

Through this experience, Roscoe and Stacey got important things they needed, from each other—together they tackled a fun but daunt-ing challenge; he was thrilled by the attention and praise she gave him (not to mention the treats), and she gained patience, persistence, and a sense of responsibility. Before that, she had always thought of him as her mother's dog because he was most attached to her, probably because she fed him. This little project brought them closer. Roscoe and Stacey started spending more time together, playing fetch in the backyard and going for walks together (even though people in their neighborhood didn't walk their dogs). She also took over responsibility for his grooming. And when she would read in her room, he would often amble in, lie down on the floor, and keep her company. Their bond had solidified.

When we bring a dog into our home, many of us focus on what we can teach these furry friends through obedience training, basic com-mands, house rules, or skills training. And there's certainly a place for all of that. But less recognized is the role that our canine companions can have in imparting valuable lessons to us at any age or in helping children learn and thrive, at home or in school. Through their calm,

---

*Interestingly, research suggests that when dogs learn new tricks, they use human-like learning abilities—interpreting what they're supposed to do with problem-solving and social attentiveness skills, rather than just copying a move.

reassuring presence, dogs can help kids improve their reading, writing, and gross motor skills and break through anxiety-based barriers in these areas, as you've seen. Without any conscious effort on their part, these canine coaches also help kids develop compassion, emotional awareness, communication skills, self-regulation, and a sense of responsibility.

As writer Susan Cheever noted, "Dogs are great teachers. They are at home in the world. They live in the moment, and they force us to stay there with them." That's really all it takes for us to learn and thrive together. *Class dismissed!*

CHAPTER ELEVEN

Anchoring Forces

How Dogs Serve as Stabilizing Influences in Our Lives

Once they're established as part of the household, dogs become constants in our lives, and they can help us deal with the myriad changes and transitions life may throw our way. Whether this means moving to a new home, dealing with a divorce or death in the family, raising children as they grow up and move away, or being deployed or returning home as a military service member, our loyal canine companions provide us with comfort and consistency along the way. They can lend a sense of stability and permanency when life feels chaotic. They serve as a bright, integral thread in the fabric of our lives. And this mutually beneficial bond reminds us of the good things in life, even when our everyday circumstances feel unsettled.

As you've read in previous chapters, the bond between dogs and their people can have profound biopsychosocial benefits on humans' health and well-being—namely, by reducing our biological reactivity to stress, calming or steadying our moods, and helping to broaden or deepen our relationships with others, both inside and outside our homes. Research has found that when people view their dogs as members of the family, they tend to have a better sense of well-being. In addition, the concept of social support plays a role in this anchoring effect, especially in times of stress. A considerable body of scientific evidence shows that having strong social support from friends and family members can improve your ability to cope with stressful circumstances, ease the effects of psychological and emotional distress, enhance your self-esteem, and encourage healthy lifestyle behaviors, according to experts at the Mayo Clinic. Your canine companion can provide some of these perks.

Indeed, the attachment you feel with your beloved pooch can help you weather life's changes more easily. As you saw earlier in the book, attachment theory describes connections where people (or people and their dogs) want to be together, feel distressed when they're apart, and rely on each other for consistency, security, and comfort in times of stress. Having secure attachments is also key for developing psychological resilience—the ability to successfully deal with adversity, disruption, and stressful periods in life. Taken together, attachment and resilience offer us the psychological support to get through transitions and difficult times in life.

Claire's family experienced a sudden, tragic loss in their lives when their Northern California house was destroyed by a wildfire in 2017. They had to evacuate their home at 1 a.m., live in their travel trailer for a month, followed by a rental house, before they were able to build a new house on the same property and move in fourteen months later.

Throughout the stressful ordeal, "our family dog, Katie, was a rock in our family—she kept us grounded and stable through the whole grieving and rebuilding process," says Claire, who was a teenager at the time. "She helped us make our different living situations feel like *home*."

In the spring of 2020, during the early part of the COVID-19 pandemic, researchers at Kingston University London surveyed 495 people about how having a pet affected their well-being. It turned out that 95 percent reported that their pets, most of which were dogs, provided them with emotional comfort, and 88 percent said their pets improved their lives during the pandemic. Among people who had lower resilience scores, having a pet also improved their sense of well-being. When the researchers repeated the study with 243 participants in the fall of 2021, they found similar results.

Similarly, research led by Cori Bussolari, PhD, found that dogs brought stabilizing effects to their owners during the early part of the COVID-19 pandemic. Besides distracting people from the worry about COVID and reducing their sense of loneliness and isolation, dogs provided people with routines of feeding, walking, and playing, which also made people feel physically and psychologically better. As one subject put it, "I couldn't have asked for a better quarantine partner!" These relatively mundane, day-to-day aspects of life with a dog may not be remarkable on their own, but taken together, these studies show that even in life-changing times, they can be just what we need to maintain a sense of safety and stability. These findings are echoed more generally in research from the University of Hong Kong, which found that people who consider their pets to be family members find security in those relationships: As the researchers noted, dogs become "security supplements," providing their humans with the security benefits of an attachment and supplementing what they get from other people. In other words, our relationships with our dogs provide us with safe havens from the stress of the outside world.

When it comes from people, social support usually takes the form of emotional support (having someone listen to and validate your feelings), having a sense of belonging (such as in a friend group or sense of community), sharing advice or other useful information (about whatever you may be dealing with), or receiving tangible support (such as someone offering to do favors, run errands, or help with resources like money). While your dog can't offer some of these forms of support—they're not going to give you advice if you're dealing with a break-up, pack boxes if you're moving, or bring you a casserole if you're grieving—your beloved canine certainly can offer plenty of emotional support and a sense of belonging. Your dog can listen, without interrupting, when you feel like venting your frustrations. They can snuggle, go on walks, and give you sloppy kisses when you crave affection. And they can keep you company wherever you are and whatever you're doing, serving as a constant, loyal presence.

By way of example, consider Bailey, who adopted Olive, a border collie mix, fifteen years ago. In the intervening years, Bailey got married, moved to a new city, got divorced, and moved home to take care of her mother as she was dying. After her mother passed away, Bailey went to graduate school and then moved again for a new job. "Whether each transition was good or bad, having Olive there as my constant companion made things feel normal and helped me feel rooted," says Bailey, now in her late thirties and a banker in Tennessee. Even when times were tough, having Olive to consider and care for helped Bailey stay focused on their day-to-day life and keep moving forward.

 Life Changes, Personality Shifts

When people undergo major changes in their lives, such as getting married or starting a new career, sometimes their personality traits and preferences may shift. Maybe they become more confident, assertive, or outgoing socially. Or maybe they become more interested in spending time at home with their honey than going out in the evenings. It turns out that if they have dogs, their pups' personalities may change in ways that are in sync with their owners.

In a study involving owners of more than sixteen hundred dogs, ranging from a few weeks old to fifteen years old, William Chopik, PhD, and Jonathan Weaver, PhD, had people evaluate their dogs' personalities and behavioral history, as well as answering a survey about their own personalities. As the researchers noted, "Because humans and dogs spend a considerable amount of time together, it is plausible that there might be some degree of similarity in human and dog personality." They did indeed find this to be true. In particular, people who were extroverted rated their dogs as more active and excitable, whereas people who were more anxious or downbeat rated their dogs as fearful or more aggressive.

There are several possible explanations for these correlations, according to the researchers. For one thing, people might select dogs whose personalities seem to match theirs. There also might be a socialization effect, in which activities that are shared by people and their dogs might influence the dogs' personalities. In addition, "there is a degree of emotional and personality contagion among humans who share similar social environments, further suggesting that shared environments might contribute to a correlation between owners and their dog," the researchers noted.

"When humans go through big changes in life, their personality traits can change. We found that this also happens with dogs—and to a surprisingly large degree," explained Chopik, a professor of psychology at Michigan State University. "We expected the dogs' personalities to be fairly stable because they don't have the wild lifestyle changes humans do, but they actually change a lot. We uncovered similarities to their owners."

An Evolving Sense of Normalcy

As time goes on, the way dog-owners and their pups interact may shift somewhat, but the connection between them may continue to have a powerful anchoring effect. The circumstances of their life may change, but the bond between people and their dogs helps connect the dots from one phase to another, thanks to the dogs' continuous presence. Wherever you go or wherever you live, there you and your dog are. *Together.* Research suggests that single adults may be particularly likely to benefit from dog ownership as they navigate significant changes in their lives, since having a dog provides an alternative (as in, non-human) source of social support. This is especially helpful because a considerable body of scientific research shows that having strong emotional support and a sense of belonging is associated with lower stress and better health. And these factors are essential to helping people get through personal crises (such as the death of a loved one) or major life transitions (such as moving to a new state).

Mike and his wife Kara got their dog Murphy from a golden retriever rescue group when another family no longer had the bandwidth to care for the lively sixteen-month-old pup. Murphy fit into their Virginia household seamlessly—and they forged a mutual adoration society that saw them through four household moves, various job changes, the birth of two kids, and the loss of older family members. At the age of thirteen and a half, Murphy died quickly from a recurrence of cancer he'd had in his abdomen the year before. "As weird as it sounds, one last gift Murphy gave us is a way to help explain grief and loss to our children in a way they haven't been able to understand before," says Mike, who works for the federal government.

The element of social support from dogs plays a significant role in their ability to serve as stabilizing forces as people's lives change in dramatic ways. To investigate this effect, Jonathan Bowen and colleagues conducted a study in which they surveyed 501 dog-owners in Spain before the COVID-19 pandemic and 794 respondents during the initial pandemic lockdown. They found that most participants reported that their dogs helped them get through "tough times." Specifically, they were comforted by physical contact with and hugging their dogs, they engaged in shared activities (like playing games) with their pooches, and they turned to them as confidants—all of which are key aspects of social support. As the researchers noted, "dogs offer the advantage of being more available than human sources of support."

This is especially true during periods of isolation like the pandemic or major life transitions such as moving to a different state where access to your usual (human) social support networks is disrupted.

After all, availability—being able to easily access a source of support—and closeness—not in terms of proximity but as it relates to mutual dependence—are essential components of valuable social support—and a companion dog checks all of these boxes. Another meaningful element: When you're interacting with each other, your pet dog is likely to be fully present in body and mind. They're not distracted by a previous conversation or what's left to tackle on today's to-do list. Your dog's attention is likely to be on you, which can be emotionally gratifying. As a participant in the Spanish study reported, "If everyone else left me, my dog would still be there for me"—a sentiment that's shared by many dog-lovers.

Amanda, an attorney in her late thirties, has counted on her dog Mirabelle, a keeshond, to help her navigate numerous transitions in recent years. In 2018, Amanda moved from the East Coast to Los Angeles to go to law school. After she lost her housing in the 2018 wildfires, she and Mirabelle lived in one temporary situation after another; they also drove across the country together ten times. "Without her being consistently there, I would not have been willing to make so many changes, because I can be pretty timid," admits Amanda, who is single and recently moved again from Virginia back to Los Angeles for work. "I get things from her [like] undivided attention to my every motion and word that it would be insane to demand from another human."

When your life feels like it's in a state of upheaval or you're navigating a major transition, the constant, supportive presence of your beloved dog can help you take comfort in knowing that some things *aren't* changing. Your dog's love and devotion to you will remain as steadfast as ever. So will your dog's needs. In the midst of a divorce, a death in the family, a job change, or adult kids leaving home to start independent lives, dogs still need to be fed, walked, brushed, bathed, and played with. Those needs and responsibilities can lend a welcome sense of routine, order, and purpose to a period of time that may feel largely unsettled. And if you find yourself in a new work setting or an unfamiliar town or neighborhood, your beloved canine companion can help ease any loneliness you may feel.

For five years, Laura, a pastor, had to live in rural areas because of her job. During those stints, she didn't have any immediate social support and felt extremely isolated, which was particularly difficult for her because she's naturally an extrovert. "I adopted my dog Dooley, a heeler mix, five months into this situation, and I'm convinced he is the only reason I survived," says Laura, who is single and in her late thirties. "While my job itself and my situation were really hard, coming home to this overexcited puppy love could literally dry my tears." Besides appreciating his complete devotion to her, Laura felt safer living alone in places where she didn't know her neighbors. Now that that bleak period is behind her and she has moved into a work position that gives her joy, Laura's relationship with her pup has evolved. "He still gives me a sense of safety and comfort, but he's also a source of joy and fun and fitness," she says. Laura has also made new friends in her community and on Dog Twitter, thanks to Dooley. This isn't surprising given that our canine companions often serve as conduits for getting to know people, making friends, and finding social support in the neighborhood.

 Divorce and Dog Custody

It's no secret that nearly half of marriages in the U.S. end in divorce. When couples split, we're accustomed to hearing about custody fights over kids, but dogs are increasingly part of the conversation. Sometimes it's a no-brainer about who should keep the dog; these days, however, custody disputes related to pets are on the rise.

Traditionally, dogs were considered property to be divided between splitting spouses like anything else they owned. But courts are increasingly recognizing that dogs are much more like family members than property, and some states are considering changing their divorce laws to reflect this.

An interesting solution: When Andrea's parents divorced, she and her sister were in elementary school. As part of the divorce agreement, which included joint custody, it was specified that their dog, a Lab they'd brought into their home as a rescue after Hurricane Katrina, would go wherever the two daughters stayed. So when the girls were at Mom's house, the dog was there, too; when the girls went to Dad's house, the dog did, too. This was very helpful, Andrea says, because "my dog quickly became one of the few reliable things in my life."

Lifelong Anchoring Effects

These dog-driven stabilizing effects are present for kids and adults alike and in a variety of situations. A case in point: When kids have a parent deployed in the military, their stress levels are much higher than otherwise. A study by Megan Mueller, PhD, and Kristina Schmid Callina, PhD, from Tufts University, found that having a strong bond with a dog or other pet helps children who have a deployed parent in the military better cope with challenges that arise and develop resiliency, especially when they have a role in their dog's care. It wasn't the presence of a pet in the home that was significant, but the level of the kids' attachment and engagement with their pet that seemed to make the difference. "Strong attachments to pets may foster a more proactive attitude about handling stressful problems and could serve as a bridge to developing and maintaining peer relationships during stressful circumstances," says Mueller.

Some of these benefits persist through various ages and stages of life. More often than not, kids come to perceive their pets as steadying influences in their lives, which in turn helps children develop stronger coping skills. When kids go off to college and the family home suddenly feels oddly still and quiet, dogs provide a valued sense of vibrancy and playfulness for the kids' parents who are suddenly empty nesters. And research has found that when older adults experience the loss of a spouse due to divorce or a partner's passing, having a canine companion helps buffer the loneliness and depressive symptoms that might otherwise occur.

If anyone knows this, it's Debbie, an underwriter for an insurance company in Illinois, who rescued Lexie, a Lab/golden mix, in 2011 to celebrate one year of sobriety. For much of her adult life, Debbie used alcohol to cope with her personal frustrations at work and at home, as well as major stressors like her divorce. While Debbie had always wanted a dog, she recognized that she wasn't responsible enough to take good care of one when she was drinking—so she waited until she quit alcohol for good. Not only was Lexie something of a reward for Debbie's sobriety, but she came at just the right time. "She filled a void for me since my sons were away at college, and she helped me improve my emotional state and my health with our walks," says Debbie, who's in her sixties. Their relationship was so gratifying that eight years ago Debbie decided to rescue a pit bull mix named Zelda. "Having both dogs made me feel comfortable living by myself," says Debbie. "They have become my world."

Shelby echoes this experience, from her parents' point of view. When she was growing up as an only child on a grain farm run by her parents and grandparents in Ohio, Shelby's family got a golden retriever they named Carlo, when Shelby was in sixth grade. Both she and her father had anxiety, and Carlo helped. Within a year, Shelby and her mother noticed that the dog's presence made a huge difference in the dad's demeanor, transforming him from someone who said few words in the morning to a man who smiled and had entire conversations within half an hour of waking up. Carlo would be at his side all day on the farm then come home with him when the work was done. Since Shelby moved away to go to college, Carlo has been a godsend to her parents. "Often I will get pictures from my mom of my dad lying on the floor next to Carlo, petting him," says Shelby, now a crop insurance adjuster in Nebraska. Later in the evening, another picture will arrive on her phone of her dad and Carlo sound asleep together.

The Joys of Reuniting

When previously present family members, such as college kids or military service members, come home after a long time away, it's often a thrilling moment for the humans and the family dog alike. Some dogs might do a happy dance, jumping up or standing on their hind legs, or running in circles. These days, when Stacey's young adult sons come home to visit, Sadie swings into full circus-dog mode, jumping up on them, spinning around, going into a play bow, then repeating the moves while squealing with delight. Other dogs, especially older ones, might seem to shun their owners after a long absence, either because they don't recognize them right away or because they were upset at them for leaving. The good news is that the shunning will be short-lived because, unlike humans, dogs don't hold lasting grudges. As long as a pup associates the absent family member with happy memories and loving encounters, you're likely to soon see pure, unadulterated joy, with wags and wiggles, expressed by your furry friend.

Besides adding richness, support, and joy to our days and nights, our trusted canine companions play leading roles in the ongoing stories of our lives. More than ever, uncertainty is a fact of modern life. Thanks to their enduring love, affection, and attention, our canine companions can help us feel grounded during times of flux. When life feels unsettled and the future ambiguous, your canine companion is likely to provide a sense of stability, continuity, and comfort from day to day and week to week. With your furry friend as your steadfast companion, you can focus on the here and now and create routines and rituals that work for both (or all) of you. You can bask in the mutual lovefest between you on good days and tough ones. And you can count on your dog's continuous presence and attention to bolster your spirits and your resolve to move forward in life confidently and steadily.

Part Four

APPRECIATING A LIFE
WELL LIVED TOGETHER

CHAPTER TWELVE

Maturing Together

Living with an Aging Dog

Toward the end of her life, Jen's dog Maggie, who was then eleven and a half, developed a clot that blocked most of the blood flow to her back legs. This didn't stop her from being her usual joyful self—at home, she didn't seem to realize anything was wrong—but suddenly Maggie wasn't able to go on the walks that she loved so much. When Jen and Maggie would go for a stroll in their tree-lined neighborhood, Maggie could only make it a few houses down the block before her legs would give out and she'd have to be carried home. Jen didn't want Maggie to lose the joy of their walks, so she bought a heavy-duty steel garden wagon, a dog crate pad to fit inside it, and created what cringingly became known as the Maggie Waggie. Jen would lift Maggie into the wagon and take her on walks around the block. Along the way, Maggie could check out the neighborhood and even get out and sniff if a spot seemed particularly attractive.

Jasmine, whom Jen had rescued along with Maggie as a bonded pair, would come on some of these walks, trotting alongside the wagon. Once, in pursuit of efficiency, Venkman (then four years old) came on the walk as well. It seemed like a fun idea to hook Venk's leash to the handle of the wagon and let her help pull it. Venk agreed this was really fun and took off at a full run, almost overturning the wagon in a crosswalk before dragging it straight into a neighbor's wall of hedges. That was Maggie's fastest wagon ride ever—and the end of Venk's very brief career as a sled dog.

While Jen and Maggie both would have preferred taking their usual beloved strolls together, the wagon provided a way to keep that bonding time going even as Maggie developed physical limitations in her older years. As Jen discovered, when your dog gets older, the activities you're going to be able to do together will change, in small ways and large ones. But that doesn't mean your bond needs to weaken. On the contrary, you can make it stronger than ever by tending to your dog's shifting needs and finding new ways to spend time with each other. Part of this bond enhancement stems from the trust and closeness that have developed between you over the years, and part of it may result from the extra time you're spending together now that your canine companion is older and has slowed down. It also may stem from your furry friend's appreciation of the TLC you provide them as their health and conditioning level change.

Paula got her golden retriever Molly as an eight-week-old puppy, and they bonded immediately. Between their mutual trust and adoration and their frequent moments of fun and affection, they were closer than close. Molly was super-healthy until age eleven when she developed an enlarged esophagus due to myasthenia gravis, an autoimmune disorder. Paula's husband built Molly a special chair for feeding her, and the couple found other ways to manage her health for another two and a half years, until 2017. When it became clear that Molly couldn't go on, Paula had a vet come to their home to release her from her suffering, on their deck. "I still feel her with me, and I wear her neck bandannas as hair kerchiefs and a bracelet with a little M and paw print that keeps her close," says Paula, an election inspector and family caregiver who lives in Poughkeepsie, New York. "I loved her her whole life. I'll miss her the rest of mine."

As Nicholas Dodman, BVMS, a veterinary behaviorist and professor emeritus at the Tufts Cummings School of Veterinary Medicine, notes in *Good Old Dog: Expert Advice for Keeping Your Aging Dog Happy, Healthy, and Comfortable,* "During checkups and other visits, we see the closeness in the way people interact with their more senior [canine] companions. There's a comfort level, a something that can be taken for granted, that isn't yet present between people and their younger dogs."

Getting older is an inevitable fact of life for humans and their beloved canines. But even though we're aging together, the rate is faster for a dog, given the relative differences in our life spans. *When* exactly a dog gains senior status depends largely on its breed. Smaller dogs (such as Yorkshire terriers and Pomeranians) aren't considered "older" until they're in their double digits, whereas big dogs (like mastiffs and Great Danes) may be considered "senior" at age eight. So while *you* may not yet be waking up feeling stiff or having sprouted gray hair, your canine companion may have developed aching joints and a whitish muzzle before you expect such changes.

On some level, most people realize there's a limit to their dog's health span and life span, though they may wish there weren't. Thanks to improvements in veterinary care and nutrition and dietary approaches, many dogs are now leading longer, healthier lives than in the past. But a time is likely to come when age-related conditions begin to affect your older dog. It's important to view aging and the challenges that come with it as a normal and unavoidable process, just as it is for humans. As Lynn Buzhardt, DVM, a veterinarian affiliated with VCA Animal Hospitals, wrote in a blog post: "With age comes lots of loss, but there is also a lot of fulfillment looking back on a life—human or canine—that was well lived. The joy you share with your pet should never get old."

As our dogs get older, develop age-related health conditions, and can no longer do many previously regular activities with us, we may have to give up some of our shared traditions. Maybe they can't run or play fetch or Frisbee anymore because they have arthritis. Maybe they can't jump onto the couch or locate their toys as easily due to problems with their strength or vision. These changes can be sad and upsetting for dogs and their owners. But there are new activities people can do with their dogs, as long as they remain observant, flexible, and encouraging.

To that end, it's important to monitor changes in your dog's energy level, expressions of discomfort, sensory acuity, and moods. You'll want to pay attention to their gait, mobility, breathing, appetite, sleep, and demeanor and bring any concerning changes to your vet's attention. Remember, too, that older dogs often need more cleaning, grooming, and oral care. They may benefit from an altered diet, with senior-formula kibble or more wet food, and certain supplements, such as glucosamine, fish oil, and probiotics, to address health conditions like arthritis or immune function; you should discuss these issues with your vet, too.

As dogs get older, their habits and interests may change, which doesn't necessarily mean their lives are worse; they may just be different. Older dogs might walk more slowly or want to go for fewer or shorter walks, content to sniff a bit and call it a day. They may not enjoy socializing with other dogs as much or may be less cuddly with their humans than they used to be. They may become more sensitive to significant temperature changes, as a result of changes in their metabolism. As a dog-owner, you'll want to stay attuned to these changes and consider how you can adapt your routines so that you and your dog can continue to enjoy activities you've always done together. If your dog enjoys being outside but doesn't care about movement or changes in scenery, you could bring them to sit outside with you on a sunny day while you read or work, as long as there's access to shade and a water bowl. The key is to think about what your aging pup would enjoy, then find ways to make it happen.

That's what Talia, a data analyst in Indianapolis, has done with Sophie, the now thirteen-year-old Jack Russell/Lab mix that she and her boyfriend Sam adopted three years ago from his family. Sophie's energy isn't what it used to be, and she has some stiffness in her back legs (she now takes a supplement to help her joint health). While Sophie still loves to go on walks twice a day, she walks more slowly these days—unless a squirrel gets into her sights, at which point she'll stalk them and then bolt into a run. As her energy and activity levels have mellowed with age, Talia says, "we have grown to really appreciate her sleeping on our bed or couch with us while we're hanging out."

Similarly, Anne, an IT project manager in Rochester, New York, has adjusted her routine to accommodate the needs of her golden retriever Chumley as both of them get older. She got Chumley when he was eight weeks old—and the bond between Anne, who's now in her fifties, and Chumley has grown closer every year. The two of them used to be avid walkers, but they can't go as far as they used to. Anne had a hip replacement last year and Chumley, now fifteen, has slowed down due to arthritis in his own hips. In his younger days, he would wrestle and play with bigger dogs; these days, he is content to snuggle up to Anne while she's working, which is just fine with her. "I am taking each and every day with him as a gift," says Anne. "While I'm working, Chums makes any stressful moments better just by letting me stroke his sweet head."

The reality is, dogs suffer from many of the same maladies and diseases that we humans do. Research led by Jessica M. Hoffman, PhD, from the University of Alabama at Birmingham, examined data from more than 112,000 humans and nearly 74,000 dogs in an attempt to look for similarities in patterns of aging. They found that obesity, arthritis, hypothyroidism, diabetes, and other chronic conditions that commonly occur in aging humans are "also associated with similarly high levels of comorbidity in companion dogs. We also find significant similarities in the effect of age on disease risk in humans and dogs."

Some of these parallels may be influenced by the fact that we live in the same home and breathe the same air. But some of these risks also are affected by genetic factors and lifestyle habits such as diet and exercise. Given the differences in the life spans of humans and dogs, signs of various medical conditions in our canine companions often catch people off-guard because they can seem to appear suddenly. For these reasons and others, the dynamic of care can shift at this point in your relationship. As your dog reaches middle age or older status, it's likely that you'll need to do more to take care of and attend to your pup than you did when they were younger. "It's a kind of altruistic love," says Chris Blazina, PhD, a psychologist in New Mexico and author of *When Man Meets Dog*. "It's about giving back."

 The Perks of Aging with a Dog

In previous chapters you read about the myriad ways that your dog can benefit *your* physical, emotional, and social well-being. There isn't an expiration date to these perks because having a companion dog can continue to enhance your overall well-being as you get older. Besides reducing feelings of loneliness and isolation, growing older with a canine companion helps people stay physically and cognitively active and socially engaged, not only with their furry friend but with other people and neighbors when they go out for walks.

As Ardra Cole, PhD, of Mount Saint Vincent University in Nova Scotia, wrote in a research article about the meaning of dogs in a 2019 issue of the *International Journal of Community Well-Being*, companion dogs "have been found to help elderly people gain a renewed sense of purpose and an increased sense of self-worth and well-being . . . as well as a stronger sense of independence and agency." In addition, older adults who live with furry friends have better morale; they tend to be more optimistic and better able to cope with everyday challenges; and they're more interested in planning for the future, according to Cole, who created a charity called ElderDog Canada.

Meanwhile, a 2019 national poll on healthy aging found that 70 percent of adults over age fifty reported that their pets help them cope with physical or emotional symptoms related to aging. Among the participating adults, ages fifty to eighty, the majority of pet owners indicated that their pets help them enjoy life, make them feel loved, reduce their stress, provide a sense of purpose, and help them adhere to a routine. In addition, the participants said their dogs help them connect with other people, stay physically active, and cope with physical and emotional symptoms, including pain. Some respondents even said they prioritize their pet's needs over their own.

A Sense of Engagement

Growing older with a dog you've shared a life with for many years can bring you a sense of comfort and peace. As Nicholas Dodman, BVMS, notes, "There's something more serene, wiser, about an older dog, even one who still has plenty of energy. A dog you've had for more than just a handful of years can simply understand you better, accommodate your moods better."

As your dog gets older, you'll want to find ways to accommodate changes in *their* temperament and functionality, too. Some older dogs want to stay close to their beloved humans, shadowing their movements throughout the home. Others may want to have more personal space. And some older dogs vacillate between these patterns. These shifts can be confusing and can sometimes be misinterpreted; the key is to pay attention to your dog's body language and adjust *your* love language accordingly.

Researchers led by Borbála Turcsán, PhD, from the Clever Dog Lab at the Messerli Research Institute at the University of Veterinary Medicine in Vienna, Austria, analyzed personality changes in 217 border collies, between the ages of six months and fifteen years old. The dogs were put through a variety of tests that were videotaped. In one, the dog was allowed to explore a room and objects on the floor while the owner ignored them. In another test, a stranger entered the room and petted the dog. In another test, designed to gauge frustration tolerance, the owner dangled a large piece of sausage in front of the dog's nose, just out of reach, for a minute. The researchers found that changes in personality occurred unevenly among dogs throughout their lives, but they did find some general patterns. Young and older dogs were more independent with activities than middle-aged dogs (between three and six years old) were; novelty-seeking decreased steadily from middle age on; the dogs' attentiveness and ability to solve problems increased in adolescence and early adulthood; and their frustration tolerance increased slightly with age. Some of these changes may be associated with a natural age-related decline in sensory and motor functions, according to the researchers.

If an older dog can't see, smell, or hear well, they may become more easily startled or even nippy if they're surprised by people or noises. Or if they're in pain and you don't realize it, they may be uncharacteristically irritable or standoffish. Or it could be that your older dog feels ill at ease with changing circumstances. Research led by Paolo Mongillo, DVM, PhD, at the University of Padua found that later-in-life dogs don't cope as well in emotionally distressing situations as younger pups do. When separated from their owners, older dogs behaved more passively and were less interested in interacting with a stranger; they also had a significant increase in salivary levels of cortisol (a stress hormone) afterward. Even though the older dogs seemed calm and composed on the surface, their internal responses to the upsetting situation were amped up.

Cognitive changes may contribute to changes in your dog's demeanor or behavior, as well. As it happens, our canine companions can experience age-related cognitive changes, dementia, or Alzheimer's disease, just as people we love can and sometimes do as they get older. In the case of our pooches, this is often referred to as canine cognitive dysfunction syndrome (CCDS), which is marked by a constellation of behavioral and neurological symptoms—such as disorientation, changes in social interactions with people or pets, altered sleep-wake cycles, house soiling, changes in activity levels, and increased anxiety— that become more common with advancing age. Unfortunately, this syndrome is usually progressive and there aren't effective treatments for it—but you should bring symptoms of it to your vet's attention.

As your dog ages and changes, the challenge is to find new ways to nurture your pooch and your relationship. "I don't know that dogs realize they're getting older—it's up to the human side of the partnership to recognize that," says Clive Wynne, PhD, a professor of psychology and founder of the Canine Science Collaboratory at Arizona State University in Tempe. "Dogs enjoy and appreciate being engaged with you at whatever level they can respond to." What they most want is the gift of time—mostly time with you but also time to relax. It's up to us, the humans, to make accommodations for their changing needs.

When Stacey's dog Inky was twelve, he would often get restless during the night. He'd walk around and whine, which made Stacey and her husband John think he had to go outside to pee. So one of them would let Inky out in the backyard—only to have him promptly lie down on the flagstone patio so he could survey his domain and gaze at the night sky. It was often really hard to get him to come back inside before he wanted to; sometimes treats couldn't even entice him back in. When Stacey mentioned this to their vet, she said that sometimes older dogs suffer from "sundowner syndrome," which can be manifested as restlessness and agitation during the night. Stacey and John learned to roll with it as best they could—by trying to shush and soothe Inky during the night so he'd go back to sleep. If that didn't work, John would sometimes let Inky out in the yard in the middle of the night and sleep on the sofa in the basement until their sweet, disoriented guy was ready to come back inside.

Something similar happened with Jen's rescued labradoodle St. Patrick, who was an old man—maybe thirteen years old—when he was found at the side of the road near some woods. He was one of the skinniest dogs Jen and Ingo had ever seen, and it was hard to get him to eat when he first arrived. The only thing he *would* eat was fast food, so Jen and Ingo would go to Burger King every couple of days and buy ten plain cheeseburgers that they would feed to him in the days that followed, until he finally started to eat normal dog food. Jen often had to make spaghetti or mix in some French fries with his dog food, though. He was a picky eater.

St. Patrick was also partly blind and deaf, and he had advanced dementia. Most of the time, he was in his own world, but he was a sweet and happy guy. At night, he would pace the house on his old, unsteady legs. They got used to waking up a few times every night to the sound of his big paws, clad in their traction booties, shuffling back and forth across the living room floor. They had to carry him on occasion because his mobility was bad. And there were a few times where he would half-heartedly snap at them, not to do damage but to express his crankiness—something their normally mellow boy never would have done. Jen and Ingo knew not to take it personally.

 Anticipatory Loss: When Grief Feels Imminent

If your dog is diagnosed with a terminal illness or struggling with mobility or breathing problems, you can have a sense of the ending of their life before it arrives. This can be accompanied by symptoms of anticipatory grief, which can include sleep and appetite changes, anxiety, sadness, a sense of guilt or helplessness, or difficulty concentrating, remembering things, or staying organized. These are the usual symptoms of grief, but in this case they begin before you actually say goodbye to your beloved dog. Not only are you grieving what your dog has already lost in terms of their good health and vitality and the joyful activities you could do together, but you're also anticipating the final loss of your canine companion while they're still with you.

These feelings can be painful and uncomfortable. And they can lead you to start to disengage from your pet because of how sad you feel. Don't do it. Don't let your sadness about their impending departure prevent you from enjoying your last days or weeks together. Try to accept your feelings of anticipatory grief while maximizing the quality time you can spend with your beloved pooch—cuddling, snuggling, and doing whatever activities you can still do together even if that's just going on a car ride to the grocery store.

On the upside, experiencing anticipatory grief can actually strengthen the bond and closeness between you and your treasured pooch later in their life. You might find yourself dedicating more time and energy to caring for your dog and enjoying their company, which can deepen your love and affection for each other. Even so, it's important to acknowledge your feelings about the anticipated loss of your fur baby without judgment. It can help to give yourself an outlet for expressing your feelings by writing about them, talking to someone you trust, or doing something physical to release your feelings. While you're experiencing anticipatory grief, don't sacrifice your own self-care for your dog's sake; make a concerted effort to get plenty of sleep, eat a balanced diet, exercise, and practice relaxation techniques such as yoga, meditation, or deep breathing. You need to take good care of yourself in order to be able to tend to your dog's growing needs.

Even when sadness seeps into the picture, it may help to remember that the intensity of your feelings is a testament to how much you love your dog and how much they love you. The wonder and joy that comes from the mutual lovefest you've cultivated will stay with you long after your dog has passed away.

The Long Reach of Canine Caregiving

When you bring a dog into your life, you commit to caring for them for the long haul. Sometimes that requires making difficult and potentially expensive decisions about their health care. Monitoring your dog's quality of life can help in this respect (we've included a scale in the Appendix that will help you gauge your dog's quality of life at any given time and your ability to address it). Unless your dog is bottoming out on the scale, meaning they are truly suffering, this is not intended to let you know that it's time to put them down; rather, this is a tool to be used over time to gauge how their quality of life is changing.

That said, this becomes especially important when your dog receives a diagnosis of a life-threatening or terminal illness, and you need to weigh the costs of keeping them alive versus the likely outcome of their condition and decide when to release them from their suffering. "It can be startling because you've stumbled upon the end of the road," says Blazina, who has had seven dogs, usually in pairs, during his adult life. "Sometimes people try to explain away symptoms—it's a bad weather day, not arthritis in the hips." People often think or hope or pray that they can do something to reverse the descent toward death, but at a certain point this just isn't possible.

While modern veterinary medicine offers many treatment options for improving and extending the lives of our beloved dogs, there are limits. And deciding what to do or not do can be challenging. We may want to do as much as we can to help our dogs feel and function better, but we don't want to put them through aggressive treatments or surgeries that may be painful, involve difficult recoveries, and may not prolong their quality of life. Of course, cost is often a factor, too, because even diagnostic interventions, such as magnetic resonance imaging (MRI) and computed tomography (CT) scans, can be expensive (we're talking thousands of dollars, not hundreds). It's a complicated calculus in every single situation, depending on your resources, the age and overall health of your dog, the difficulty of the procedure, and the possible outcomes.

If you had an otherwise healthy, energetic middle-aged dog who developed a cancerous tumor that could be surgically removed without the need for chemotherapy, you might opt in if you could afford to and your vet expected this would give you many more happy years with your pooch. On the other hand, if an older dog with diabetes developed cancer that could be treated with surgery and chemotherapy that would likely compromise their remaining quality of life, you might decide not to go down that path. Your vet should be able to tell you the average life expectancy range for dogs who receive a particular treatment, as well as a prognosis for your individual pet based on their age and health status. Weighing these issues against each other can give you some insight into whether it's worth pursuing certain treatments.

It's also important to consider whether the results of a diagnostic test, biopsy, or exploratory surgery would change what you do. These can cost thousands of dollars, and while they might reveal a lot about your dog's condition, would the results substantially change how you're likely to treat your dog? If the answer is yes, it may be worth having the test or procedure. But if the results are unlikely to change what you would do for your pooch—say, because they're already old and have multiple health problems—you might opt out of the tests.

While most of us would like our old dogs to pass away peacefully in their sleep, it doesn't usually happen that way. There's a good chance that you may need to decide how their life will end, which can be stressful and absolutely heartrending. You are likely to feel guilty no matter what you decide to do and when you decide it. But it is your duty, as a dog-owner, to make that decision. This is a time to be brave. It's a time for you, your dog's BFF, to make decisions that are in *their* best interest.

 Very Old Dogs and Hospice Cases

Because Jen and Ingo take in so many dogs who are old and sick, people often remark that they don't think they could handle the strain of the loss. But just because a dog doesn't have much time left to live doesn't mean they can't be a loving companion for the time that you do have them! Giving a dog a gentle, joyful, loving end-of-life chapter is profoundly rewarding. It allows you to connect on a level with no expectations beyond sharing some peace with one another. Here are stories of three Golden Ratio dogs who joined the squad for their last months, along with some of Jen's favorite memories of them:

Swizzle was a fourteen-year-old whose owner had advanced dementia, forgetting to feed both herself and her dogs. When Swizzle arrived to Jen and Ingo, she weighed only twenty-five pounds. They eventually got her up to around sixty pounds, and she never turned down food of any kind. In fact, in the time they had her, Jen and Ingo only ate one meal without her barking and begging for their (human) dinner; she had fallen asleep, and they crept outside with their food to enjoy one quiet, uninterrupted meal together. Swizzle was a sweet old lady who enjoyed every minute of the last months she spent in the Golden Ratio squad.

Manchego arrived to Jen and Ingo as a hospice case. He was a blind diabetic who couldn't walk well. They bought him a wagon that was specially sized to fit in their house's elevator, which goes from their balcony to the ground floor since the house is elevated. Four or five times a day, they would carry him into the cart, head down in the elevator, wheel him into the front yard, and then stand him up so he could have a few sniffs and take care of his business. Jen's favorite moment with him was taking him for his first swim: She and Ingo live in the Florida Keys and their backyard is the ocean. Manchego had turned his face to the setting sun, so Jen picked him up and carried him into the warm water, where he melted against her; as he lay in her arms, he relaxed and seemed to enjoy the feeling of floating and having the water soothe his old bones.

Parmesan was another hospice case. He had been a breeder dog in Sweden and made his way to the U.S. when he was adopted by a family after he retired. When he developed a large abdominal tumor, he was turned over to a rescue group. Jen and Ingo took him in and did their best to give him a happy last few months. They even learned to say "good boy" in Swedish, just in case he remembered it from his earlier years (it's "*duktig pojke*," pronounced DOOK-teeg POY-keh). He was mostly deaf and didn't like to move much, so when he couldn't see Jen or Ingo, he'd let out whispery barks until they waved their arms from the couch to let him know where they were.

When the time comes, humane euthanasia is a way for owners to save their dogs from days that are filled with unnecessary confusion, pain, and suffering. "The best gift you can give your dog at the end is to make sure they have a good goodbye," Blazina says. Making that choice, however, can be incredibly difficult, both emotionally and logistically, because it's sometimes hard to know *when* it's the right time for our dogs to pass away.

Because Jen and her husband rescue old and sick dogs, they have had to go through this decision-making process more often than most people do. Jen still cries about her sweet golden retriever Riley, whom she called "Boyfren." Jen's connection with him was one of the deepest she has ever had with a dog, and since he was only seven, she had so many plans for the years they were going to spend together. She wanted them to go running, to go on long car rides, and to play in the waves and swim together in the ocean. He was a dog she thought she could be carefree with, which she can't with all their other dogs because of their medical needs. Because they got him in the prime of his life, it seemed like there were no limits to what they could do together.

That turned out not to be true. Riley had a broken tooth when they got him, and during a visit to the vet to do routine bloodwork before having his tooth fixed, they discovered his blood levels for kidney function were a bit off. They decided to alter his diet and repeat the test a few weeks later. During a couple of repeat tests and a subsequent visit to a veterinary internal medicine specialist, it became clear that he had severe kidney disease as a result of Lyme disease, which he had contracted before they rescued him. Sadly, there's no cure for this type of eventual kidney failure (Lyme nephritis), so Riley was on a lot of medicine to try to slow the progression. The process of watching it unfold was terrible. Eventually, Riley stopped eating. Jen and Ingo tried giving him special prescription food, then they tried cooking at home. When that didn't work, they literally bought one of every kind of canned food at the pet store to find something he would eat. They bought burgers and fries from fast-food joints, hoping he would eat them. If they stumbled upon a snack he *would* eat, they would buy bags of it, though he usually would only eat it for a day or two. Then it got to the point where he could barely stand. He was in pain, unhappy, and suffering. Jen would have to carry him out to the yard to do his business. She knew it was time to let him go, but she kept hoping that maybe he would get a bit better and they would have a few more days together.

By the time they had him put down, it was past the "right time" to do it. Riley ended up suffering needlessly and intensely for two days longer than he should have. Jen will never forgive herself for making her poor Boyfren suffer unnecessarily for those last two days. He was the best dog she ever had and she had him for only seven months. She still cries when she thinks or talks about him—not only because she misses him but because she feels like she let him down.

With the benefit of experience, Jen can tell you this: There is rarely a "perfect time" to let your dog go gently over the rainbow bridge; there is a gray zone between "they are okay" and "it is absolutely time right now" in which either decision is probably all right. But waiting too long is the worst thing to do. Jen would absolutely prefer to euthanize a dog two weeks before it would have gotten really bad than to wait two days too long. She has felt guilty about every dog she and Ingo have lost, but the only soul-crushing guilt has come from letting one of their dogs suffer unnecessarily because she failed to make the choice on time.

When your aged dog is declining or you're in that gray zone where you're not sure whether it's time to put your dog down, there are specific signs to take into account. If a dog pants all night and is obviously having trouble breathing, night after night, their quality life may be over. If a dog consistently stops drinking or won't eat even the most delicious foods, they have crossed the line. If a dog doesn't know where they are or can't control their bodily functions, or if they are unable to stand up or are obviously in constant pain, it's time to let them go. In these instances, ending a dog's life is the last act of kindness and grace we can offer as a thanks for all they have given us.

At that point, the goal is to have the best last day with your dog that you can. When you know your beloved pup's life is about to come to an end, you have the freedom to do whatever you want with your dog without worrying about the consequences. Think about something they love or have always wanted to try and let them have it in the last few hours of their lives. For around half the dogs that Jen and Ingo have lost, they've been able to put together a best last day. Your vet may be willing, like theirs have always been, to give you medicine to help relieve your dog's pain and perk up your pal's energy enough to enjoy a few nice things. Jen and Ingo have spent some of these best last days, or even best last weekends, lying in the sun in the grass, providing all kinds of foods they never would have let the dogs have when they were healthy, or sleeping together on the floor. They have gently rolled a tennis ball to dogs who loved to play fetch but could no longer run. They made waffles and piled them high with whipped cream and sprinkles and put the whole plate in front of a dog. Manchego, a diabetic, got to eat as many chocolate chip cookies as he wanted. For their dog Jasmine, who was as passionate about the car as any dog ever was, they spent her last days going for drives together, stopping at beaches so she could take a brief sniff around, and then getting back into the car to drive to another spot. It was a wonderful farewell tour for her.

For us humans these sendoffs are bittersweet—lovely, sad, heartbreaking, and heartwarming all at the same time. For the dogs, it's a joy, even if a mellow one, to have *your* undivided attention and unbridled love focused on them during their final hours. Even if we've had many amazing years together, most of us are never quite ready to say goodbye to our precious pooches. The end of their aging comes far too quickly, to our way of thinking.

CHAPTER THIRTEEN

The Broken Bond

Coping with Grief and Sorrow

For Stacey, the death of her beloved dog Inky in August 2020 shook her to the core. In the weeks that followed, Stacey could barely focus or think clearly. She'd get teary throughout the day, often without any provocation. She'd simply start missing Inky's soulful face or the way he'd wriggle and make Chewbacca-like sounds to signal her to come over and pet him—and Stacey would start sobbing again. It felt like a piece of her heart had been ripped out. Part of her devastation stemmed from the suddenness of his death. Late one night Inky collapsed while trying to stand and cried out in pain; three hours later, an ER doctor at the twenty-four-hour pet hospital informed Stacey and her husband that Inky, thirteen, had internal bleeding from a cancerous tumor (a hemangiosarcoma) that had ruptured. Until that moment, they'd had no idea that something so deadly was growing inside him. It was untreatable, and they were told that humane euthanasia was in order.

The hospital vet loaded Inky up with painkillers so they could bring him home. The next afternoon they had a kind, compassionate veterinarian who did house calls come over and put Inky to sleep at home, so he could pass away peacefully among the people who loved him. It was the gentlest, most loving send-off imaginable, under the circumstances. But Stacey was devastated to lose her canine angel (which is what she called him). Inky was her constant companion as she worked in her home office. He slept on the floor next to Stacey's side of the bed and he'd wag and wiggle whenever he caught her eye. For weeks, Stacey was such a sad, weepy mess that one day her teenage son Nick said he thought she should consider getting another dog soon because he was worried about her emotional health. He added, "Let's face it, Mom, you don't know how to live without a dog."

Losing a cherished canine companion can be an incredibly painful experience. Most people consider their dogs members of the family, holding nearly as valued a place as human family members do. And some people are as emotionally attached to their dogs as they are to their human relatives because the dog-human bond provides the same, and sometimes an even greater, sense of comfort, support, and affection as close human relationships do. The death of a dog can lead to a complex constellation of emotions including sorrow, anger, and guilt.

Society doesn't always give dog-lovers permission to feel the depth of sadness and grief that comes with this loss, but for most of us this is the loss of a close member of our families. It's important for people to allow themselves to feel however they feel as they process this painful change in their lives. They may experience a profound void, including the loss of a schedule around which to organize their time. They may have trouble eating, sleeping, or concentrating the way they usually do. They may miss the unbridled joy that used to greet them when they returned home after a trip to the store, or the random bouts of affection they got from their fur baby throughout the day. They may struggle with the reality that their home suddenly feels eerily quiet and still or that they don't quite know what to do with themselves when the usual dog-walking hours roll around.

The loss of a pet is so significant that it can disrupt the other relationships in our lives, with our partners, family members, friends, neighbors, and coworkers. You may end up being short-fused or impatient with other people or you may withdraw from others because you're so steeped in your own grief. You may be less willing to get together with people because your grief may make it harder to enjoy activities you normally relish. And you may fear that you'll dissolve in a tsunami of tears at any given moment. Initially, it can feel like you will never get through the grief and that the pain will overwhelm you. Psychologists recognize that this is a natural response to losing a pet—as a group of researchers led by Paul T. Clements, PhD, at the University of New Mexico put it, "the shock, numbness, searching, yearning, and disorientation are all appropriate and necessary parts of the grieving process."

For those who have very strong connections with their dogs, the loss is similar to losing a person they love. But our society doesn't have rituals or ceremonies like funerals or memorial services that bring the community together to support you or help you process the loss when your dog dies. That is why researchers have described grieving the death of a beloved dog as a form of "disenfranchised grief," meaning one that isn't acknowledged as legitimate by society.

Those who have studied grief in response to the loss of a pet have found that the way others in our lives respond to our loss can impact how we grieve. In a year-long study involving forty-four people who had recently had a pet die, the researchers found that people "struggled with the contradiction between how they felt after their pet had died and the perceived absence of support for their feelings from others, or society in general." This led to them feeling like they should hide their grief and distress (sometimes going so far as to wear dark sunglasses to hide their puffy eyes) or distract themselves with other activities. This lack of support, sympathy, or even acknowledgment can make it more difficult to process our grief, and it can be profoundly isolating. It can also complicate our feelings by making us feel ashamed or embarrassed about how saddened we are by the loss of an adored dog.

Several weeks after Inky died, Stacey and her husband went out for lunch with her mother and stepfather. They had just ordered when Stacey's mother turned to her and said, "Are you still upset about the dog?" Shocked by the question, Stacey said, "Of course!" As her stepfather chastised Stacey's mom for asking such a tone-deaf question and as her mother looked at her blankly, Stacey sputtered, "You don't understand—I loved that dog more than I *like* most people!"*

Receiving social support is important to help us get through grief. It allows us to process our feelings, handle the confusion of loss, and feel less alone. It protects us from both psychological stress and physical illness. When we don't receive that support, as often happens when we lose pets, it can have a profoundly negative impact on our sense of well-being.

Jen has experienced this social awkwardness firsthand. Maggie was an extra-special dog, and when she died in 2019, Jen cried non-stop for six months. Then her dog Riley died and Jen just kept crying. Losing both dogs so close together was devastating. At that point, Jen was doing group Pilates classes every day, and as soon as she'd lie on her back on the Reformer, under the studio's calming blue lights, she would get teary and would cry the entire fifty minutes. The instructor never said anything to her but at one point, Jen felt the need to explain, "Somebody very close to me just died and this is the place where my

---

*Apparently, Stacey isn't alone in this feeling. In a study involving 573 participants, Richard Topolski, PhD, and colleagues presented a moral dilemma about being forced to decide whether to save a human or their pet dog from imminent death and found that 44 percent of women would choose to save their dog over a human they didn't know. As the researchers noted, these findings indicate that people have a powerful sense of psychological kinship with their pet dogs.

body releases the sadness." Sometimes you have to be careful whom you tell the truth to about these things.

Stacey's neighbor Erin is personally familiar with the heartbreak of losing two dogs in a short span of time. Maisey, a spirited fox terrier/poodle mix, and Weeman, a gentle Cavalier King Charles/poodle mix, had been together their whole lives. Erin, who hadn't grown up with pets, got the two dogs as puppies during her first marriage. They were there for the birth of her two children, and she kept the dogs after her divorce. The pups later became pivotal points of interest as she and her current partner blended their families, now with a total of five kids. Throughout it all, the dogs were inseparable. "They were each other's permanent companions—they were in love with each other and they slept wrapped around each other every night," recalls Erin, who works for a nonprofit organization in Washington, D.C.

The two dogs died, three months apart, in 2021. After Maisey passed away at fourteen and a half, Erin is convinced that Weeman died of a broken heart. "Without Maisey, he didn't know what to do with himself—he was lost without her; she was his everything," she recalls. Suddenly, Weeman became listless and began having trouble breathing. "I did whatever I could to keep him alive because I couldn't stand the thought of losing both of them," she recalls. But when Weeman could no longer stand up by himself and was struggling for breath, Erin took him to the vet to be put to permanent rest. Knowing that Weeman, the perfect dog in her eyes, had died with a broken heart, compounded the grief Erin felt from losing both pups. "I was traumatized and cried for days—I couldn't function," she recalls. "Before this, I couldn't have imagined in a million years how hard that level of grief would be."

The Benefits of Having Our Feelings Validated

Because Jen rescues old dogs, sick dogs, and hospice cases, she has a lot of experience losing dogs—and it's always painful. These bonds with the dogs run deep, and there isn't any magical way to make it hurt less when they pass away. But Jen says there can be a silver lining: When one of the Golden Ratio dogs dies and she posts about it on social media, she receives an outpouring of love, support, and sadness from the online community. Jen has always felt that *this* is the magnitude of response this kind of loss deserves, because losing a beloved dog can disrupt our lives in ways that we want the whole world to acknowledge. The Golden Ratio community allows her to know that tens of thousands of people are sharing in her sadness, which at least makes her feel supported and understood and takes away the sense of emotional isolation. Her sadness is not met with any judgment or social shame. This helps mitigate some of the unfortunate ways society imposes expectations on us for how we should feel and deal with our grief.

Of course, very few people have a situation like Jen's, but it's important to find social support to cope with the loss of a dog you love. There are social media groups on many platforms that exist so that grieving pet owners can support one another; you can join online support groups like the Rainbow Bridge Pet Loss and Grief Support or Pet Soul Grief and Loss Support. If you don't have the support you need in your life, don't feel like you need to tamp down your sadness and go it alone. One of the greatest benefits of the internet is that it allows us to find different communities; you can find one to help you through your grief.

In 2019, Jen's friend Kathy lost her eight-year-old English shepherd Scout to a hemangiosarcoma, an extremely aggressive cancer that can produce massive tumors seemingly overnight, the kind Stacey's dog Inky died from. A day after his diagnosis, Scout died. His suffering was over, but Kathy's was just beginning. Scout had been her soulmate dog; he went with her to work at the university where she teaches in Maryland, did therapy sessions with her in hospitals, and always let her know what he was thinking. (When he got bored with agility classes, he made eye contact with Kathy, walked over to a jump, and peed on it to express his displeasure.) "I wanted to take care of him into old age and help him grow old gracefully, and we lost him too early," says Kathy. Her grief was overwhelming. She went through periods of numbness and anger. She was overcome with guilt, as she wondered what she could have or should have done to prevent or catch his cancer early.

Recognizing how distraught she was, Kathy started looking for help. She went to group therapy briefly, before it was interrupted by the pandemic. Watching the people there, she noticed that they didn't want to let go of their grief because they felt it was like letting go of their dog—a feeling she understood. She tried individual therapists; it was important to her that she find someone who would not try to make her let go of her guilt but who could still help her get to the next level of grieving. Kathy pushed back against the stigma surrounding grief counseling for the loss of a pet. "It's okay to say *I am really miserable because I lost the best thing in my life,*" she says. Nearly three years later, Kathy still cries when she talks about losing Scout, but she feels like counseling gave her the tools she needed to start feeling better and to remember and appreciate the overall goodness of their life together.

Researchers from several universities in Europe developed a tool called the Mourning Dog Questionnaire to evaluate the mourning process in those who have lost a dog. Among the factors that were found to influence the level of distress people felt after the death of their dog were the nature and quality of their human-dog attachment, how much social support they experienced from people in their lives, the extent to which people perceived emotional and spiritual differences between humans and dogs, the circumstances surrounding the dog's death, and the people's overall outlook on life and death. Interestingly, some of the primary emotional factors that are related to grieving the loss of a person you love—such as feelings of guilt or anger or having intrusive thoughts—are often present after the death of a beloved dog, according to the researchers.

The element of guilt may come as a surprise, but it is an unfortunately common aspect of this particular loss. If a dog got lost or dies suddenly, we might wonder if we could have done something more to protect them and feel guilty that we didn't. If we lose them after an illness, we either have made the choice to euthanize them and can feel guilty for being the one to decide the moment of their death, *or* if they died naturally, we can feel guilt for not sparing them unnecessary suffering. And sometimes—such as when there's a diagnosis of terminal cancer or heart disease—we may feel angry at ourselves for not recognizing early signs of the disease *and* guilty for not getting it treated when there may have been a chance of saving our beloved dog. There's no question: These are complicated, uncomfortable feelings to navigate.

On social media, Jen is often asked *How long is this sadness, heartache, or pain going to last?* The answer is, it varies widely between people, depending on their personality and the intensity and duration of the relationship they had with their dog. The typical grieving period lasts from six months to a year, with an average of around ten months, according to research led by Thomas A. Wrobel, PhD, a professor of psychology at the University of Michigan-Flint. After six months, most people start to see a decrease in their symptoms of grief, as well as crying jags, feelings of guilt, depression, despair, and anger. But after a year, approximately 22 percent of people will still have some symptoms of grief. Women tend to have more symptoms of grief and more intense symptoms than men do—perhaps because we, women, are raised and socially encouraged to be in tune with our emotions, and thus we have permission to fully feel these fraught feelings.

Creating Rituals for Grieving

Aside from finding social support, the onus is on each of us to find ways to grieve the loss of our pets that feel right to us. Creating rituals or channels for your grief can help. To make the mourning process easier as you grapple with the painful loss of your pet, it can help to write in a journal about what your dog meant to you or how you feel without them, or to create a scrapbook or collage with photos and other mementos of your dog to honor their life. It can help to reach out to kindred dog-lovers who can lend a sympathetic ear as you talk about how you feel. You could hold a memorial service and write a poem or eulogy to acknowledge your loss and your dog's place in your life, or you could do something symbolic to honor your dog like planting a special tree or bush in your yard.

For Jen, solace can be found in projects. She has created photo books, torn up her garden and planted a new weeping cherry tree in honor of her dog Pi after she passed, created memorial boxes (with their collars and favorite things), and painted rooms of her house while grieving. She needs to *create* tangible things to deal with her grief. Other people write poems or stories. Scholars have specifically looked at the benefits that come from writing poetry to help with grieving the loss of pets. For example, writing poetry can help you embrace the paradox of grieving: understanding that when you love a dog, this means you will eventually suffer grief when they die, but that avoiding the grief would require avoiding the love, which would rob you of the joy of the life you shared together. Most of us wouldn't want that! Writing poetry has long been used as a way to help people process their grief, because it really can help.

After Stacey's Australian shepherd Wolfy died at age thirteen and a half, she and her sons read the comforting book *Dog Heaven*, written and illustrated by Cynthia Rylant, together. Then they expressed their own sadness through writing or art. Nicky, then four, drew a picture with Magic Markers of a gravestone with Wolfy's name on it. Nate, then nine, wrote a poem about Wolfy, describing him as his "furry brother," and read it to the family. And Stacey wrote Wolfy a private letter that ended with:

> *I miss you terribly, Wolfy, but as my intense grief begins to fade into a bittersweet sadness, I mostly appreciate how much we had together. You had a long and mostly happy life with us and for that I'm grateful. We grew up through our adulthoods together, and you knew how much we loved you every single day of your life, for which I am also grateful. You were so much more than a pet; you were always a true member of our family, as beloved as any. Which is why a piece of my heart broke when you died. . . .*

I wasn't ready to say goodbye to you. But the truth is, I never would be. I really wanted you to be a part of my life forever—it's unrealistic, I know, but it's how I felt without realizing it until you were gone.

Yours,
Stacey

Granted, none of these activities will necessarily make you feel less sad, but channeling the sadness into something tangible can help you comprehend the enormity of the loss and at least feel some ownership of your grief. It may help to remember, too, that even though your dog's death has brought about a permanent physical separation, the love and connection you shared can be sustained. This idea relates to a concept called "continuing bonds," the notion that even though death has physically separated you, the emotional connection between you can be sustained in your heart, mind, and soul. Based on four specific expressions—having fond memories, sharing those memories, creating a legacy of the deceased, and using photographs of the departed loved one—the attachment to your beloved pup can continue after the dog dies, just as your attachment would to a person you loved and lost.

Research led by Wendy Packman, PhD, at Palo Alto University in California found that the use of expressions of continuing bonds by bereaved pet owners was more comforting than distressing. What's more, it led them to have thoughts about being reunited or to sense their pet's presence or to have dreams about their pet. It also helped them cope with their grief and better regulate their emotions in general.

There are many ways to forge and manifest continuing bonds—whether it's through writing or drawing, getting a tattoo in your pet's honor, preserving a special photograph of your dog, or perhaps donating a bench to a park you used to visit together, where you can sit and reminisce about your pooch. If you want to do something really special, there are artists who will take a small sample of your dog's cremains and turn them into marbles, glass art, or diamonds. Jen wears a necklace almost every day that contains a diamond made from the collected fur from her original squad of six dogs. Its sparkle reminds her of the joy she had with those dogs who changed her life.

Above all, it's important to give yourself ample time to mourn. It can take months or years to reach a level of acceptance where the sadness decreases substantially.* Some studies have found that the period of grief that's associated with the loss of a canine companion may be even longer than the one associated with the death of a person, perhaps because people's feelings toward their dogs are so unequivocally positive. In the meantime, it's important to be patient and compassionate toward yourself. Also, honoring your dog's memory by volunteering with rescue organizations or foster care groups or an animal welfare organization can help ease the pain you feel after your dog's death, because you'll be channeling it toward a worthy cause.

Eventually, the overwhelming grief will subside and you *will* be able to return to a new-normal life (albeit, without your cherished canine companion). That said, the sadness can creep back in, sometimes when you least expect it. One of the most helpful strategies that Jen heard was shared with her after she lost Maggie in 2019. It involves imagining a box. On the inside surface of the box, there is a "pain button" that when pushed triggers an intense amount of pain and sadness; there's also a ball that gets jiggled around inside the box and has the potential to hit the pain button. In the early stages of grief, the ball is very large, which means the pain button continually gets pushed, causing you nearly nonstop sadness. Eventually, the ball gets smaller. It can still hit the button, and it's not that the pain is lessened, but the hurt is triggered less often. But on some days the ball can become big again. Even

---

*In her 1969 book *On Death and Dying*, psychiatrist Elisabeth Kübler-Ross, MD, proposed that there are five stages of grief—denial, anger, bargaining, depression, and acceptance—that people typically experience as they come to terms with the reality that they have a terminal illness. The stages were later applied to family members and friends as they grieved the loss of a loved one (or a beloved pet) and moved through it. Now there's growing recognition among experts that grief is less predictable and more complicated than the five-stage model suggests, which can lead people to feel that the way they're experiencing grief is wrong. In the current thinking, grief is more like a loop-de-loop roller coaster that goes around and around than a linear progression that comes to a definitive end.

years later, when the ball is generally much smaller, you can still experience the intense pain from the loss, but it becomes easier to manage as the ball gets smaller. And yet, even when you think you've gotten past it, something will happen—that ball in the box will hit the button—and that grief can hit you hard again.

Looked at another way, it can feel as though you're living in a snow globe. Things can be calm and peaceful and you may be feeling and functioning just fine after your loss; then, something happens to shake up the snow globe, triggering your feelings of grief and loss all over again. The magnitude of the shaking—and your feelings—can vary from one day or situation to another. This is all normal, but it can be confusing as you navigate a period of time where thoughts of your dog may bring joy one minute and cause you to get teary later the same day.

Over time, you're likely to experience fewer blizzards in your snow globe of grief and more light flurries. And eventually your grief will ease to the point where memories of your dog will bring you comfort and happiness rather than only sadness. One of the signs that you have forged a continuing bond occurs when you have dreams about your dog, notes Chris Blazina, PhD, a psychologist in New Mexico and author of *When Man Meets Dog*. In 2015, his dog Sadie—a border collie who was the best friend he'd ever have—died. About two weeks later, Blazina had a dream where Sadie was in the woods by herself and he wondered if she'd be all right; then, she began howling at the moon, transformed into a white wolf, and went on her way. That's when "I knew she would be okay," he recalls. For him, the dream was a moment of sweetness mixed with sorrow, a feeling that remains with him to this day when he thinks about her.

Losing a dog you love "can be an incredibly rich and painful opportunity to face life in a way that some of us have not," Blazina says. "Dogs are a wonderful existential reminder that *we're* not going to be here forever."

After you've processed the loss of your treasured dog, your memories and dreams about your pup may elicit mixed emotions. The sadness over their loss doesn't ever go away, but it fades somewhat with time, as you remember all the sweet, goofy, affectionate, frustrating, and mystifying moments you had together. These feelings serve as a powerful reminder of how much your dog meant to you and how deeply they affected your life. If you look at it this way, would you really want to get rid of those bittersweet feelings?

Lessons from Our Dogs

After coming this far, we hope that you have gained profound insights into the incredible bond that exists between humans and dogs, that you have come to value this relationship more than ever before, or that you have decided to take the plunge and get a(nother) dog of your own if you were considering it. One of the greatest gifts the universe has given humans is the companionship of dogs. In many people's experience, few relationships in life are as gratifying and unconditionally loving as the human-canine connection. Our dogs enrich our lives in too many ways to count—and we do the same for them.

In exchange for us feeding, loving, and caring for them, they pay us back many times over. They are safe havens that we can turn to in times of stress. They cheer us up when we're feeling down and make us want to become better versions of ourselves. They improve and inspire our connections with friends, family, neighbors, and partners. They get us up when we want to stay in bed, out when we want to stay inside, and moving when we want to stay on the couch. Our physical, mental, emotional, and spiritual health is consistently better, thanks to the company of our furry friends.

From the day we bring a dog home, whether they enthusiastically bound through the door or cry throughout their first night, we begin to forge this purest bond. If we are lucky, we will spend more than a decade learning about their quirks and how to make them happy. We will learn about the weird snacks they like—maybe you get a dog who steals whole heads of iceberg lettuce off the counter or who craves tater tots—and the games they like to play. We will comfort them through fireworks and thunderstorms, injuries and illnesses, and the taunts of squirrels in the yard. And we will take them on adventures, whether it's camping in the wilderness, road trips across the country, or a daily outing to that weirdly, but consistently, intriguing patch of grass one block over.

Eventually, our dogs will slow down. We will massage their backs and hips and buy them orthopedic beds, cook them dinner and feed it to them by hand. And eventually, in exchange for their lifetime of good days, we will endure one of our worst when we have to say goodbye. It will be painful to do, but we know that giving them a gentle, loving send-off is a profound responsibility and the last, great kindness we can do for them. And even though we will be left with a permanent crack in our hearts, we won't spend one minute regretting that we loved them so completely.

Throughout our time together, our dogs will serve as role models for how we can be better humans. Sometimes human beings make life more complicated than it should be and lose sight of what's truly important in the grand scheme of things. Our beloved canine companions don't do that; in fact, they have so much to teach us about friendship, commitment, loyalty, and caring for others. We all can benefit from the lessons they provide, especially the importance of:

• Loving others without judgment or conditions

• Appreciating the here and now, rather than always focusing on the future

• Taking advantage of small moments of pleasure

• Basking in the joy of being outside, no matter what the weather is

• Showing our loved ones how happy we are to see them

• Letting others know when we want to play

• Showering our loved ones with affection

• Realizing that simply keeping someone who's upset company is often consoling enough (words aren't always necessary)

By tuning in to and practicing what our dogs do naturally, we can start to feel more grounded and present-minded, focused on what's genuinely important, and resilient in the face of life's turbulence. We will be able to hold on to enduring reminders of what our canine companions mean to us and a lasting legacy for how to lead a happier life, today, tomorrow, and thereafter. Our dogs fill our days and nights with love, comfort, affection, play, joy, and so many other wonderful things. As photographer and writer Roger Caras put it, "Dogs are not our whole life but they make our lives whole." *What more could you ask for from any relationship?*

ACKNOWLEDGMENTS

It's often said that it takes a village to raise a child. Well, the same could be said about giving birth to a book. In the case of *The Purest Bond*, multiple villages played a role in bringing it to life—including the Golden Ratio community, people in Jen's and Stacey's everyday orbits, the scientists who study dog behavior and the emotional connections between people and their pooches, as well as key people in the publishing world.

This book would not have been possible if it weren't for the creativity and keen insights of literary agent Todd Shuster, who during the early days of the pandemic identified an untapped desire for a book about the joys of the human-canine connection and with fellow agents Daniella Cohen and Jane von Mehren helped us shape the content for this book. Todd, Daniella, and Jane, we are incredibly grateful for your support and wisdom while bringing this project to life.

We are also deeply indebted to our talented editor Stephanie Hitchcock, who immediately appreciated the need for a "feel-good book" like this and brought warmth, clarity, and compassion to the topic and the process. At Atria, we would also like to thank Lindsay Sagnette, Libby McGuire, Lisa Sciambra, Emma Van Deun, Erica Siudzinski, Maudee Genao, Megan Rudloff, and Morgan Hoit for their contributions. And we want to extend a huge thank-you to the brilliant illustrator Mark Ulriksen, who happens to be a dog-lover and immediately embraced the spirit behind this book with his evocative and whimsical illustrations.

Acknowledgments

We are deeply grateful to the online Golden Ratio community for their support and trust. You shared over seven hundred heartfelt stories about dogs you love as well as those you've loved and lost, including the support they provided and the joy they brought into every day that you knew them. Many of the personal stories in this book came from you, and we are honored that you trusted us with these intimate, beautiful glimpses into the connections you've had with the precious pups in your lives.

We are also grateful to the scientists and experts whose research we relied on or who provided important insights we incorporated in the book. In particular, we would like to thank Clive Wynne, PhD, of the Canine Science Collaboratory at Arizona State University; Julia Meyers-Manor, PhD, of Ripon College in Ripon, Wisconsin; Chris Blazina, PhD, a psychologist in New Mexico; and Krista Geller, PhD, an organizational psychologist in Virginia. Of course, we want to thank our families—especially Ingo, John, Nate, and Nick—for all of their support as we wrote this book. And we are eternally indebted to the various canine companions who have enriched our lives.

The truth is, writing this book was a labor of love for us. It provided a chance for us to celebrate the meaningful connections between people and their pooches, learn more about the unexpected ways dogs can benefit our physical, emotional, and social well-being, and understand what lies beneath the profound connections we have with our pups. We hope that this book will open your eyes even wider to the many ways dogs can enrich *your* life and allow you to bask in the lovefest that has developed—or has the potential to develop—between you. This purest of bonds really is one of the greatest gifts life has to offer.

APPENDIX 1

ISO THE RIGHT DOG FOR YOU:

WHAT TO KNOW

If you're hoping to get a puppy, make sure you find a reputable source. Puppy mills are far too common and sometimes hard to recognize. These commercial dog-breeding operations are characterized by high-volume breeding and poor conditions that neglect the welfare of all the dogs involved. Jen and Ingo have rescued both male and female dogs that were breeders at puppy mills, and they can be among the hardest to build attachments with. They have usually been denied any human love, were often kept in crates and in filth, and provided with little medical care beyond what was necessary for them to keep breeding. The puppies also suffer, as they are often infected with preventable diseases and have been living in unsanitary conditions.

The reality is, puppy mills supply many pet stores that sell puppies. They also turn up in some less expected situations—for example, many puppy mills in states like Ohio and Pennsylvania are run by people in Amish communities. These idyllic-looking country farms often hide poor treatment of these dogs that are used for breeding; they are often kept in stacked crates and continuously put into service until they cannot breed anymore.

Some better options: Whether you're looking for an adult dog or a puppy, rescue groups are a great place to start. If you are interested in a specific breed, there are often breed-specific rescue groups that you can work with. If you want to buy a dog directly from a breeder, check out the Humane Society's checklist of what to look for in responsible breeders: humanesociety.org/breeders. A good breeder will make sure that your whole family meets the puppy before you adopt. A good breeder will produce only a few litters per year, and they will provide documentation about the parents and why they were chosen. These outfits will also have veterinarian records for your specific puppy and the treatments and shots it has had.

APPENDIX 2

THE QUALITY-OF-LIFE SURVEY

You can use the survey that follows to gauge your dog's quality of life at any given time and your ability to address it. Being able to do this becomes especially important with older pooches and dogs that are battling life-threatening illnesses.

Read each of the following statements, then choose the response that most accurately reflects your dog's experience, on a scale from 1 to 5. We've provided some guidelines for responses 1, 3, and 5 to help you judge.

1. How well is your pet engaging with you and your family?
☐ 1 – My dog does not want to engage, is irritated by things they used to enjoy, and wants to be left alone.
☐ 3 – My dog sleeps more than they used to and isn't up for all the usual fun games, but they enjoy seeing the people they love.
☐ 5 - My dog engages with me, wants to play, and seeks out company from me and other members of the squad.

2. Does your dog seem to be enjoying life these days?
☐ 1 – My dog seems depressed, dull, and withdrawn.
☐ 3 – My dog sleeps a lot and is mellower than they used to be, but still shows frequent bouts of happiness.
☐ 5 – My dog wants to play and shows joy and interest in various activities.

3. Is your dog in pain?

☐ 1 – Yes, even with pain medication, they seem to be uncomfortable or in pain (e.g., they are panting even though it isn't hot and they haven't been exercising; they may wince, shake, or tremble at random times).

☐ 3 – They are on pain medicine and it seems to help most of the time.

☐ 5 – No, they do not seem to be in any pain.

4. How well is your dog eating and drinking?

☐ 1 – They do not want any food and sometimes it's hard to get them to drink.

☐ 3 – Their appetite is not great, but they will usually eat treats and at least part of a meal if I make it extra-appetizing. They are drinking normally.

☐ 5 – They have a great appetite and are eating and drinking normally.

5. Can your dog stand and move okay?

☐ 1 – They need help to stand up and are unsteady on their feet.

☐ 3 – Standing can be tough, but once they are on their feet, they can move around even if it's a bit stiffly at times.

☐ 5 – They can run and play and enjoy their usual activities.

6. How are your dog's elimination habits?

☐ 1 – They often have diarrhea or cannot always control their urination or defecation, and/or they may lie in their own excrement.

☐ 3 – They have occasional problems or accidents, but are usually able to control their bodily functions until they are let outside.

☐ 5 – Everything seems normal in this department.

Now add up the numeric value of your responses to determine your dog's total score on the quality-of-life scale, which ranges from 5 (poor quality of life) to 30 (a high quality of life). If your dog has low scores on many of these items, it may be time to have a candid conversation with your vet about their quality of life. The purpose of this tool is *not* to give you a sense of when it is time to say goodbye. Rather, this survey will help you track the changes in your dog's quality of life and think about which areas are improving or worsening for them; then the goal is to find ways to make your dog's life as comfortable and enjoyable as possible for the duration.

APPENDIX 3

PUPCAKES

These easy-to-make cupcakes have healthy, recognizable ingredients. Dogs love them—and so do some humans (like Stacey's husband).

Makes 8–10

> 2 tablespoons peanut butter
> 2 tablespoons vegetable oil
> 1 medium-to-large banana, mashed
> 2 tablespoons honey
> ½ cup white or whole-wheat flour
> ½ teaspoon baking soda
> ¼ teaspoon baking powder

Preheat oven to 350° F. Line a muffin pan with paper liners or spray it with cooking spray.

In a large mixing bowl, stir together the peanut butter, vegetable oil, mashed banana, and honey.

Mix in the flour, baking soda, and baking powder until well combined. Spoon the batter evenly into the muffin tins until they are half to two-thirds full and bake for 15 to 20 minutes, until a fork inserted in the center of a pupcake comes out clean. Cool the pupcakes completely before serving.

NOTES

Introduction

1 *In the face of having* Megan McCluskey, "Rescue Animals Are TIME's 2020 Pet of the Year," *TIME*, December 9, 2020.

1 **Human relationships are being strained** American Psychological Association, "Patients with Depression and Anxiety Surge as Psychologists Respond to the Coronavirus Pandemic" (2020).

2 **This isn't surprising, given that** Lauren Powell et al., "Companion Dog Acquisition and Mental Well-Being: A Community-Based Three-Arm Controlled Study," *BMC Public Health* 19, no. 1 (2019): 1–10.

2 *In fact, research shows that* Tilly Alexander, "People with Dogs Are Happier Than Cat Owners," Wales online, October 2021, https://www.walesonline.co.uk/news/uk-news/people-dogs-happier-cat-owners-21739776.

5 *As researchers found in a* Lori Kogan, PhD, et al., *Pet Dogs During the Time of COVID* (Fort Collins, CO: FIDO Fort Collins, 2020), https://fidofortcollins.org/covid-dog-owner-survery-results/.

Chapter One

9 *Why do we take in new dogs* Michael Gerson, "Why I Will Never Live Without a Dog Again," *Washington Post*, July 4, 2022.

14 *But scientific evidence shows that* Márta Gácsi et al., "Attachment Behavior of Adult Dogs (Canis Familiaris) Living at Rescue Centers: Forming New Bonds," *Journal of Comparative Psychology* 115, no. 4 (2001): 423.

23 *Research has found that when* David S. Tuber et al., "Dogs in Animal Shelters: Problems, Suggestions, and Needed Expertise," *Psychological Science* 10, no. 5 (1999): 379–386.

24 *However, a study published in* James G. Heys and Daniel A. Dombeck, "Evidence for a Subcircuit in Medial Entorhinal Cortex Representing Elapsed Time During Immobility," *Nature Neuroscience* 21, no. 11 (2018): 1574–1582.

25 *Other research with dogs has* Krista Macpherson and William A. Roberts,

"On the Clock: Interval Timing and Overshadowing in Domestic Dogs (Canis Familiaris)," *Journal of Comparative Psychology* 131, no. 4 (2017): 348.

26 *Whenever you can, take a* Helen Harvie et al., "Does Stress Run Through the Leash? An Examination of Stress Transmission Between Owners and Dogs During a Walk," *Animal Cognition* 24, no. 2 (2021): 239–250.

27 *New research has found, for* Ana Catarina Vieira de Castro et al., "Does Training Method Matter? Evidence for the Negative Impact of Aversive-Based Methods on Companion Dog Welfare," *PLOS One* 15, no. 12 (2020): e0225023.

28 *Dogs communicate their wants, needs* Juliane Kaminski et al., "Human Attention Affects Facial Expressions in Domestic Dogs," *Scientific Reports* 7, no. 1 (2017): 1–7.

30 *When dogs saw their owners* A. Quaranta, M. Siniscalchi, and G. Vallortigara, "Asymmetric Tail-Wagging Responses by Dogs to Different Emotive Stimuli," *Current Biology* 17, no. 6 (2007): R199–R201.

30 *In another study, Elena Gobbo* Elena Gobbo and Manja Zupan Šemrov, "Neuroendocrine and Cardiovascular Activation During Aggressive Reactivity in Dogs," *Frontiers in Veterinary Science* (2021): 902.

32 *An aggressive or angry dog's ears forward and erect* "Reading Canine Body Postures," accessed August 12, 2022, https://jointanimalservices.org/wp -content/uploads/2015/07/Body-Language-Packet.pdf.

32 *An alert dog has a tail* Stanley Coren, "How to Read Your Dog's Body Language," *Modern Dog Magazine*, accessed August 12, 2022, https://moderndogmagazine .com/articles/how-read-your-dogs-body-language/415.

Chapter Two

33 *A fearful or nervous dog* San Francisco SPCA, "Dog: Body Language," accessed August 12, 2022, https://www.sfspca.org/sites/default/files/dog_body -language.pdf.

38 *For example, a study by* Wendie Bodsworth and G. J. Coleman, "Child– Companion Animal Attachment Bonds in Single and Two-Parent Families," *Anthrozoös* 14, no. 4 (2001): 216–223.

38 *In research led by Sabrina* Sabrina Karl et al., "Exploring the Dog–Human Relationship by Combining fMRI, Eye-Tracking and Behavioural Measures," *Scientific Reports* 10, no. 1 (2020): 1–15.

39 *In a study led by* Chiari Mariti et al., "Owners as a Secure Base for Their Dogs," *Behaviour* 150, no. 11 (2013): 1275–1294.

39 *In a tangentially related study* Lisa Horn et al., "The Importance of the Secure Base Effect for Domestic Dogs—Evidence from a Manipulative Problem-Solving Task," *PLOS One* 8, no. 5 (2013): e65296.

39 *In a study designed to* John Archer and Jane L. Ireland, "The Development and Factor Structure of a Questionnaire Measure of the Strength of Attachment to Pet Dogs," *Anthrozoös* 24, no. 3 (2011): 249–261.

40 *Heartwarmingly, researchers have found that* Miho Nagasawa et al., "Oxytocin-

Gaze Positive Loop and the Coevolution of Human-Dog Bonds," *Science* 348, no. 6232 (2015): 333–336.

40 *In the study, the pairs* Gregory S. Berns, Andrew M. Brooks, and Mark Spivak, "Scent of the Familiar: An fMRI Study of Canine Brain Responses to Familiar and Unfamiliar Human and Dog Odors," *Behavioural Processes* 110 (2015): 37–46.

41 *After a positive interaction, you* Johannes S. J. Odendaal and Roy Alec Meintjes, "Neurophysiological Correlates of Affiliative Behaviour Between Humans and Dogs," *Veterinary Journal* 165, no. 3 (2003): 296–301.

41 *This is just one factor* Kyle Kittleson, "The 5 Love Languages (for Your Dog)," KyleKittleson.com, November 8, 2017, accessed August 12, 2022, https:// kylekittleson.com/5-love-languages-dog/.

42 *A 2019 study by Ann-Sofie* Ann-Sofie Sundman et al., "Long-Term Stress Levels Are Synchronized in Dogs and Their Owners," *Scientific Reports* 9, no. 1 (2019): 1–7.

42 *Between humans, the transmission of* Carolina Herrando and Efthymios Constantinides, "Emotional Contagion: A Brief Overview and Future Directions," *Frontiers in Psychology* 12 (2021): 712606.

42 *Incremental muscle movements that are* James M. Kilner and Roger N. Lemon, "What We Know Currently About Mirror Neurons," *Current Biology* 23, no. 23 (2013): R1057–R1062.

42 *This "rapid mimicry"* Elisabetta Palagi, Velia Nicotra, and Giada Cordoni, "Rapid Mimicry and Emotional Contagion in Domestic Dogs," *Royal Society Open Science* 2, no. 12 (2015): 150505; see also Elisabetta Palagi and Giada Cordoni, "Intraspecific Motor and Emotional Alignment in Dogs and Wolves: The Basic Building Blocks of Dog-Human Affective Connectedness," *Animals* 10, no. 2 (2020): 241.

42 *A 2017 study by Elisabetta* Elisabetta Palagi, Velia Nicotra, and Giada Cordoni, "Rapid Mimicry and Emotional Contagion in Domestic Dogs," *Royal Society Open Science* 2, no. 12 (2015): 150505.

43 *Numerous studies have shown that* Karine Silva, Joana Bessa, and Liliana De Sousa, "Auditory Contagious Yawning in Domestic Dogs (Canis Familiaris): First Evidence for Social Modulation," *Animal Cognition* 15, no. 4 (2012): 721–724.

43 *In one particular study, twenty-nine* Ramiro M.Joly-Mascheroni, Atsushi Senju, and Alex J. Shepherd. "Dogs catch human yawns." *Biology Letters* 4, no. 5 (2008): 446-448.

43 *develop lower heart rate variability* Julia E. Meyers-Manor and Marijo L. Botten, "A Shoulder to Cry On: Heart Rate Variability and Empathetic Behavioral Responses to Crying and Laughing in Dogs," *Canadian Journal of Experimental Psychology/Revue canadienne de psychologie expérimentale* 74, no. 3 (2020): 235.

43 *increased cortisol levels* Min Hooi Yong and Ted Ruffman, "Emotional Contagion: Dogs and Humans Show a Similar Physiological Response to Human Infant Crying," *Behavioural Processes* 108 (2014): 155–165.

43 *Dogs also have "affective empathy"* Monica Mazza et al., "Affective and Cognitive Empathy in Adolescents with Autism Spectrum Disorder," *Frontiers in Human Neuroscience* 8 (2014): 791.

43 *A 2018 study by Marcello* Marcello Siniscalchi, Serenella d'Ingeo, and Angelo Quaranta, "Orienting Asymmetries and Physiological Reactivity in Dogs' Response to Human Emotional Faces," *Learning & Behavior* 46, no. 4 (2018): 574–585.

44 *an ability to distinguish between happy faces* Sanni Somppi et al., "Nasal Oxytocin Treatment Biases Dogs' Visual Attention and Emotional Response Toward Positive Human Facial Expressions," *Frontiers in Psychology* 8 (2017): 1854.

44 *When it comes to sounds* Annika Huber et al., "Investigating Emotional Contagion in Dogs (Canis Familiaris) to Emotional Sounds of Humans and Conspecifics," *Animal Cognition* 20, no. 4 (2017): 703–715.

44 *It may be, as some* Miho Nagasawa, Kazutaka Mogi, and Takefumi Kikusui, "Attachment Between Humans and Dogs," *Japanese Psychological Research* 51, no. 3 (2009): 209–221.

45 *A 2019 study found that* Maki Katayama et al., "Emotional Contagion from Humans to Dogs Is Facilitated by Duration of Ownership," *Frontiers in Psychology* (2019): 1678.

45 *What's more, "for dogs, humans"* Elyssa Payne, Pauleen C. Bennett, and Paul D. McGreevy, "Current Perspectives on Attachment and Bonding in the Dog–Human Dyad," *Psychology Research and Behavior Management* 8 (2015): 71.

45 *On the human side of* Michael J. Dotson and Eva M. Hyatt, "Understanding Dog–Human Companionship," *Journal of Business Research* 61, no. 5 (2008): 457–466.

47 *Interestingly, research has found that* Iris Smolkovic, Mateja Fajfar, and Vesna Mlinaric, "Attachment to Pets and Interpersonal Relationships: Can a Four-Legged Friend Replace a Two-Legged One?," *Journal of European Psychology Students* 3, no. 1 (2012).

47 *One way sociologists describe the* Mark S. Granovetter, "The Strength of Weak Ties," *American Journal of Sociology* 78, no. 6 (1973): 1360–1380.

48 *Ardra Cole, PhD, a professor* Ardra Cole, "Grow Old Along with Me: The Meaning of Dogs in Seniors' Lives," *International Journal of Community Well-Being* 2, no. 3 (2019): 235–252.

49 *It offers intrinsic rewards such* Iris Smolkovic, Mateja Fajfar, and Vesna Mlinaric, "Attachment to Pets and Interpersonal Relationships: Can a Four-Legged Friend Replace a Two-Legged One?," *Journal of European Psychology Students* 3, no. 1 (2012).

49 *In addition to these constructs . . .* Michael J. Dotson and Eva M. Hyatt, "Understanding Dog–Human Companionship," *Journal of Business Research* 61, no. 5 (2008): 457–466.

49 *In an eye-opening study, Michael* Ibid.

Chapter Three

54 *These days, most of us* Katie Burns, "Pet Ownership Stable, Veterinary Care Variable," American Veterinary Medical Association, December 31, 2018, accessed August 12, 2022, https://www.avma.org/javma-news/2019-01-15/pet -ownership-stable-veterinary-care-variable.

54 *In some families, people even* "National Companion Animal Owner Survey Finds People Prefer Animal Companionship Over Human," *Faunalytics*, April 12, 2010, accessed August 12, 2022, https://faunalytics.org/national-pet-owner -survey-finds-people-prefer-pet-companionship-over-human/#.

55 *Without any conscious effort on* Froma Walsh, "Human-Animal Bonds II: The Role of Pets in Family Systems and Family Therapy," *Family Process* 48, no. 4 (2009): 481–499.

55 *Kids often describe their dogs* Lawrence A. Kurdek, "Young Adults' Attachment to Pet Dogs: Findings from Open-Ended Methods," *Anthrozoös* 22, no. 4 (2009): 359–369.

55 *They also teach children responsibility* Cassandra Leow, "It's Not Just a Dog: The Role of Companion Animals in the Family's Emotional System," master's thesis, University of Nebraska, 2018.

56 *In an in-depth study into* Krista Scott Geller, "The Power of Pets: How Animals Affect Family Relationships," PhD dissertation, Virginia Tech, 2002.

56 *A study by Ann Ottney* Ann Ottney Cain, "A Study of Pets in the Family System," *New Perspectives on Our Lives with Companion Animals* (1983): 72–81.

56 *In a study of ninety-nine tweens* Kathryn A. Kerns et al., "Preadolescents' Relationships with Pet Dogs: Relationship Continuity and Associations with Adjustment," *Applied Developmental Science* 21, no. 1 (2017): 67–80.

57 *Sam Carr, Ph.D., and Ben* Sam Carr and Ben Rockett, "Fostering Secure Attachment: Experiences of Animal Companions in the Foster Home," *Attachment & Human Development* 19, no. 3 (2017): 259–277.

58 *In a fascinating study, Deborah* Deborah Tannen, "Talking the Dog: Framing Pets as Interactional Resources in Family Discourse," *Research on Language and Social Interaction* 37, no. 4 (2004): 399–420.

58 *Rather than venting his frustration* Alex Benjamin and Katie Slocombe, "'Who's a Good Boy?!' Dogs Prefer Naturalistic Dog-Directed Speech," *Animal Cognition* 21, no. 3 (2018): 353–364.

59 *Interestingly, when people talk directly* Ibid.

59 *A preliminary study of military veterans* Christine E. McCall et al., "'A Part of Our Family'? Effects of Psychiatric Service Dogs on Quality of Life and Relationship Functioning in Military-Connected Couples," *Military Behavioral Health* 8, no. 4 (2020): 410–423.

60 *In a study of seventy* Hannah Wright et al., "Pet Dogs Improve Family Functioning and Reduce Anxiety in Children with Autism Spectrum Disorder," *Anthrozoös* 28, no. 4 (2015): 611–624.

60   *A separate study by Hannah* H. F. Wright et al., "Acquiring a Pet Dog Significantly Reduces Stress of Primary Carers for Children with Autism Spectrum Disorder: A Prospective Case Control Study," *Journal of Autism and Developmental Disorders* 45, no. 8 (2015): 2531–2540.

60   *In a study of 126* Jessica Bibbo, Kerri E. Rodriguez, and Marguerite E. O'Haire, "Impact of Service Dogs on Family Members' Psychosocial Functioning," *American Journal of Occupational Therapy* 73, no. 3 (2019): 7303205120p1–7303205120p11.

61   *Indeed, research by Carri Westgarth* Carri Westgarth et al., "Functional and Recreational Dog Walking Practices in the UK," *Health Promotion International* 36, no. 1 (2021): 109–119.

61   *A pilot study by Katie* Katie Potter et al., "Examining How Dog 'Acquisition' Affects Physical Activity and Psychosocial Well-Being: Findings from the Buddystudy Pilot Trial," *Animals* 9, no. 9 (2019): 666.

62   *Research also has found that* Cassandra Leow, "It's Not Just a Dog: The Role of Companion Animals in the Family's Emotional System," master's thesis, University of Nebraska, 2018.

63   *A study by Jennifer Applebaum* Jennifer W. Applebaum and Barbara A. Zsembik, "Pet Attachment in the Context of Family Conflict," *Anthrozoös* 33, no. 3 (2020): 361–370.

Chapter Four

65   *It's been dubbed "the pet factor" by Lisa Wood* Lisa Wood et al., "The Pet Factor: Companion Animals as a Conduit for Getting to Know People, Friendship Formation and Social Support," *PLOS One* 10, no. 4 (2015): e0122085.

65   *Interestingly, having a dog has* Lisa Wood et al., "Social Capital and Pet Ownership: A Tale of Four Cities," *SSM-Population Health* 3 (2017): 442.

66   *For starters, dogs encourage people* Emma R. Power, "Dogs and Practices of Community and Neighboring," *Anthrozoös* 26, no. 4 (2013): 579–591.

66   *For example, a pair of* June McNicholas and Glyn M. Collis, "Dogs as Catalysts for Social Interactions: Robustness of the Effect," *British Journal of Psychology* 91, no. 1 (2000): 61–70.

66   *Kelly Ann Rossbach and John* Kelly Ann Rossbach and John P. Wilson, "Does a Dog's Presence Make a Person Appear More Likable? Two Studies," *Anthrozoös* 5, no. 1 (1992): 40–51.

67   *In a study by Deborah* Deborah L. Wells, "The Facilitation of Social Interactions by Domestic Dogs," *Anthrozoös* 17, no. 4 (2004): 340–352.

67   *The dog-as-social-catalyst effect is so* June McNicholas and Glyn M. Collis, "Dogs as Catalysts for Social Interactions: Robustness of the Effect," *British Journal of Psychology* 91, no. 1 (2000): 61–70.

67   *Research led by Sigal Tifferet, PhD* Sigal Tifferet et al., "Dog Ownership Increases Attractiveness and Attenuates Perceptions of Short-Term Mating Strategy in Cad-like Men," *Journal of Evolutionary Psychology* 11, no. 3 (2013): 121–129.

68 *Sociologist Erving Goffman, PhD, coined* Erving Goffman, *Relations in Public* (Transaction Publishers, 1963).

69 *In a series of experiments* Akiko Takaoka et al., "Do Dogs Follow Behavioral Cues from an Unreliable Human?," *Animal Cognition* 18, no. 2 (2015): 475–483.

70 *In one research project, led* John Rogers, Lynette A. Hart, and Ronald P. Boltz, "The Role of Pet Dogs in Casual Conversations of Elderly Adults," *Journal of Social Psychology* 133, no. 3 (1993): 265–277.

71 *Besides getting us out of* Emma R. Power, "Dogs and Practices of Community and Neighboring," *Anthrozoös* 26, no. 4 (2013): 579–591.

72 *Interestingly, research led by Gillian* Gillian M. Sandstrom and Elizabeth W. Dunn, "Social Interactions and Well-Being: The Surprising Power of Weak Ties," *Personality and Social Psychology Bulletin* 40, no. 7 (2014): 910–922.

72 *Her experience is hardly unusual* Max Bulsara et al., "More Than a Furry Companion: The Ripple Effect of Companion Animals on Neighborhood Interactions and Sense of Community," *Society & Animals* 15, no. 1 (2007): 43–56.

73 *Research by Nicolo Pinchak and* Nicolo P. Pinchak et al., "Paws on the Street: Neighborhood-Level Concentration of Households with Dogs and Urban Crime," *Social Forces* (2022).

73 *In a series of studies* Stephen M. Colarelli et al., "A Companion Dog Increases Prosocial Behavior in Work Groups," *Anthrozoös* 30, no. 1 (2017): 77–89.

74 *In another study, led by* Randolph T. Barker et al., "Preliminary Investigation of Employee's Dog Presence on Stress and Organizational Perceptions," *International Journal of Workplace Health Management* 5, no. 1 (2012): 15–30.

74 *When speaking to the American* Jen Reeder, "The Many Benefits of Pets in the Workplace," *Pets Matter*, May 10, 2016, accessed August 12, 2022, https://web .archive.org/web/20160720174952/http:/www.aaha.org/blog/petsmatter/post /2016/05/10/317030/The-many-benefits-of-pets-in-the-workplace.aspx.

74 *Fortunately, pet-friendly policies are becoming* Elisa Wagner and Miguel Pina e Cunha, "Dogs at the Workplace: A Multiple Case Study," *Animals* 11, no. 1 (2021): 89.

74 *A study led by Lynette A.* Lynette A. Hart, Benjamin L. Hart, and Bonita L. Bergin, "Socializing Effects of Service Dogs for People with Disabilities," *Anthrozoös* 1, no. 1 (1987): 41–44.

74 *Similarly, research has found that* Melanie C. Steffens and Reinhold Bergler, "Blind People and Their Dogs: An Empirical Study on Changes in Everyday Life, in Self-Experience, and in Communication," *Companion Animals in Human Health* (1998).

74 *deaf people with hearing dogs* Lynette A. Hart, R. Lee Zasloff, and Anne Marie Benfatto, "The Socializing Role of Hearing Dogs," *Applied Animal Behaviour Science* 47, no. 1–2 (1996): 7–15.

75 *Our canine companions help us* Kirk Warren Brown and Richard M. Ryan, "The Benefits of Being Present: Mindfulness and Its Role in Psychological Well-Being," *Journal of Personality and Social Psychology* 84, no. 4 (2003): 822.

Chapter Five

79 *Only 53 percent of adults* Centers for Disease Control and Prevention, *Exercise or Physical Activity*, June 11, 2021, accessed August 12, 2022, https://www.cdc.gov/nchs/fastats/exercise.htm.

80 *Dog ownership has been referred* Carri Westgarth et al., "Dog Owners Are More Likely to Meet Physical Activity Guidelines Than People Without a Dog: An Investigation of the Association Between Dog Ownership and Physical Activity Levels in a UK Community," *Scientific Reports* 9, no. 1 (2019): 1–10.

80 *According to a 2019 study* Ibid.

80 *The simple act of walking* "The Benefits of Walking," *NIH News in Health*, March, 2016, accessed August 12, 2022, https://newsinhealth.nih.gov/2016/03/benefits-walking; *Walking: Trim Your Waistline, Improve Your Health*, Mayo Clinic, May 19, 2021, accessed August 12, 2022, https://www.mayoclinic.org/healthy-lifestyle/fitness/in-depth/walking/art-20046261.

80 *In a survey of more* Hayley Cutt et al., "Understanding Dog Owners' Increased Levels of Physical Activity: Results from RESIDE," *American Journal of Public Health* 98, no. 1 (2008): 66–69.

81 *Research by Yue Liao, PhD* Yue Liao, Olga Solomon, and Genevieve F. Dunton, "Does the Company of a Dog Influence Affective Response to Exercise? Using Ecological Momentary Assessment to Study Dog-Accompanied Physical Activity," *American Journal of Health Promotion* 31, no. 5 (2017): 388–390.

81 *In a 2017 study by* Carri Westgarth et al., "I Walk My Dog Because It Makes Me Happy: A Qualitative Study to Understand Why Dogs Motivate Walking and Improved Health," *International Journal of Environmental Research and Public Health* 14, no. 8 (2017): 936.

81 *There was an element of* Pierre-Yves Oudeyer and Frederic Kaplan, "What Is Intrinsic Motivation? A Typology of Computational Approaches," *Frontiers in Neurorobotics* (2009): 6; Stefano I. Di Domenico and Richard M. Ryan, "The Emerging Neuroscience of Intrinsic Motivation: A New Frontier in Self-Determination Research," *Frontiers in Human Neuroscience* 11 (2017): 145; and Marie Flannery, "Self-Determination Theory: Intrinsic Motivation and Behavioral Change," *Oncology Nursing Forum* 44, no. 2 (2017).

82 *Research has found that kids* Hayley Christian et al., "Understanding the Relationship Between Dog Ownership and Children's Physical Activity and Sedentary Behaviour," *Pediatric Obesity* 8, no. 5 (2013): 392–403.

82 *And a study by Philippa* Philippa Margaret Dall et al., "The Influence of Dog Ownership on Objective Measures of Free-Living Physical Activity and Sedentary Behaviour in Community-Dwelling Older Adults: A Longitudinal Case-Controlled Study," *BMC Public Health* 17, no. 1 (2017): 1–9.

82 *Interestingly, research by Wilma L.* Wilma L. Zijlema et al., "Dog Ownership, the Natural Outdoor Environment and Health: A Cross-Sectional Study," *BMJ Open* 9, no. 5 (2019): e023000.

83 *calming us down* Margarita Triguero-Mas et al., "Natural Outdoor Environments and Mental Health: Stress as a Possible Mechanism," *Environmental Research* 159 (2017): 629–638; Margarita Triguero-Mas et al., "Natural Outdoor Environments and Mental and Physical Health: Relationships and Mechanisms," *Environment International* 77 (2015): 35–41; Emi Morita, "Psychological Effects of Forest Environments on Healthy Adults: Shinrin-Yoku (Forest-Air Bathing, Walking) as a Possible Method of Stress Reduction," *Public Health* 121, no. 1 (2007): 54–63.

83 *improving our memory and cognitive function* Kathryn E. Schertz and Marc G. Berman, "Understanding Nature and Its Cognitive Benefits," *Current Directions in Psychological Science* 28, no. 5 (2019): 496–502.

83 *reducing our blood pressure* Bum Jin Park et al., "The Physiological Effects of Shinrin-Yoku (Taking in the Forest Atmosphere or Forest Bathing): Evidence from Field Experiments in 24 Forests Across Japan," *Environmental Health and Preventive Medicine* 15, no. 1 (2010): 18–26.

83 *improving our immune function* Qing Li et al., "Effect of Phytoncide from Trees on Human Natural Killer Cell Function," *International Journal of Immunopathology and Pharmacology* 22, no. 4 (2009): 951–959.

83 *During the pandemic, many people* "Nearly 40% of Dogs May Have Gained Weight During the COVID-19 Pandemic, Survey Shows," *Inside Edition*, June 2, 2021; and Maria Morava and Scottie Andrew, "It's Not Just You. Your Pets Are Also Putting on the Pounds During the Pandemic," CNN, March 8, 2021.

83 *In an intriguing pair of* J. Rebecca Niese et al., "Evaluating the Potential Benefit of a Combined Weight Loss Program in Dogs and Their Owners," *Frontiers in Veterinary Science* (2021): 378.

84 *Similarly, a weight-loss program at* Robert F. Kushner et al., "The PPET Study: People and Pets Exercising Together," *Obesity* 14, no. 10 (2006): 1762–1770.

86 *A study by Kate Campbell* Kate Campbell et al., "How Does Dog-Walking Influence Perceptions of Health and Wellbeing in Healthy Adults? A Qualitative Dog-Walk-Along Study," *Anthrozoös* 29, no. 2 (2016): 181–192.

87 *In a study by Angela* Angela L. Curl, Jessica Bibbo, and Rebecca A. Johnson, "Dog Walking, the Human-Animal Bond and Older Adults' Physical Health," *Gerontologist* 57, no. 5 (2017): 930–939.

87 *In a study by Joan* Joan Wharf Higgins et al., "Walking Sole Mates: Dogs Motivating, Enabling and Supporting Guardians' Physical Activity," *Anthrozoös* 26, no. 2 (2013): 237–252.

89 *In a small study of* Catherine M. Smith, Gareth J. Treharne, and Steve Tumilty, "All Those Ingredients of the Walk: The Therapeutic Spaces of Dog-Walking for People with Long-Term Health Conditions," *Anthrozoös* 30, no. 2 (2017): 327–340.

Chapter Six

91 *Research has also found that* Gill Mein and Robert Grant, "A Cross-Sectional Exploratory Analysis Between Pet Ownership, Sleep, Exercise, Health and

Neighbourhood Perceptions: The Whitehall II Cohort Study," *BMC Geriatrics* 18, no. 1 (2018): 1–9.

92 **Bruce Headey, PhD, conducted a** Bruce Headey, "Health Benefits and Health Cost Savings Due to Pets: Preliminary Estimates from an Australian National Survey," *Social Indicators Research* 47, no. 2 (1999): 233–243.

92 **James Serpell, PhD, conducted a** James Serpell, "Beneficial Effects of Pet Ownership on Some Aspects of Human Health and Behaviour," *Journal of the Royal Society of Medicine* 84, no. 12 (1991): 717720.

92 **In China, a study by** Bruce Headey, Fu Na, and Richard Zheng, "Pet Dogs Benefit Owners' Health: A 'Natural Experiment' in China," *Social Indicators Research* 87, no. 3 (2008): 481–493.

93 **American thriller writer Dean Koonz** Lauren Garcia, *The 101 Best Dog Quotes* (June 13, 2022), accessed August 12, 2022, https://www.care.com/c/the -101-best-dog-quotes/.

93 **These microbes are a** Ron Sender, Shai Fuchs, and Ron Milo, "Revised Estimates for the Number of Human and Bacteria Cells in the Body," *PLOS Biology* 14, no. 8 (2016): e1002533.

93 **This may sound problematic but** Marilyn Hair and Jon Sharpe, *Fast Facts About the Human Microbiome* (University of Washington Center for Ecogenetics & Environmental Health, accesed December 6, 2015, http://depts .washington.edu/ceeh/downloads/FF_Microbiome. pdf; and M. Hasan Mohajeri et al., "The Role of the Microbiome for Human Health: From Basic Science to Clinical Applications," *European Journal of Nutrition* 57, no. 1 (2018): 1–14.

93 **Research by Rob** Se Jin Song et al., "Cohabiting Family Members Share Microbiota with One Another and with Their Dogs," *elife* 2 (2013): e00458.

94 **A study by Albert Barberán** Albert Barberán et al., "The Ecology of Microscopic Life in Household Dust," *Proceedings of the Royal Society B: Biological Sciences* 282, no. 1814 (2015): 20151139.

94 **In a study by Alexandra** Alexandra R. Sitarik et al., "Dog Introduction Alters the Home Dust Microbiota," *Indoor Air* 28, no. 4 (2018): 539–547.

94 **allergies, eczema, or asthma** Kei E. Fujimura et al., "Man's Best Friend? The Effect of Pet Ownership on House Dust Microbial Communities," *Journal of Allergy and Clinical Immunology* 126, no. 2 (2010): 410–412; Claudio Pelucchi et al., "Pet Exposure and Risk of Atopic Dermatitis at the Pediatric Age: A Meta-Analysis of Birth Cohort Studies," *Journal of Allergy and Clinical Immunology* 132, no. 3 (2013): 616–622; J. D. Bufford et al., "Effects of Dog Ownership in Early Childhood on Immune Development and Atopic Diseases," *Clinical & Experimental Allergy* 38, no. 10 (2008): 1635–1643.

95 **Research by Bill Hesselmar, MD** Bill Hesselmar et al., "Pet-Keeping in Early Life Reduces the Risk of Allergy in a Dose-Dependent Fashion," *PLOS One* 13, no. 12 (2018): e0208472.

95 **This is an example of** Dennis R. Ownby et al., "Exposure to Dogs and Cats in

the First Year of Life and Risk of Allergic Sensitization at 6 to 7 Years of Age," *JAMA* 288, no. 8 (2002): 963–972.

96 **Research led by Mary Janevic** Mary R. Janevic et al., "The Role of Pets in Supporting Cognitive-Behavioral Chronic Pain Self-Management: Perspectives of Older Adults," *Journal of Applied Gerontology* 39, no. 10 (2020): 1088–1096.

96 **As Janevic noted in an** University of Michigan School of Public Health, *Q&A: How Pets Can Help Older Adults Manage Chronic Pain* (July 1, 2019), accessed August 12, 2022, https://sph.umich.edu/news/2019posts/how-pets-can-help-older-adults-manage-chronic-pain.html.

96 **These findings were echoed in** April DuCasse et al., "The Effects of Pets on Chronic Pain," *AJOT: American Journal of Occupational Therapy* 74, no. S1 (2020).

96 **In another study, led by** Eloise CJ Carr, et al., "Exploring the Meaning and Experience of Chronic Pain with People Who Live with a Dog: A Qualitative Study," *Anthrozoös* 31, no. 5 (2018): 551–565.

97 **When it comes to the** Chayakrit Krittanawong et al., "Pet Ownership and Cardiovascular Health in the US General Population," *American Journal of Cardiology* 125, no. 8 (2020): 1158–1161.

97 **These effects may partly explain** Caroline K. Kramer, Sadia Mehmood, and Renée S. Suen, "Dog Ownership and Survival: A Systematic Review and Meta-Analysis," *Circulation: Cardiovascular Quality and Outcomes* 12, no. 10 (2019): e005554.

97 **In a study by Erika** Erika Friedmann et al., "Social Interaction and Blood Pressure: Influence of Animal Companions," *Journal of Nervous and Mental Disease* 171, no. 8: (1983): 461–465.

97 **Similarly, in a study by** Julia K. Vormbrock and John M. Grossberg, "Cardiovascular Effects of Human-Pet Dog Interactions," *Journal of Behavioral Medicine* 11, no. 5 (1988): 509–517.

98 **In a study by Karen** Karen Allen, Jim Blascovich, and Wendy B. Mendes, "Cardiovascular Reactivity and the Presence of Pets, Friends, and Spouses: The Truth About Cats and Dogs," *Psychosomatic Medicine* 64, no. 5 (2002): 727–739.

98 **A case in point** Karen Allen, Barbara E. Shykoff, and Joseph L. Izzo Jr., "Pet Ownership, but Not ACE Inhibitor Therapy, Blunts Home Blood Pressure Responses to Mental Stress," *Hypertension* 38, no. 4 (2001): 815–820.

99 **Among people who have heart** Mary M. Herrald, Joe Tomaka, and Amanda Y. Medina, "Pet Ownership Predicts Adherence to Cardiovascular Rehabilitation 1," *Journal of Applied Social Psychology* 32, no. 6 (2002): 1107–1123.

99 **What's more, research by Mwenya** Mwenya Mubanga et al., "Dog Ownership and Survival After a Major Cardiovascular Event: A Register-Based Prospective Study," *Circulation: Cardiovascular Quality and Outcomes* 12, no. 10 (2019): e005342.

99 **Many other studies support these** Caroline K. Kramer, Sadia Mehmood,

and Renée S. Suen, "Dog Ownership and Survival: A Systematic Review and Meta-Analysis," *Circulation: Cardiovascular Quality and Outcomes* 12, no. 10 (2019): e005554.

99 **One of the early explorations** Erika Friedmann and Sue A. Thomas, "Pet Ownership, Social Support, and One-Year Survival After Acute Myocardial Infarction in the Cardiac Arrhythmia Suppression Trial (CAST)," *American Journal of Cardiology* 76, no. 17 (1995): 1213–1217.

100 **Having social support doesn't just** R. Gurung, B. Sarason and I. Sarason, "Close Personal Relationships and Health Outcomes: A Key to the Role of Social Support," *Handbook of Personal Relationships: Theory, Research and Interventions* (1997): 547–573.

100 **In fact, a meta-analysis by** Hsiu-Hung Wang, Su-Zu Wu, and Yea-Ying Liu, "Association Between Social Support and Health Outcomes: A Meta-Analysis," *Kaohsiung Journal of Medical Sciences* 19, no. 7 (2003): 345–350.

101 **As Erika Friedmann and colleagues** Erika Friedmann et al., "Animal Companions and One-Year Survival of Patients After Discharge from a Coronary Care Unit," *Public Health Reports* 95, no. 4 (1980): 307.

Chapter Seven

105 **A dog's sense of smell** Ellen Furlong, "Your Dog's Nose Knows No Bounds— And Neither Does Its Love for You," *The Conversation*, October 26, 2020, accessed August 12, 2022, https://theconversation.com/your-dogs-nose-knows -no-bounds-and-neither-does-its-love-for-you-148484.

105 **canines have 200 million** Alexandra Horowitz, *Being a Dog: Following the Dog into a World of Smell* (Simon & Schuster, 2016), p. 48.

105 **roughly forty times larger** Ryan Llera and Lynn Buzhardt, "How Dogs Use Smell to Perceive the World," *VCA Animal Hospitals*, accessed August 12, 2022, https:// vcahospitals.com/know-your-pet/how-dogs-use-smell-to-perceive-the-world.

105 **That's why dogs can tell** Alexandra Horowitz, *Being a Dog: Following the Dog into a World of Smell* (Simon & Schuster, 2016).

106 **Their bodies have evolved to** Laura Mueller, "9 Dogs with Long Ears," The Spruce Pets, March 12, 2022, accessed August 12, 2022, https://www.thesprucepets.com /dogs-with-long-ears-5095574.

106 **Take bloodhounds, for example. When** Alexandra Horowitz, *Being a Dog: Following the Dog into a World of Smell* (Simon & Schuster, 2016).

106 **When their noses are pointing** Amanda Mull, "How Your Dog Knows When You're Sick," *Atlantic*, March 12, 2019.

107 **"Dogs are preternaturally sensitive to"** Amanda Mull, "How Your Dog Knows When You're Sick," *Atlantic*, March 12, 2019.

107 **In the fall of 2020** Holly Else, "Can Dogs Smell COVID? Here's What the Science Says," *Nature* 587, no. 7835 (2020): 530–531; and Khan Sharun et al., "Biodetection Dogs for COVID-19: An Alternative Diagnostic Screening Strategy," *Public Health* 197 (2021): e10.

107 *A recent study by Edward* E. H. Maa, J. Arnold, and C. K. Bush, "Epilepsy and the Smell of Fear," *Epilepsy & Behavior* 121 (2021): 108078.

107 *Similarly, dogs can be trained* Sankalpa Neupane et al., "Exhaled Breath Isoprene Rises During Hypoglycemia in Type 1 Diabetes," *Diabetes Care* 39, no. 7 (2016): e97-e98.

107 *Pet dogs can sometimes sense* A. E. Stocks, "Can Dogs Help Patients with Hypoglycaemia?," in *Diabetologia* 45 (2002): A79; and K. Lim et al., "Type 1 Diabetics and Their Pets," *Diabetic Medicine* 9, no. 2 (1992): S3–S4.

107 *Researchers suspect that changes in* Deborah L. Wells, "Dogs as a Diagnostic Tool for Ill Health in Humans," *Alternative Therapies in Health & Medicine* 18, no. 2 (2012).

108 *The theory is that the* Mika Shirasu and Kazushige Touhara, "The Scent of Disease: Volatile Organic Compounds of the Human Body Related to Disease and Disorder," *Journal of Biochemistry* 150, no. 3 (2011): 257–266.

108 *Chemical analyses have found 1,840* Mika Shirasu and Kazushige Touhara, "The Scent of Disease: Volatile Organic Compounds of the Human Body Related to Disease and Disorder," *Journal of Biochemistry* 150, no. 3 (2011): 257–266.

108 *Untrained dogs may notice that* Federica Pirrone and Mariangela Albertini, "Olfactory Detection of Cancer by Trained Sniffer Dogs: A Systematic Review of the Literature," *Journal of Veterinary Behavior* 19 (2017): 105–117.

108 *Scientists first hypothesized that dogs* Hywel Williams and Andres Pembroke, "Sniffer Dogs in the Melanoma Clinic?," *Lancet* 333, no. 8640 (1989): 734.

108 *Dogs that were trained to* Duane Pickel et al., "Evidence for Canine Olfactory Detection of Melanoma," *Applied Animal Behaviour Science* 89, no. 1–2 (2004): 107–116.

109 *In a study by Gianluigi* Gianluigi Taverna et al., "Olfactory System of Highly Trained Dogs Detects Prostate Cancer in Urine Samples," *Journal of Urology* 193, no. 4 (2015): 1382–1387.

109 *One dog found 100 percent* Ibid.

109 *In a study by Hideto* Hideto Sonoda et al., "Colorectal Cancer Screening with Odour Material by Canine Scent Detection," *Gut* 60, no. 6 (2011): 814–819.

109 *In their review of the* Federica Pirrone and Mariangela Albertini, "Olfactory Detection of Cancer by Trained Sniffer Dogs: A Systematic Review of the Literature," *Journal of Veterinary Behavior* 19 (2017): 105–117.

110 *During the prodromal phase, some* Epilepsy Foundation, *Seizure Phases*, accessed August 12, 2022, https://epilepsyfoundation.org.au/understanding -epilepsy/seizures/seizure-phases/.

111 *A study by Edward Maa* Edward Maa et al., "Canine Detection of Volatile Organic Compounds Unique to Human Epileptic Seizure," *Epilepsy & Behavior* 115 (2021): 107690.

111 *In a review of research* Amélie Catala et al., "Dog Alerting and/or Responding to Epileptic Seizures: A Scoping Review," *PLOS One* 13, no. 12 (2018): e0208280.

111 **Previously, research by Val Strong** Val Strong, Stephen W. Brown, and R. Walker, "Seizure-Alert Dogs—Fact or Fiction?," *Seizure* 8, no. 1 (1999): 62–65.

112 **"Patients reported benefits arising from"** Val Strong et al., "Effect of Trained Seizure Alert Dogs® on Frequency of Tonic–Clonic Seizures," *Seizure* 11, no. 6 (2002): 402–405.

Chapter Eight

115 **Anxiety disorders affect 48 million** "Mental Health By the Numbers," National Alliance on Mental Illness, 2020, accessed August 12, 2022, https://www.nami.org/mhstats.

115 **Meanwhile, it's estimated that nearly** "Data and Statistics on Children's Mental Health," Centers for Disease Control and Prevention, accessed September 13, 2019, https://www.cdc.gov/childrensmentalhealth/data.html.

115 **The presence of a dog** Sandra B. Barker et al., "Effects of Animal-Assisted Therapy on Patients' Anxiety, Fear, and Depression Before ECT," *Journal of ECT* 19, no. 1 (2003): 38–44.

116 **And therapy sessions in which** Inbar Nathans-Barel et al., "Animal-Assisted Therapy Ameliorates Anhedonia in Schizophrenia Patients," *Psychotherapy and Psychosomatics* 74, no. 1 (2005): 31–35.

116 **Being with a friendly or** "Study Finds Evidence Emotional Support Animals Benefit Those with Chronic Mental Illness," *AAAS EurekAlert*, May 20, 2021, accessed August 12, 2022, https://www.eurekalert.org/news-releases/846610.

117 **A study by Cheryl Krause-Parello** Cheryl A. Krause-Parello and Kristie A. Morales, "Military Veterans and Service Dogs: A Qualitative Inquiry Using Interpretive Phenomenological Analysis," *Anthrozoös* 31, no. 1 (2018): 61–75.

117 **Research by Atilla Andics, PhD** Attila Andics et al., "Voice-Sensitive Regions in the Dog and Human Brain Are Revealed by Comparative fMRI," *Current Biology* 24, no. 5 (2014): 574–578.

118 **PTSD, bipolar disorder, and major depression** Matthew Price et al., "An Examination of Social Support and PTSD Treatment Response During Prolonged Exposure," *Psychiatry* 81, no. 3 (2018): 258–270; Lars Johnson et al., "Social Support in Bipolar Disorder: Its Relevance to Remission and Relapse," *Bipolar Disorders* 5, no. 2 (2003): 129–137; Tracey D. Wade and Kenneth S. Kendler, "The Relationship Between Social Support and Major Depression: Cross-Sectional, Longitudinal, and Genetic Perspectives," *Journal of Nervous and Mental Disease* 188, no. 5 (2000): 251–258.

118 **In a fascinating study by** Helen Brooks et al., "Ontological Security and Connectivity Provided by Pets: A Study in the Self-Management of the Everyday Lives of People Diagnosed with a Long-Term Mental Health Condition," *BMC Psychiatry* 16, no. 1 (2016): 1–12.

119 **In a meta-analysis of twenty-one** Javier Virués-Ortega et al., "Effect of Animal-Assisted Therapy on the Psychological and Functional Status of Elderly

Populations and Patients with Psychiatric Disorders: A Meta-Analysis," *Health Psychology Review* 6, no. 2 (2012): 197–221.

120 ***Loneliness is often a factor*** Helen Brooks et al., "Ontological Security and Connectivity Provided by Pets: A Study in the Self-Management of the Everyday Lives of People Diagnosed with a Long-Term Mental Health Condition," *BMC Psychiatry* 16, no. 1 (2016): 1–12; Carol Opdebeeck et al., "What Are the Benefits of Pet Ownership and Care Among People with Mild-to-Moderate Dementia? Findings from the IDEAL Programme," *Journal of Applied Gerontology* 40, no. 11 (2021): 1559–1567; and Nancy E. Richeson, "Effects of Animal-Assisted Therapy on Agitated Behaviors and Social Interactions of Older Adults with Dementia," *American Journal of Alzheimer's Disease & Other Dementias* 18, no. 6 (2003): 353–358.

120 ***A study by Carol Opdebeeck*** Carol Opdebeeck et al., "What Are the Benefits of Pet Ownership and Care Among People with Mild-to-Moderate Dementia? Findings from the IDEAL Programme," Journal of Applied Gerontology 40, no. 11 (2021): 1559–1567.

120 ***In addition, research by Nancy*** Nancy E. Richeson, "Effects of Animal-Assisted Therapy on Agitated Behaviors and Social Interactions of Older Adults with Dementia," *American Journal of Alzheimer's Disease & Other Dementias* 18, no. 6 (2003): 353–358.

120 ***For example, a study by*** Jonathan D. Prince, Adashima Oyo, Olivia Mora, Katarzyna Wyka, and Andrew D. Schonebaum, "Loneliness Among Persons with Severe Mental Illness," *Journal of Nervous and Mental Disease* 206, no. 2 (2018): 136–141.

120 ***In fact, research by Janet*** Janet Hoy-Gerlach et al., "Exploring Benefits of Emotional Support Animals (ESAs): A Longitudinal Pilot Study with Adults with Serious Mental Illness (SMI)," *Human-Animal Interaction Bulletin*, 2022.

121 ***The sense of touch is*** Tiffany Field, "Touch for Socioemotional and Physical Well-Being: A Review," *Developmental Review* 30, no. 4 (2010): 367–383.

121 ***Touch deprivation, on the other*** Tiffany Field et al., "Touch Deprivation and Exercise During the COVID-19 Lockdown April 2020," *Medical Research Archives* 8, no. 8 (2020).

122 ***Research has found that in*** Uta Sailer and Siri Leknes, "Meaning Makes Touch Affective," *Current Opinion in Behavioral Sciences* 44 (2022): 101099.

122 ***In other words, petting or*** Janette Young et al., "Pets, Touch, and COVID-19: Health Benefits from Non-human Touch Through Times of Stress," *Journal of Behavioral Economics for Policy* 4 (2020): 25–33.

122 ***Green Chimneys is a residential*** Gerald P. Mallon, "Some of Our Best Therapists Are Dogs," *Child and Youth Care Forum* 23, no. 2 (1994): 89–101.

123 ***Not surprisingly, the study by*** Cheryl A. Krause-Parello and Kristie A. Morales, "Military Veterans and Service Dogs: A Qualitative Inquiry Using Interpretive Phenomenological Analysis," *Anthrozoös* 31, no. 1 (2018): 61–75.

124 ***In a study of 107*** Melissa G. Hunt and Rachel R. Chizkov, "Are Therapy Dogs

Like Xanax? Does Animal-Assisted Therapy Impact Processes Relevant to Cognitive Behavioral Psychotherapy?," *Anthrozoös* 27, no. 3 (2014): 457–469.

124 *For example, in one study* Sandra B. Barker and Kathryn S. Dawson, "The Effects of Animal-Assisted Therapy on Anxiety Ratings of Hospitalized Psychiatric Patients," *Psychiatric Services* 49, no. 6 (1998): 797–801.

125 *Another study, conducted by Sandra* Sandra B. Barker, Anand K. Pandurangi, and Al M. Best, "Effects of Animal-Assisted Therapy on Patients' Anxiety, Fear, and Depression Before ECT," *Journal of ECT* 19, no. 1 (2003): 38–44; and "What Is Electroconvulsive Therapy (ECT)?," American Psychiatric Association, July 2019, accessed August 12, 2022, https://www.psychiatry.org/patients -families/ect.

125 *Ideally, the positive feelings that* Jonathan W. Kanter et al., "What Is Behavioral Activation? A Review of the Empirical Literature," *Clinical Psychology Review* 30, no. 6 (2010): 608–620.

125 *Research by Mary Janevic, PhD* Mary R. Janevic et al., "The Role of Pets in Supporting Cognitive-Behavioral Chronic Pain Self-Management: Perspectives of Older Adults," *Journal of Applied Gerontology* 39, no. 10 (2020): 1088–1096.

126 *In a study involving 119* Roxanne D. Hawkins, Emma L. Hawkins, and Liesbeth Tip, "'I Can't Give Up When I Have Them to Care For': People's Experiences of Pets and Their Mental Health," *Anthrozoös* 34, no. 4 (2021): 543–562.

Chapter Nine

130 *What's more, being in the* Dasha Grajfoner et al., "The Effect of Dog-Assisted Intervention on Student Well-Being, Mood, and Anxiety," *International Journal of Environmental Research and Public Health* 14, no. 5 (2017): 483.

130 *A study by Molly K. Crossman* Molly K. Crossman, Alan E. Kazdin, and Krista Knudson, "Brief Unstructured Interaction with a Dog Reduces Distress," *Anthrozoös* 28, no. 4 (2015): 649–659.

130 *Another study, by Dasha Grajfoner* Dasha Grajfoner et al., "The Effect of Dog-Assisted Intervention on Student Well-Being, Mood, and Anxiety," *International Journal of Environmental Research and Public Health* 14, no. 5 (2017): 483.

131 *Research shows that people tell* Aislinn S. Evans-Wilday et al., "Self-Disclosure with Dogs: Dog Owners' and Non–Dog Owners' Willingness to Disclose Emotional Topics," *Anthrozoös* 31, no. 3 (2018): 353–366.

132 *A study by Lawrence Kurdek* Lawrence A. Kurdek, "Pet Dogs as Attachment Figures for Adult Owners," *Journal of Family Psychology* 23, no. 4 (2009): 439.

132 *They are a dependable source* Mary D. Salter Ainsworth, "Attachments and Other Affectional Bonds Across the Life Cycle," in *Attachment Across the Life Cycle* (Routledge, 2006), 41–59.

132 *Further research, conducted by Aislinn* Aislinn S. Evans-Wilday et al., "Self-Disclosure with Dogs: Dog Owners' and Non–Dog Owners' Willingness to Disclose Emotional Topics," *Anthrozoös* 31, no. 3 (2018): 353–366.

134 *Scientists have sought to understand* Andrea M. Beetz, "Theories and Pos-

sible Processes of Action in Animal Assisted Interventions," *Applied Developmental Science* 21, no. 2 (2017): 139–149.

135 *Indeed, a study by Lauren* Lauren Powell et al., "Companion Dog Acquisition and Mental Well-Being: A Community-Based Three-Arm Controlled Study," *BMC Public Health* 19, no. 1 (2019): 1–10.

135 *Research by Ilona Papousek, PhD* Ilona Papousek et al., "The Impacts of the Presence of an Unfamiliar Dog on Emerging Adults' Physiological and Behavioral Responses Following Social Exclusion," *Behavioral Sciences* 10, no. 12 (2020): 191.

135 *In an experiment by Christina* Christina M. Brown, Selena M. Hengy, and Allen R. McConnell, "Thinking About Cats or Dogs Provides Relief from Social Rejection," *Anthrozoös* 29, no. 1 (2016): 47–58.

136 *A study by Johannes Odendaal* Johannes S. J. Odendaal and Roy Alec Meintjes, "Neurophysiological Correlates of Affiliative Behaviour Between Humans and Dogs," *Veterinary Journal* 165, no. 3 (2003): 296–301.

137 *In a study by Natalia* Natalia Albuquerque et al., "Dogs Recognize Dog and Human Emotions," *Biology Letters* 12, no. 1 (2016): 20150883.

138 *A study by Emily Sanford* Emily M. Sanford, Emma R. Burt, and Julia E. Meyers-Manor, "Timmy's in the Well: Empathy and Prosocial Helping in Dogs," *Learning & behavior* 46, no. 4 (2018): 374–386.

138 *Another study, by Joshua Van* Joshua Van Bourg, Jordan Elizabeth Patterson, and Clive D. L. Wynne, "Pet Dogs (Canis Lupus Familiaris) Release Their Trapped and Distressed Owners: Individual Variation and Evidence of Emotional Contagion," *PLOS One* 15, no. 4 (2020): e0231742.

139 *As psychologist Stanley Coren, PhD* S. Coren, "Canine Empathy: Your Dog Really Does Care If You Are Unhappy," *Psychology Today, Canine Corner* (2012).

Chapter Ten

142 *A significant body of research* Sophie Susannah Hall, Nancy R. Gee, and Daniel Simon Mills, "Children Reading to Dogs: A Systematic Review of the Literature," *PLOS One* 11, no. 2 (2016): e0149759.

142 *All of these factors help* Claudia Fugazza et al., "Word Learning Dogs (Canis Familiaris) Provide an Animal Model for Studying Exceptional Performance," *Scientific Reports* 11, no. 1 (2021): 1–9.

144 *In a 2007 study, they* Nancy R. Gee, Shelly L. Harris, and Kristina L. Johnson, "The Role of Therapy Dogs in Speed and Accuracy to Complete Motor Skills Tasks for Preschool Children," *Anthrozoös* 20, no. 4 (2007): 375–386.

144 *In other studies, the kids* Nancy R. Gee, Elise N. Crist, and Daniel N. Carr, "Preschool Children Require Fewer Instructional Prompts to Perform a Memory Task in the Presence of a Dog," *Anthrozoös* 23, no. 2 (2010): 173–184.

144 *and they made fewer errors* Nancy R. Gee et al., "The Presence of a Therapy Dog Results in Improved Object Recognition Performance in Preschool Children," *Anthrozoös* 25, no. 3 (2012): 289–300.

145 *To see how kids would* Kurt Kotrschal and Brita Ortbauer, "Behavioral Effects of the Presence of a Dog in a Classroom," *Anthrozoös* 16, no. 2 (2003): 147–159.

145 *After reviewing thirty articles published* Jerri J. Kropp and Mikaela M. Shupp, "Review of the Research: Are Therapy Dogs in Classrooms Beneficial?," *Forum on Public Policy Online* 2017, no. 2.

145 *Other research has found some* Christine Grove and Linda Henderson, "Therapy Dogs Can Help Reduce Student Stress, Anxiety and Improve School Attendance," *The Conversation*, March 19, 2018, https://theconversation.com /therapy-dogs-can-help-reduce-student-stress-anxiety-and-improve-school -attendance-93073; and Christine Grove et al., "Understanding the Impact of Therapy Dogs on Children's Wellbeing in Educational Settings," in *Australian Psychological Society (APS) College of Educational and Developmental Psychologists Virtual Conference 2021: Working Together for the Future* (2021).

145 *Dogs in the classroom can* Sabrina E. B. Schuck et al., "Canine-Assisted Therapy for Children with ADHD: Preliminary Findings from the Positive Assertive Cooperative Kids Study," *Journal of Attention Disorders* 19, no. 2 (2015): 125–137.

146 *One possible explanation for some* National Institutes of Health, "The Power of Pets Health Benefits of Human-Animal Interactions," *News in Health* (2018).

146 *In any setting, a child's* Megan K. Mueller, "Human-Animal Interaction and Child Health and Development," in *Well-Being Over the Life Course* by Nancy R. Gee and Regina M. Bures (Springer Nature, 2021): 53–67.

146 *There's also some evidence that* Adele Diamond, "Executive Functions," *Annual Review of Psychology* 64 (2013): 135.

146 *working memory, mental flexibility, planning abilities, and self-control* Erika Friedmann et al., "Pet Ownership Patterns and Successful Aging Outcomes in Community Dwelling Older Adults," *Frontiers in Veterinary Science* 7 (2020): 293.

147 *Researchers found that preadolescents regularly* Aaron Honori Katcher and Alan M. Beck, "New Perspectives on Our Lives with Companion Animals," in *International Conference on the Human-Companion Animal Bond (1981: University of Pennsylvania)* (University of Pennsylvania Press, 1983); and Janet Haggerty Davis and Anne McCreary Juhasz, "The Preadolescent/Pet Bond and Psychosocial Development," *Marriage & Family Review* 8, no. 3–4 (1985): 79–94.

148 *Research suggests that children with* Sabine Doebel, Laura E. Michaelson, and Yuko Munakata, "Good Things Come to Those Who Wait: Delaying Gratification Likely Does Matter for Later Achievement (A Commentary on Watts, Duncan, & Quan, 2018)," *Psychological Science* 31, no. 1 (2020): 97–99.

148 *Multiple studies have found that* Beth Daly and Larry L. Morton, "Empathic Differences in Adults as a Function of Childhood and Adult Pet Ownership and Pet Type," *Anthrozoös* 22, no. 4 (2009): 371–382; and Vlasta Vizek-Vidović et al., "Pet Ownership in Childhood and Socio-Emotional Characteristics, Work Values and Professional Choices in Early Adulthood," *Anthrozoös* 14, no. 4 (2001): 224–231.

148 *Roughly one in five students* "Effects of Bullying," StopBullying.gov, accessed August 12, 2022, https://www.stopbullying.gov/bullying/effects.

149 *Dogs can also teach anti-bullying* Wanda J. Pearson, "The Healing Species: Animal-Assisted Character Education for Improving Student Behavior," *Journal of Youth Development* 6, no. 1 (2011): 79–93.

150 *Stacey was super-proud of* Lisa Wallis et al., "An Analysis of the Cognitive Structure of Dogs: Age, Sex and Training 1 Effects 2," conference paper: Canine Science Forum, 2016, https://www.researchgate.net/publication/305475856 _AN_ANALYSIS_OF_THE_COGNITIVE_STRUCTURE_OF_DOGS_AGE _SEX_AND_TRAINING_EFFECTS.

151 *As writer Susan Cheever noted* Caroline Knapp, "Love Among the Milk-Bones," *New York Times*, June 25, 1998.

Chapter Eleven

153 *As you've read in previous* Nancy R. Gee et al., "Dogs Supporting Human Health and Well-Being: A Biopsychosocial Approach," *Frontiers in Veterinary Science* 8 (2021): 630465.

153 *Research has found that when* R. Allen, E. Paige Lloyd, and Brandon T. Humphrey, "We Are Family: Viewing Pets as Family Members Improves Wellbeing," *Anthrozoös* 32, no. 4 (2019): 459–470.

153 *A considerable body of scientific* "Social Support: Tap This Tool to Beat Stress," Mayo Clinic, 2012.

153 *Having secure attachments is also* Sam Carr and Ben Rockett, "Fostering Secure Attachment: Experiences of Animal Companions in the Foster Home," *Attachment & Human Development* 19, no. 3 (2017): 259–277.

154 *In the spring of 2020* Ece Beren Barklam and Fatima Maria Felisberti, "Pet Ownership and Wellbeing During the COVID-19 Pandemic: The Importance of Resilience and Attachment to Pets," *Anthrozoös* (2022): 1–22.

154 *Similarly, research led by Cori* Cori Bussolari et al., "I Couldn't Have Asked for a Better Quarantine Partner!" Experiences with Companion Dogs During Covid-19," *Animals* 11, no. 2 (2021): 330.

154 *These findings are echoed more* Hiu Wo Chan and Daniel Fu Keung Wong, "Effects of Companion Dogs on Adult Attachment, Emotion Regulation, and Mental Wellbeing in Hong Kong," *Society & Animals* 1, no. aop (2022): 1–21.

154 *When it comes from people* Hsiu-Chia Ko, Li-Ling Wang, and Yi-Ting Xu, "Understanding the Different Types of Social Support Offered by Audience to A-List Diary-Like and Informative Bloggers," *Cyberpsychology, Behavior, and Social Networking* 16, no. 3 (2013): 194–199.

156 *In a study involving owners* William J. Chopik and Jonathan R. Weaver, "Old Dog, New Tricks: Age Differences in Dog Personality Traits, Associations with Human Personality Traits, and Links to Important Outcomes," *Journal of Research in Personality* 79 (2019): 94–108.

156 *We found that this also* "Good Dog? Bad Dog? Their Personalities Can Change," *MSU Today*, February 21, 2019.

157 *Research suggests that single adults* Clark Cline and Krista Marie, "Psychological

Effects of Dog Ownership: Role Strain, Role Enhancement, and Depression," *Journal of Social Psychology* 150, no. 2 (2010): 117–131.

157 ***This is especially helpful because*** Kimberly S. Bowen et al., "The Stress-Buffering Effects of Functional Social Support on Ambulatory Blood Pressure," *Health Psychology* 33, no. 11 (2014): 1440; and Debra Umberson and Jennifer Karas Montez, "Social Relationships and Health: A Flashpoint for Health Policy," *Journal of Health and Social Behavior* 51, no. 1 suppl (2010): S54–S66.

157 ***To investigate this effect*** Jonathan Bowen, Antonio Bulbena, and Jaume Fatjó, "The Value of Companion Dogs as a Source of Social Support for Their Owners: Findings from a Pre-Pandemic Representative Sample and a Convenience Sample Obtained During the COVID-19 Lockdown in Spain," *Frontiers in Psychiatry* 12 (2021): 622060.

159 ***This isn't surprising given that*** Lisa Wood et al., "The Pet Factor: Companion Animals as a Conduit for Getting to Know People, Friendship Formation and Social Support," *PLOS One* 10, no. 4 (2015): e0122085.

159 ***It's no secret that nearly*** "Research on Marriage and Divorce," American Psychological Association, accessed August 12, 2022, https://www.apa.org/topics/divorce-child-custody.

159 ***Sometimes it's a no-brainer about*** Melissa Chan, "Pets Are Part of Our Families. Now They're Part of Our Divorces, Too," *TIME*, January 22, 2020.

159 ***But courts are increasingly recognizing that*** Ibid.

160 ***A study by Megan Mueller*** Megan Kiely Mueller and Kristina Schmid Callina, "Human–Animal Interaction as a Context for Thriving and Coping in Military-Connected Youth: The Role of Pets During Deployment," *Applied Developmental Science* 18, no. 4 (2014): 214–223.

161 ***And research has found that*** Dawn C. Carr et al., "Psychological Health Benefits of Companion Animals Following a Social Loss," *Gerontologist* 60, no. 3 (2020): 428–438.

Chapter Twelve

167 ***When exactly a dog gains*** Ryan Llera and Lynn Buzhardt, "How Old Is Old? Comparing Dog Age to Human Age," VCA Animal Hospitals, accessed August 12, 2022, https://vcahospitals.com/know-your-pet/how-old-is-old-comparing-dog-age-to-human-age.

167 ***As Lynn Buzhardt, DVM*** Ibid.

168 ***They may become more sensitive*** "Helping Your 'Good Old Dog' Navigate Aging," *Fresh Air*, WLRN, November 23, 2010.

169 ***Research led by Jessica M.*** Jessica Hoffman et al., "The Companion Dog as a Model for Human Aging and Mortality," *Aging Cell* 17, no. 3 (2018): e12737.

170 ***Meanwhile, a 2019 national poll*** Mary Janevic et al., "National Poll on Healthy Aging: How Pets Contribute to Healthy Aging," 2019, https://deepblue.lib.umich.edu/bitstream/handle/2027.42/148428/NPHA_Pets-Report_FINAL-040319.pdf?sequence=3&isAllowed=y.

171 **Researchers led by Borbála Turcsán** Borbála Turcsán et al., "Individual and Group Level Personality Change Across the Lifespan in Dogs," *Scientific Reports* 10, no. 1 (2020): 1–12.

172 **Research led by Paolo Mongillo** Paolo Mongillo et al., "Does the Attachment System Towards Owners Change in Aged Dogs?," *Physiology & Behavior* 120 (2013): 64–69.

172 **Cognitive changes may contribute to** Durga Chapagain et al., "Cognitive Aging in Dogs," *Gerontology* 64, no. 2 (2018): 165–171.

172 **In the case of our** Zuzana Vikartovska et al., "Novel Diagnostic Tools for Identifying Cognitive Impairment in Dogs: Behavior, Biomarkers, and Pathology," *Frontiers in Veterinary Science* 7 (2021): 551895; Durga Chapagain et al., "Cognitive Aging in Dogs," *Gerontology* 64, no. 2 (2018): 165–171; and "Cognitive Decline in Aging Dogs: What to Know," *Texas A&M School of Veterinary Medicine & Biomedical Sciences*, April 15, 2021, accessed August 12, 2022, https://vetmed.tamu.edu/news/pet-talk/cognitive-decline-in-aging-dogs/.

174 **This can be accompanied by** Andria Corso, "Anticipatory Grief: What It Is and How to Cope," June 21, 2020, accessed August 12, 2022, https://www.vetvine.com/forums/topic/1195/anticipatory-grief-what-it-is-and-how-to-cope.

Chapter Thirteen

184 **Psychologists recognize that this is** Paul T. Clements, Kathleen M. Benasutti, and Andy Carmone, "Support for Bereaved Owners of Pets," *Perspectives in Psychiatric Care* 39, no. 2 (2003): 49–54.

184 **In a year-long study involving** Cindy L. Adams, Brenda N. Bonnett, and Alan H. Meek, "Owner Response to Companion Animal Death: Development of a Theory and Practical Implications," *Canadian Veterinary Journal* 40, no. 1 (1999): 33.

185 **Apparently, Stacey isn't alone in** Richard Topolski et al., "Choosing Between the Emotional Dog and the Rational Pal: A Moral Dilemma with a Tail," *Anthrozoös* 26, no. 2 (2013): 253–263.

185 **It protects us from both** Inger Benkel, Helle Wijk, and Ulla Molander, "Family and Friends Provide Most Social Support for the Bereaved," *Palliative Medicine* 23, no. 2 (2009): 141–149.

188 **Researchers from several universities** Stefania Uccheddu et al., "Pet Humanisation and Related Grief: Development and Validation of a Structured Questionnaire Instrument to Evaluate Grief in People Who Have Lost a Companion Dog," *Animals* 9, no. 11 (2019): 933.

189 **The typical grieving period lasts** Thomas A. Wrobel and Amanda L. Dye, "Grieving Pet Death: Normative, Gender, and Attachment Issues," *OMEGA—Journal of Death and Dying* 47, no. 4 (2003): 385–393.

190 **Scholars have specifically looked at** Louis Hoffman, Michael Moats, and Tom Greening, eds., *Our Last Walk: Using Poetry for Grieving and Remembering Our Pets* (University Professors Press, 2020).

191 **Research led by Wendy Packman** Wendy Packman et al., "Continuing Bonds

and Psychosocial Adjustment in Pet Loss," *Journal of Loss and Trauma* 16, no. 4 (2011): 341–357.

192 ***In her 1969 book*** Donald Oken, "On Death and Dying: What the Dying Have to Teach Doctors, Nurses, Clergy and Their Own Families," *Archives of General Psychiatry* 21, no. 5 (1969): 639–640.

192 ***Now there's growing recognition among*** Lucy Burns, "Elisabeth Kübler-Ross: The Rise and Fall of the Five Stages of Grief," BBC News, July 3, 2020.

192 ***It involves imagining a box*** The "ball in the box" analogy helps to explain how feelings of grief change over time and can continue to be triggered at random moments. Accessed August 12, 2022, https://www.hospiscare.co.uk/how-we -help/advice-support/talking-about-death-and-dying/why-grief-is-like-a-ball -in-a-box/.

Appendix 1

202 ***If you want to buy*** "How to Find a Responsible Dog Breeder," Humane Society of the United States, accessed August 12, 2022, https://www.humanesociety .org/sites/default/files/docs/find-responsible-dog-breeder.pdf.

INDEX

ABOUT THE AUTHORS

Jen Golbeck is the "internet's dog mom" and creator of the social media sensation *The Golden Ratio*. A professor at the University of Maryland's College of Information Studies, she is a popular science communicator on issues related to her research on social media and dogs. Her TED Talks have been viewed by millions, and she is a popular keynote speaker who has appeared on NPR, *The 11th Hour*, and more. Her writing has appeared in the *Washington Post, The Atlantic*, and *Wired*. She and her husband rescue golden retrievers who are seniors or who have special medical needs, and give them a safe and comfortable life. Find out more at JenGolbeck.com.

Stacey Colino is an award-winning writer specializing in health and psychological issues. Her writing has appeared in *US News & World Report, National Geographic*, the *Washington Post, Newsweek, Parade, Sports Illustrated*, and more. She is the coauthor of numerous books, including *Count Down, Emotional Inflammation*, and *Disease Proof*. Stacey is a lifelong dog lover and has owned three rescue dogs. Follow her on Twitter @ColinoStacey.